OUTSIDE THE BOX

OUTSIDE THE BOX

The Life and Legacy of Writer Mona Gould

The Grandmother I Thought I Knew

MARIA MEINDL

MCGILL-QUEEN'S UNIVERSITY PRESS   Montreal & Kingston • London • Ithaca

Legal deposit third quarter 2011
Bibliothèque nationale du Québec

Printed in Canada on acid-free paper that is 100% ancient forest free
(100% post-consumer recycled), processed chlorine free.

McGill-Queen's University Press acknowledges the support of the Canada Council for
the Arts for our publishing program. We also acknowledge the financial support of the
Government of Canada through the Canada Book Fund for our publishing activities.

©Noël Coward, "I'll See You Again" from *Bitter Sweet*, published by Methuen Drama,
an imprint of Bloomsbury Publishing Plc. I'LL SEE YOU AGAIN copyright © NC Aventales
AG 1929 by permission of Alan Brodie Representation Ltd www.alanbrodie.com

"Love is not all; it is not meat or drink" ©1931, 1958 by Edna St. Vincent Millay and
Norman Millay Ellis. Reprinted by permission of Holly Peppe, Literary Executor,
The Millay Society

Library and Archives Canada Cataloguing in Publication

Meindl, Maria, 1959–
Outside the box : the life and legacy of writer Mona Gould : the
grandmother I thought I knew / Maria Meindl.
Includes bibliographical references and index.
ISBN 978-0-7735-3911-2
1. Gould, Mona, 1908–1999. 2. Poets, Canadian (English)–20th
century–Biography. 3. Broadcasters–Canada–Biography. I. Title.

PS8513.0739Z57 2011   C811'.52   C2011-902637-6

Designed and typeset by studio oneonone in Sabon 10/14

In memory of my father

Contents

Acknowledgments   ix
Preface   xi

1	Spring Cleaning 3
2	Past Forgetting 11
3	The Vicissitudes of Life 30
4	Introducing Mona Gould 47
5	Full Circle 65
6	A Grand Surprise 73
7	This Was My Brother 84
8	Demobilization 99
9	Daily-ness 119
10	A Good, Wide Wonderful Business 125
11	Did You Notice? 144
12	A Talent to Amuse 149
13	This Bleak Design 167
14	Social Pages 173
15	Diminished but Not Licked 182
16	Liberty Hall 196
17	The Heart Alone 205
18	Displaced 223
19	Who Sink and Rise, and Sink Again 237
20	The Walnut-Shell Game 245
21	Everest 259
22	Bones 275

Afterword   279
Notes   281
Bibliography   299

Acknowledgments

Working on this project has been a long and painstaking process, but I have encountered generosity and kindness at every turn. I'll do my best to list the many people who deserve thanks.

Mona McTavish Gould, for never throwing anything away.

The Toronto Arts Council and the Ontario Arts Council for their financial support of this project.

The staff at the Fisher Library, including Anne Dondertman, Edna Hajnal, Richard Landon, and Jennifer Toews for many forms of assistance and encouragement – and above all their patience – through the years it has taken to complete this work.

John Aylesworth, Jean Aylesworth, Elizabeth Barry, Maija Beeton, Phyllis Benner, Leonard Brooks, Robert Coulter, Martha Feilding, Edra Ferguson, Marjorie Harris, John Ide, Douglas McTavish, James McTavish, Dodi Robb, Herbert and Carolyn Rowell, Fraser Sutherland, and Hetty Ventura for interviews, information and – once again – patience.

Special thanks to Ingi and John Gould for sharing their memories.

Gret Staats for generously permitting the use of his photograph of Mona's hands. Paul Armstrong of the University of Toronto for his excellent services in digital reproduction. Diana Kiesners and Robert Coulter for the loan of photographs.

The staff of the Toronto Public Library, the Public Library of London Ontario, the archives at McMaster University, Tony Glen of the National War Museum of Canada, as well as Stephen Francom and the staff of the Elgin County Archives.

Terri Favro, Andrea Johnston, Diana Kiesners, Karen Mulhallen, Julia Steinecke, and Nancy Wesson for negotiating the confusing territory between friendship, editing, and impromptu psychotherapy with aplomb. Thanks also to Elisabeth Raab Yanowski for her attentive and encouraging reading when I needed it most, and for the example she has set in her own work.

Karen Connelly for her help through the Toronto Public Library Writer in Residence program, and the Salonistas, for encouraging me to "get it all out."

My friends, for seeing me through many ups and downs and ups and downs.

This book is immeasurably stronger for the editorial attention I received from McGill Queen's University Press. I would especially like to thank Mark Abley for his faith in this project, and for the sensitive, insightful, and thorough comments which helped me see new possibilities in the manuscript I thought I knew. My thanks also to Susan Glickman, who miraculously managed to keep both the big and the small picture in her sights, and whose diligent editing and ingenious suggestions served to refine not only my prose but my thoughts.

And – last but by no means least – thanks to my dear husband, Rolf Meindl, for supporting me in ways I never knew were possible, and believing in me even when I don't believe in myself.

Preface

This book includes excerpts from Mona Gould's poetry, journals, personal notes, radio scripts, and prose. Some of these have been previously published; others have been transcribed from rough typescript and manuscript documents in her archives.

Mona's punctuation was flamboyant at best. At worst, it rendered her work unintelligible. In later years, she marked her drafts with circles, crossings-out, marginal comments, and emphasis marks above and below the text that may have been meant as guidelines for how the work should be read on radio. These layerings sometimes obscured the original text, and were probably influenced by her drinking and her eventual loss of vision. Her poetry is easier to decipher than her prose, but it, too, is subject to idiosyncrasies of punctuation, including two dots for ellipses and commas in ungrammatical places.

In this book, I draw on Mona's own words to tell the story of her life and to give insight into her thoughts and feelings, rather than for any critical purpose. Therefore, some judicious editing has been done, with the aim of preserving her style as much as possible while reducing any inconsistencies and errors that might prove distracting.

In her lifetime, Mona depended heavily on her editors. Despite her claims of near-divine inspiration, it is unlikely she would ever have wanted her work seen without some moderating influence on what *Saturday Night*'s editor B.K. Sandwell once called her "infernal rows of dots." She submitted her writing to his corrections, and those of other magazine editors, as well as to those of subsequent editors in all three of her published volumes of work. In accordance with this precedent, poems cited in this book have been emended to conform to ordinary English usage.

Nonetheless, it is never comfortable to edit the work of someone who cannot consent to its alteration, particularly a writer as headstrong and devoted to the sanctity of inspiration as Mona. Her idiosyncratic punctuation was an extension of her personality. Journal entries and letters have therefore been edited as little as possible. In a couple of cases, Mona's journals and scripts have been reproduced as well as typesetting will allow, and a poetry draft is recreated below. For those interested in Mona Gould's completed and polished work, her three published books are available for free on Project Gutenberg.

Promise

It's Far Too Late ....

It's far too late for "kissing and making it better" .. you see
It's far too late for kissing ..and making it well ..
And I know now if you love .. and it's a good LONG love ..
The Perimeter .. is .. hell!

Fill my hand with flowers . . speak to me tenderly
Have every consideration under the sun
And I shall thank you .. and appreciate and duly write you
But .. I am .. done.

I can manage to smile in the marketplace
Display my courage
My medals are obvious~~ly~~ pinned on my breast ---
By midnight .. I am .. nothing]* in my own house
Cry, I .. for rest!

Who was it said "Time is a great healer?"
Ah .. but can I WAIT?
Easy .. and s*w*eet and *s*imple and ~~quick~~
To slip the latch of the gate

So tho' I feed on ashes* . taste, clay*
I shall see it out* to the long* night .
I shall stay* .. I shall stay*.

It will come – right! –

Some*thing keeps me .. something whispers "<u>Not</u> now*" ---
Once there was a marriage that WAS <u>marriage</u>*
a long* vow!

NOTE
Italics indicate handwriting.
Asterisk indicates words that are circled.
    There is an arrow from the word "marriage" up to the lightly crossed-out
word "quick."

OUTSIDE THE BOX

1

Spring Cleaning

"Remember, Darling, when we all used to love *The New Yorker*?" Nanna pauses in her story long enough to take a sip of her drink: whiskey and milk, over ice. I murmur in agreement. At the age of six, I understand that my job is to stay with Nanna, to sit very quietly while she talks, sometimes until my parents arrive to pick me up, or sometimes – if I'm staying all night – until the candles have burned down and TV set shines its cool gray light from the corner of the room.

I understand Nanna's way of speaking. I know that loving *The New Yorker* means Nanna was part of the magazine in some way. That she belonged there, the way I belong to my family or my class at school. I don't know who she means by "we all," but I act like I do. I have a picture in my mind of a lot of people – famous, like Nanna herself – gathered around Nanna at a big party or all living together in the same house. That was a long time ago. Before my grandfather died, before my mother came along and married my father. Before Nanna was alone. It's a dark and blurry picture. I don't know who the people are or what they're doing, but I can't ask Nanna for any details. There are some things I must never ask. Knowing what these things are is what makes me special. I am an old soul. Nanna calls me "my ancient one."

I say I remember what Nanna remembers, because it's my part of the conversation. I nod and say yes whenever she pauses. Nanna tells me about the days when she was on the radio, and wore four-inch heels and something called a picture hat, and opened bazaars and spoke to groups of silly, trivial women. Nanna's stories put a kind of spell on me. They make me feel glued to my chair. If I need to go to the bathroom, I hold it. If I'm tired, I don't say I want to go to bed. There are certain times for me to talk, certain things for me to say; otherwise it's as if my mouth were stuck together and there were no way for the words to come out. Anyway, I don't really notice that I'm tired or have to go to the bathroom – at least, not in the usual way. When Nanna is talking, I don't *feel* myself. It's as if these things were happening to somebody else, somebody whose arms and legs I see when I look down at my own body. Nanna's stories pull my attention out of me. I become just eyes and ears, watching and listening to her.

It's still afternoon, not time to start cooking dinner yet. Nanna settles back against the colourful shawls that cover her couch. She bought them in Mexico when she lived there with my grandfather. The shawls are – as she puts it – "upholstered" with hair from Mister Chi Chi Bu the Second, her cat. Chi Chi is a seal point Siamese. He eats ground meat which Nanna feeds him by hand, in little balls. He leaves greasy fur on everything. Nanna got Mister Chi Chi Bu the Second just after my grandfather died, and she loves him very much because he comforted her during that time. She loves me very much, too, for the same reason. The first Mister Chi Chi Bu had to be put to sleep. When cats get old, Nanna tells me, they stop eating and drinking. They feel very light when you lift them, because their little organs have dried up inside. Then you take them to the vet and have them put to sleep. I know this means that the vet kills them, but I don't say so.

Nanna's lips and nails are painted red, and show in brilliant contrast to her white skin. Jungle Red: that's the name of her favourite colour. Her shoulder-length gray hair is clipped back from her face with bobby pins. She always wears black – now that she's a widow – alternating between two "good" suits which she fastens with safety pins at the waist and hem. When I stay overnight, I see her stretch her girdle over the back of a chair before getting into bed. She never wears socks or shoes in the house, and when she sits down on the couch she lifts her feet to show off their tough and blackened soles. "I love to walk barefoot," she says, "I'm a gypsy at heart."

Nanna lives at Number Thirty Nine, Farnham Avenue, lower duplex. This is what she tells me to say when we get in a cab together. I tell the driver the address; she just says "Home, James." The front door of Nanna's house is just a few steps up from the ground, but in the back you step out onto a wooden porch built high above the sloping garden. At the very end of the garden is an enormous elm tree. Soon it will get sick, Nanna, says. Like all the other elms in the world, it will get a disease and will have to be cut down.

Nanna's apartment is made up of a series of narrow, adjoining rooms. The living room is at the front. Books cover every surface. There are piles of them on the coffee table, on the arms of the chair and love seat, and on a round antique dining table which takes up one whole corner of the living room. The walls are covered in drawings, mostly by my father, but some by his friends. One is of goats grazing on a hillside. Old Man Varley gave it to her, Nanna tells me, to apologize for getting drunk and being rude to her one night. The longest wall is taken up by a single, enormous drawing of a woman. The lower part of her body is draped in thin fabric which clings to her belly and legs. The top of her is completely naked. I'm embarrassed to look at the picture, but must never say so. Only trivial people are embarrassed by naked-ness. We Goulds are not trivial people.

Nanna's apartment is heated by radiators piled with *New Yorkers* several inches deep. They are crisp with the heat that comes from the rads below them and with the rain and snow that pour in the windows. The magazines also act as coasters for Nanna's drinks. Each layer gathers its own pattern of circles for the month or two that it is on top. Nanna keeps her windows open winter and summer. There are hanging plants draped in front of them in-stead of curtains. One is particularly green and healthy. "I'm trying to kill that thing," she says, from time to time, "but it just keeps on growing. Do you want it? Take it away, will you?"

The dining room is next. In the middle of the room sits Nanna's Big Black Table, surrounded by four captain's chairs. There is a telephone stand in the corner. A heavy typewriter migrates from the end of the table to the tele-phone stand and back again. Nanna doesn't know how to change a type-writer ribbon. She uses each one until the black ink is gone, then switches to the red part and uses that up too. She tries to change the ribbon herself but it gets tangled, and all her clothes get covered in ink. Then the typewriter sits unused, with loops of ribbon spilling out of the top, until someone who knows how to replace it comes over and she can start writing again. Nanna types with two fingers, the middle finger of each hand. Her elbows raised high in the air, she stabs the keys so quickly that the typewriter rattles on the table. When she types, you can hardly see her lipstick because she closes her mouth in a firm line.

All along one wall of the dining room is a closet, closed off by a set of louvered doors. The closet is full of cardboard boxes which Nanna says she's going to sort some day, but she doesn't know when she'll get the time. The boxes are so full that when she opens the door, papers fall in a kind of landslide into the room. She adds more papers to the boxes every so often, shutting the doors quickly to stop them from falling out again.

The next room is the kitchen. Nanna's fridge is packed with food, but it smells so terrible that I dread being asked to refill her drink or get myself a glass of orange juice. She calls the fridge her icebox, and when she defrosts it the whole kitchen floor gets wet. Nanna doesn't look in the fridge when she's about to make dinner. She likes to buy food just before serving it. Either she calls Mr Duguid down the street and gets one of his boys to deliver a few things, or we take a cab to the supermarket at St Clair. At the supermarket they have a tank of lobsters like the ones she and my grandfather used to eat in New England, all the summers when they went there on holiday. Nanna sticks one finger in the tank and strokes the heads of the lobsters with her red nail. In the next few days, she tells me, all these lobsters will be boiled alive.

For dinner, Nanna may serve a barbecued chicken that she buys ready-made, along with a salad laced with slices of raw, red onion. (Nanna loves red onions, just like Colette. Colette was Aquarius, like Nanna. It's the writers' sign.) If we don't have chicken, we'll have pork chops coated with sugar and cinnamon and baked until they're too hard to cut. It's okay if I pick them up with my hands, though. "It's not a dinner party," she assures me when we sit down to eat. There are always roast potatoes in tin foil, and for dessert, a "float" made from ice cream with ginger ale poured on top. There is no waiting for treats at Nanna's, no "After you clean your room," or "That's enough." And you don't have to be afraid of breaking anything. "Liberty hall!" she cries, when something falls on the floor. "It's just a thing, dear. Throw it in the garbage. I don't give a shit."

Nanna bakes a lot. She makes peanut butter cookies, which we roll into little balls and then press down with the back of a fork before they go into the oven. She makes another kind of cookies with Special K cereal mixed into the dough. Biting into one of Nanna's cookies is exciting and a little scary. I might find a delicious spot of uncooked dough, or a vein of pure sugar nestled inside one of the cereal flakes, but I never know when a dot of baking soda or salt will pop on my tongue. Nanna says I love her cookies, just like my father did, so when they taste bad I do my best to swallow them down without making a face. Nanna also bakes a kind of cake she calls "snip doodle." She learned how to make it in New England. The cakes are never the same; often they're toasted on the top and raw inside, at other times, sunken in the middle. She makes a snip-doodle every time I come to visit. She makes a snip doodle for every*one* who comes to visit; sometimes even the mailman.

Books, books everywhere. And in the back room, where she sleeps: more *New Yorkers* on the rads. The cat sleeps in Nanna's bed, upholstering it with dark hair. As soon as spring comes, Nanna spends her nights outside on the back porch. The porch's railing is topped with four wooden window boxes. Nanna plants them with white petunias and blue morning glories. She calls the porch her back deck. On her back deck, Nanna takes pictures. Every time a flower opens or the cat rolls on his back, every time a squirrel comes to visit, it's a special occasion. Nanna is fascinated by the shadows cast by animals. She snaps two, three, five, ten photographs as the animals move and their shadows on the floor change shape.

The photos have to wait to be developed until Nanna has some money. When a cheque arrives at Nanna's house, she proceeds straight to the telephone and calls the Metro Cab Company. "It's Mona Gould, Dear," she says, urgently. "Send one of your boys over, will you? I've got errands to do." The dispatcher doesn't need to ask Nanna's address; he sends a lot of cabs her way. Sometimes she gets in the cab herself, but more often she simply hands the driver her camera and a clump of bills. His job is to take the camera up to Black's at Yonge and St Clair, where they'll change the film for her and give her whatever pictures have been developed since her last infusion of cash. Then, he's to pick up the copy of the Sunday *New York Times* they've been holding for her at the book store, and make a final stop at the liquor store for a bottle of whiskey. If the cheque is really big, the driver will go all the way downtown to Holt Renfrew and buy Nanna some new lipstick and nail polish. When he arrives with her things, she refuses to accept the change right away. "Keep something for yourself, dear. Are you sure you've got enough?" She takes the money that's left and shoves it, uncounted, into her purse.

Today was spring-cleaning day. Every spring, Nanna paints her porch white and her furniture black. She covers everything with a fresh coat of paint, sealing dust and cat hair underneath it in bubbles which may unexpectedly pop a few months later, leaving stains on a skirt or sleeve. Nanna hates cleaning, but likes all the fresh, shiny surfaces that are left when it's done. Now that the cleaning is finished, Nanna feels good. She sets both feet up on the coffee table beside a bowl of chocolate mints, and another of salted peanuts. She puts the palms of her hands together and I know she's about to start talking. Sometimes, especially when it's late at night, Nanna tells me about how lonely she is now my grandfather is gone. How she loves my father and wants to see him all the time, but my mother won't let her. Not today though. Today Nanna feels good. She will tell a happy story, this time.

"When Graham went overseas – he was a paymaster in the army – I moved to Toronto with John. We got a little apartment in Forest Hill, in one of those four-story buildings that are all torn down now. I was working for the Red Cross. For Pat Kelly. He 'borrowed' me from MacLaren's, you see, because they wanted someone who could really write. And I could write. They used to say I could write like a man. But I worked like a dog in those days. Just like a dog. My days were so long. And of course there was John to take care of, and my mother was in London but I was the only girl so I had to see to her, as well. She was getting older, by that time. She used to say, 'You're not measuring up, my girl,' like that. Very sternly. She was a Victorian beauty, my mother. I could never do anything right as far as she was concerned. Howard was her favourite – the eldest, and a boy, of course. Mook, we used to call him. That was his nickname.

"So there I was working for Pat Kelly and going around to all the hospitals and the clinics and speaking at various functions. You know, opening bazaars. Checking the lists of prisoners of war. And I had my big four-inch heels and my red nails and my trench coat. A real working gal. And one day there I was writing up a script, a thank-you speech for a campaign, a fundraising campaign we were doing. We were about to get a million dollars. And I had to go and pick up the cheque and give it to Pat and he'd read my speech at the ceremony. And the phone rang. It was the war office, and as soon as I heard that voice on the phone, I knew something had happened to Mook. They said, 'Your brother has been killed at Dieppe. He was a hero. He fought until the end, but he was killed.' And so I sat down on the floor of the office. That's all I could do, just sat right down and looked at all the *legs* of things: the legs of my desk, the legs of my table. I couldn't stop staring at the wastebasket. And all I could think of was saying goodbye to Mook when he left on the troop train. He was a great, big strong guy with shoulders like this and a big, loud voice. I was standing there snivelling while the guys all said goodbye to their girlfriends and wives, and John was trying to hold back his tears, and Mook bounced up on the train and waved out the window and when the train was taking off he threw me a chocolate bar out the window, and I caught it, just like that. I thought it was a good sign.

"And then I remembered how, when I was little and we spent summers in Port Stanley, we used to walk down the beach and people would call us Big Mook and Little Mook. And my brother was Big Mook and I was Little Mook. He was a big, rough-and-tumble guy that you thought nothing would ever happen to. He always made everything alright. I would go up and tease the bigger kids – sauce them, you know – and they'd get mad. I'd see him coming over and I'd introduce him: 'This is my brother.' All I had to do was introduce him, and they'd back off and leave me alone, you see. And now he was dead. And all I could think to myself was 'This *was* my brother. Was.'

"But it was a work day and I had to keep going. I got up and straightened myself up and combed my hair and put on new lipstick, and I went to Pat and I said, 'Pat, my brother Mook was taken down at Dieppe.' And Pat said, 'Mona, do you want to go home? You can go home if you like.' And I said, 'No, Pat. Mook kept fighting 'til the end and so will I.' And I got in a cab, which was quite a luxury in those days, and I went over to the bank and I waited outside the manager's office to pick up that cheque. And just as I was sitting there, it came to me. *This was my brother. This was my brother.* Just like the poem was writing itself down on my forehead. I reached into my purse and I found the stub of a pencil and a cigarette package, because I used to smoke in those days, everybody smoked. Or at least you carried cigarettes even if you didn't smoke them. It was a Katie Hepburn kind of a thing to do. And I wrote it down, right there: *This was my brother at Dieppe, quietly a hero, who gave his life like a gift, withholding nothing.* The whole thing. The whole poem. Just like I was taking dictation. And then the manager came out and was about to give me the cheque and so I just shoved the poem down in my purse and I went on with my day.

"And of course you can imagine what it was like, getting through that day. I had to go home and tell John, who just adored his uncle, and I had to talk to my other brother, you know, the four-eyes one. Myopic. Of course nothing ever happened to him. He's still alive and has pots of money. He'll die in bed like the rest of the goddamned plutocrats. Anyway, there was my mother. She had to be sedated. That's what they did at the time. And by the time I finished my day I was just lying there in bed wide awake. I couldn't sleep. It was as if I'd had a pint of coffee just before I got into bed.

"Now at that time I had a habit, which was a very bad habit, but I had to keep myself organized. At the end of the day I'd just dump my purse out in the garbage and take the garbage downstairs to the bins outside. And I was lying there in bed and I thought: *My God! The poem ... the poem ... I've thrown it away!* And it was garbage night. Well I put on Graham's old bathrobe that I kept with me just to remind me of him, of his smell, and I put on a pair of John's Wellington boots – he was getting tall by then and had great big feet – and down I went to the street. Can you imagine, in Forest Hill at three in the morning, there I was picking through the garbage for that little piece of paper? And I found it. And I came inside and I typed it up right then and there at three in the morning and I typed it up about ten times and distributed copies of the poem in various places. Just so it would never get lost again. And I put one copy in an envelope and I mailed it to B.K. Sandwell, the editor of *Saturday Night.* He'd been publishing bits and pieces of my stuff from time to time. He was a very imperious man. I was terrified of him. But I decided to send him this. If nothing else, he'd be less likely to lose it than me.

"And I went on with things. There was news coming out about Dieppe, and of course my brother had distinguished himself in battle. And there were so many men killed, and lost and missing in action. Everyone had lost someone from their family or friends. It was a terrible time. The Red Cross was frantically busy. And so I forgot all about the poem. And then one day I got a call from Sandwell's secretary to come over to the office of *Saturday Night*. I went over on my lunch hour, because Pat couldn't spare me for a minute. I went over on my lunch hour and the secretary showed me in, and B.K. Sandwell was standing in front of the window with the light coming in all around his head. I couldn't see his face but I knew from his voice that he was smiling. And he said: 'Your time has come, Mona Gould. The time has come for you to have a book. Now, send a hundred of your best poems over to Ellen Elliott at Macmillan's. And I'll tell her you're to have a book.' Well, I just about dropped on the floor right there. But I didn't show how I was feeling. I just said 'Alright. I'll do it,' and I did.

"And that's how my first book came to be. And I got to choose the paper and the typeface and the design and everything. I loved it! I loved it! There's nothing better than having a book. You'll know when you have your first book, what a wonderful feeling it is."

Past Forgetting

The ward in the nursing home was enormous. Its powder blue walls seemed to recede in the dim, mid-winter afternoon light. The place was silent, and preternaturally clean. A pale woman made her way toward the window, leaning on a walker. Eventually she settled in a chair, where she gave a sigh and stared out at the featureless parking lot with its wisps of snow. There were several bent figures gathered by the window, facing out. One woman's hair hung down to her tiny shoulders: white against red. I crossed the room and crouched beside her.

"Nanna!" I said.

"They call me the lady in red," she answered, turning her hands to display perfectly manicured nails.

My grandmother's hands were still slender, undistorted by arthritis, though she was ninety-one years old. She had never had the patience to wait for her nail polish to dry, and so it was strange to see the nails' lacquered surfaces without streaks and bubbles. Her lipstick was not the usual rectangular slash, but a symmetrical cupid's bow. It must have been painted on by a nurse; Nanna didn't see well any more.

I had come to this nursing home in Collingwood to talk with my grandmother about the logistics of becoming her literary executor. Over the past two decades, Mona had moved several times, and had pared down her possessions in the process. Furniture, jewellery, drawings, and hundreds of books had all been distributed among family and friends. By the time she moved to

Barrie about ten years before, to be near my father and his wife, Ingi, she owned almost nothing. Except for the thirty-eight boxes of papers that now lined their garage. I had come to suggest that Mona donate her boxes to the Thomas Fisher Rare Book Library at the University of Toronto. In the coming months or years – as long as it took – I would sort the manuscripts, letters and photos and place them in tidy, acid-free folders, to be stored in the stacks. When it was all finished she would get a tax receipt, or my father would, if ... But we didn't have to think about that today.

I made my pitch nervously, chattering on for longer than I had things to say. When I finally finished, Mona nodded and said, "Okay."

Just "Okay"? All my life, Mona had talked constantly through our visits. Her silence left me at a loss. We stared out the window. A nurse came to the door to ask, "Does anyone want anything in here? We have Jell-o, applesauce, arrowroot cookies, and to drink, there's tea or juice."

Mona said, "Applesauce, please," and then turned to me. "May I be put to bed, now?"

"Of course, Nanna," I said. I wheeled her over to her bed, where a dusky pink melamine bowl sat waiting on the night table. I let her balance herself on my arm while she stood, then transferred her to the bed. She was very, very light. I wound a handle near the foot of the bed to raise her to a sitting position, then perched sideways beside her, spoon in hand. I tapped each spoonful on the side of the bowl, lifting and dipping it ceremoniously before bringing it towards her. She opened her mouth trustingly and swallowed with pleasure. Meticulously I scraped out the last of the applesauce.

"It's good," she said, and asked me to wind the bed down again.

She lay on top of the covers, hands folded on her chest as if in prayer. Her eyes fluttered open and closed like a baby's. I watched the shadows of sleep and consciousness play over her face ... just watched, imprinting her image in my memory: the pale, pale skin, veined at the temples, the sharp nose and green-flecked eyes, the broad cheekbones which lent her face a heart-shaped sweetness.

This would probably be the last time I'd see my grandmother. *I should feel sad,* I thought. But I didn't. Grief had come – and gone – six weeks before, when I visited her in the hospital in Barrie. She had become weak, all of a sudden, unable to manage on her own. The doctor had decided to keep her there until a bed became available in a nursing home. In the hospital I'd found her laid out on a reclining wheelchair in the geriatric common room, her head thrown back and to one side, cheeks caved in, without any lipstick or nail polish. It was the first time I had seen her this way, and I didn't recognize her. I had to ask the nurse which one of the many sleeping figures was Mona. I said I would take her back to her room, and wheeled her down the hallway while she slept. She breathed without constriction, welcoming the air into her open mouth. I sat and gazed at her that day, holding her hand, a wash of tears covering my face because I didn't want to pull my hand away to wipe them. Then I thought: *She's dying. She's doing what she's supposed to do, right now,* and I stopped.

꿏

Mona finished her nap. She looked at the ceiling, squinting a little, her eyebrows puckered, as if straining to see or hear something far away. At last she looked at me. She ruminated for a moment, as if translating what she was about to say into a foreign language. "It's a good thing you're doing," she said. "I appreciate it."

"You're ... you're welcome Nanna," I said. "I mean, I'm happy to sort your papers. And the library is happy to have them. You're giving them a gift – me – a gift ..." stammering, now, because I felt it: grief, or was it fear, or was it rage? *Do not go gentle.*

She said, "It'll be an exchange. You'll get something from it, and so will I."

It was wrong, I told myself – completely self-centred – but I still could not stop resentment from bubbling up. *What? ... What will I get?* I forced my voice to sound calm, even though calm was the last thing I felt.

"Nanna," I said, "If there's anything you don't want people to see, I can put it away. I can put things in sealed boxes. You can seal them for as many years as you like. *I* won't even look at them if you don't want me to."

She closed her lips together primly. "I have no secrets," she said.

꿏

Mona launched what I used to call her "farewell tour" in her sixties, when she survived a cancer operation. "I won't be around for much longer," she used to say with an arch sort of brightness, "But who cares, eh? I've become dispensable." At the end of each visit she would take both of my hands in a painful grip and stare hungrily into my eyes, as if she needed my gaze for sustenance. I would pull away, feeling claustrophobic but battling a sense of guilt. Maybe if I kept holding on for one more minute she would be satisfied. Then she would pull me in for goodbye kisses, leaving lipstick marks on my cheeks and glasses.

Some years later, the doctor discovered that Mona had developed a build-up of plaque in her carotid artery. He said there was no loss of blood to her brain, but Mona maintained that she was under a death sentence. She would tap a vein in her pale temple with a fingernail, and intone fatalistically, "You see this, this blue vein? It's going to get me in the end."

She talked about Death with a capital "D," and personified it in various ways. Early one morning, she phoned to tell me she had determined the true nature of Death. Death was not an old man with a sickle but a child standing at her window, inviting her out to play. I flipped through a magazine as I listened to her, determined to give her the bare minimum of attention. Mona's farewell tour was getting on my nerves by that time. She told me that she thought about death when she woke up at five every morning; that this, in fact, defined her as a writer. A writer is someone who wakes up at five in the morning, thinking about death.

At the age of eighty, Mona began to make funeral plans. She announced that the whole family was to line up at the head of the church, each of us displaying our particular talents in our tributes to her. My sister Ellen, for instance, would sing a song, accompanied by my father on the clarinet. I, of course, would write a poem in her honour and read it to the assembled crowd. She made regular phone calls to inform me of the revisions and additions she had made to the plans.

And so I had always imagined an operatic death for Mona. There would be one last round of stories, perhaps going on through the night. Then she'd summon her strength to say goodbye to each of us and fall back on the pillow with a peaceful smile. There would have to be music. Perhaps she'd even die at the piano, playing her favourite Noel Coward song. She used to come over for dinner every Sunday night when I was a teenager. After we ate, she would make her way, with sashaying steps, to the piano, a glass of milky whiskey held aloft as if to light her way. By that time of the evening we would all be worn down, steeped to the point of intoxication in Mona's relentless talk. A maudlin, foreboding atmosphere would settle over the room as she'd begin to play:

I'll see you again
Whenever spring breaks through again.

Time may lie heavy between,
But what has been
Is past forgetting ...

Mona's sense of rhythm was infallible, but she didn't particularly care where her fingers landed. The last few chords would descend in an atonal cascade:

Though the world may go awry
In my heart will ever lie
Just the echo of a sigh:
Gooooood-bye!

She would run the top of one finger all the way up the scale at the end of the song, her nail leaving red skid marks as it clicked its way across the keys. I imagined Mona falling forward at this moment. Curtain.

It didn't happen that way. Early in the morning of 8 March 1999, Mona was sent from her nursing home to the hospital in Collingwood. Stomach trouble, they thought at first, but she was suffering from congestive heart failure. She fell deeper and deeper into sleep through the day and was dead by six p.m. Mona died alone, after her son and daughter-in-law, reassured by a nurse, had gone home to supper.

My father felt abandoned. A massive stroke in 1996 had left him with aphasia. Now, he expressed himself in the language of gesture, aided by the odd stock phrase: "As a matter of fact ..." or "What do you know?" First, taking on the role of Mona, he set his face coldly and turned it away. "You see?" he asked, then demonstrated. "This is what he does," referring to himself in the third person, as he'd come to do since his stroke. He slumped as if crestfallen, taking the role of himself, the one left behind.

As for me, I didn't feel much different. For me, it was as if Mona wasn't really gone.

⸙

I once interviewed a neurosurgeon about what happens after a patient sustains a spinal cord injury. He described various medical procedures: the stabilizing of bodily functions, the surgery, the traction, the drugs.

"And of course," he said, "no injury arrives in a vacuum."

"Can you say more about that?"

"Well, it's not as if the person just appears for the first time the moment their spinal cord is severed. An injury always comes *into* something. There's a family, a job, a home. A whole set of circumstances that have to change, now ... and, as you know, no one's life is perfect to begin with."

If the person with the injury were to tell his or her story, some would call it a trauma narrative. There are scholars who look at how people construct the stories of their lives around catastrophic events, how they see their lives before and after, how they order their memories, and how the storytelling itself serves to help them recover. Often people treat the injury as a kind of birth. They begin by telling this moment: "I was walking along the dirt road listening to my headphones. I guess I didn't hear the car coming. Next thing I knew, I was in the middle of a field, propped up against a tree. My legs were stretched out in front of me. I wasn't in pain, but I knew something bad had happened." Eventually, they give you some background – the kinds of circumstances that the neurosurgeon talked about – and tell you how all those things changed. Then there are struggles, leading to some point of balance, resolution, or understanding: an ending. Sometimes, but not always, it's a happy one. That's the nature of stories. They begin somewhere. End somewhere else.

At the time Mona died, my job was to help others tell their stories. I interviewed people who'd broken their necks and people who'd contracted polio or some other, paralysing disease. I helped write reports on the experience of people with disabilities in the health care system. I edited people's writing too, with a special emphasis on memoirs. I was good at it, sifting through masses of raw, unprocessed memory to find out what was important; helping people make sense of what they were already saying. But making sense of my own story was more difficult. It still is. Is Mona's death the beginning of the story? That part is not clear.

I was forty years old when Mona died, and studying for my M.A. Week after week, I would sit with a group of people in an airless seminar room at the Ontario Institute for Studies in Education. Our number included primary school teachers, psychologists, and full-time students, all of us taking night-classes towards a degree in Philosophy of Mind. We were not a talkative group. Frowning, we stared at the photocopies on the table in front of us, occasionally venturing a few cautious words. Under discussion were questions like *How does language shape consciousness, and vice versa? How do language and meaning interact? What is meaning, anyway? What do we know, and how do we know we know it?*

Those evenings passed quickly. It would be after ten o'clock when we noticed the time. The others would hastily pack up their books and get ready to go home. A few jokes would be made about insomnia, a condition many of us shared. I didn't want the class to end. My head felt like it would burst with the effort of following my classmates' unfamiliar logic, but for a change I felt calm. With the questions that plagued me literally out on the table for discussion, my ceaseless *inner* questioning could stop. Here, everyone was doing the same thing as I was. Here, everyone understood you could lie awake at night, wondering whether you knew anything at all.

"I don't advise you to do this," said my professor when I asked to transfer from Curriculum Studies to his less popular department.

"Why not?"

"Well, you can't earn any money at it. You won't get a job."

"I don't care."

That wasn't true; I worried constantly about money. But I felt passionate about philosophy. It seemed vital, more vital to me than owning a house or saving for a pension. Philosophy was not enough, however; I sought out other forms of instruction as well. Considered "tone deaf" since my early teens, I took lessons in Extended Vocal Technique. This includes raw and inarticulate sounds like sobbing, laughing, growling, and screaming in the vocal palette, alongside what we usually consider musical sounds. My lack of a musical ear ceased to be a problem, but it also stopped mattering to me. I just liked making noise. At the same time, I was trying to overcome a case of repetitive strain injury. Rejecting physiotherapy or painkillers, I studied to become a Feldenkrais practitioner. Feldenkrais is a type of movement education which retrains the entire nervous system, leading – in my case – to figuring out which habits created the problem in the first place. In the training, we retraced the stages of human development from the earliest movements of the eyes and mouth, to creeping, crawling, sitting, and eventually standing. In those days, I felt driven to get behind language, beneath it, searching for something I could count on. Language itself seemed inherently untrustworthy to me.

I lived in the front room of a house in Toronto's Little Italy, a living room converted to a bedroom, with thin curtains for privacy and vast amounts of floor space. I had almost no furniture. The bed was a mattress on the floor. There was an old chair with one mashed arm which my parents had bought when they were still together. Somehow, it had found its way to me. There was a lamp belonging to the landlady, a spindly rack for the telephone and telephone book, a few milk crates. That was all. Socks and underwear were kept in plastic bags in the corners. My books, my computer, and all my other furniture were at the office I rented a few blocks away. My days were spent at the office, and most evenings and weekends as well.

It was winter, 1999, when it became clear that Mona could not stay in her apartment any more. She was installed in the nursing home, and Ingi gathered up all the boxes and transported them – over a series of trips – from Mona's empty apartment to the garage of their house. Record amounts of snow fell that winter. Shovelling was a downright comical undertaking, because there was nowhere to put it all. You'd fill a shovel with snow and toss it on top of a pile, but then it all tumbled down again, leaving more at your feet than when you'd started.

One night, the sky cleared and there was an enormous full moon. It was cold, but the whole neighbourhood seemed to end up outdoors at the same time, gazing up at the bright disk in the sky. It was if the earth had changed its orbit; as if the planets had been rearranged to bring us closer to the moon. That night, I slept unusually hard and long. I dreamed I was standing on a riverbank, and that Mona and many other old people were floating by on ice floes, each with a small pet. Mona was weeping.

I called out to her, "What's the matter, Nanna?"

She replied, "I'm in love with my son. It's an obsession. I can't help it."

She came to the bank of the river, and I helped her ashore. I put my arm around her shoulders and said, "You can stop now, Nanna. It's over." For a change, I had no desire to pull away from her. I woke up with a bruised feeling in my belly, as if something had been wrenched out of the centre of me.

I phoned Ingi. "I was thinking ... Could you bring me a couple of Nanna's boxes? Just whenever you happen to be in town ..." I said it casually, not wanting to betray the fear that made my heart pound as I spoke. I wanted to say, "Whatever you do, don't throw them away."

It was a lot to ask, for her to take a trip to Toronto. She had been caring full time for my father since his stroke. Now Mona needed help too, Mona, who had been viciously unkind to her daughter-in-law for years. I was too busy to contribute much, preoccupied with my mother, Hetty (my father's first wife). For over ten years she had spent most of her winters in the hospital, suffering from systemic lupus, an auto-immune disease. Her whole body was under attack from within. She had strokes and heart attacks. She fell and broke her hip, her ribs, her shoulder. She had internal bleeding. Drug-resistant infections began to proliferate in hospitals, and she caught them.

Then there was the pneumonia, which never really went away. It was just tamed, temporarily, before flaring up again.

Time was in short supply. Care was in short supply. Those were also the years when hospitals in Ontario were subject to massive cutbacks. Hospital emergency rooms became dirtier, line-ups longer, nurses angrier, patients more desperate. Everything seemed to be getting worse. In my interviewing work, I heard stories of people being discharged prematurely from the hospital, nowhere near ready to look after themselves. I lived through it with my mother. I came to feel the whole world was teeming with needs, always more than I could give. Despite pushing myself to exhaustion, I was always saying "No." Nothing I did was enough.

Ingi and I had not always seen eye to eye, yet she had begun to seem increasingly saintly to me. Graciously, she had taken on all the practical tasks in their household, making it possible for my father to continue his career as an artist and musician. We developed an unspoken solidarity. Both of us had to be sensible, and sometimes tough. When she arrived on my slippery doorstep with a box of papers, Ingi said, "Just get a recycling container and start throwing things away. It's mostly garbage." She brought a few boxes to the door, then went away in the car. She didn't come in for a visit and I didn't coax her to stay. She was busy; so was I. It went without saying that we wouldn't spend any time together. I left the boxes, untouched, in a pile by the bed for a week before I opened any of them. Sometimes, I woke in the middle of the night and drifted back to sleep looking at the tower of boxes.

One evening, imprisoned by yet another storm, I reached across and pulled a handful of papers out of one of the boxes. Maybe this is the real starting point of the story, that moment of discovery. The handful contained a note from E.J. Pratt, and another from Vera McIntosh Bell, the sister of Katherine Mansfield and Mona's close friend. I found fragile pieces of Mona's radio scripts and handwritten versions of a couple of her poems. That week I showed them to Richard Landon, the director of the Fisher Rare Book Library, and asked if he would take the boxes. He said he would, provided I agreed to sort them. I said, "Yes."

❧

Why did I say yes, when I already had so much to do? Because if I didn't do it, no one would. It was much the same reason I was looking after my mother. *Because no one else will*. It was the guiding principle of my life at that time.

Taking responsibility for the boxes was just part of the general trend. It's not that I didn't love my mother, or want to look after her. It's just that love was not the point. Being motivated by love was a luxury. It was an inconsistent, undependable motivation. My mother needed me no matter how I felt. Certainly, I felt excited by the prospect of finding out what was in the boxes. Certainly, I wanted Mona's papers to be preserved and for her to die knowing they would be. But no matter how I felt, I had agreed to sort them, anyway.

A week or so later – after I'd made arrangements for the Fisher Library to take the papers, after my visit to Mona in the nursing home – I delved deeper into the boxes and began to understand what I had taken on. The boxes contained not just evidence of Mona's past, but of my own. In Mona's notes, journals, and photographs, I saw my childhood preserved in the closest detail. Every stage of development was documented, every visit celebrated. It was like looking in a magnifying mirror, seeing wrinkles and pores I would rather not know were there. There were the letters I myself had written to Mona over the years. I wrote of overwork, anxiety, poor health, the ending of yet another temporary job ... a job I had never liked in the first place. I wrote of rents suddenly going up, of roommates becoming intolerable, of broken relationships which left me without a place to live. I never told Mona the whole story, but left enough hints that I could read my own biography in my letters to her, a biography I was deeply uncomfortable with.

Though I felt as weary as a centenarian, all the milestones of adulthood seemed to have eluded me. Here I was at forty, with no family of my own. I had a companion I spent weekends with and spoke to on the telephone every night. Our love was deep and tender, but felt ancient, a love fuelled by a lack of illusion, by a tragic acceptance of our own essential aloneness. A thread must be kept suspended between us; our contract was never to slacken it. Never to suggest the possibility of sharing a home. My career seemed to be in an even greater shambles. I grew up believing that I had a destiny. I was a writer. This was not something I had to *do* anything about. Yes, I had to work, to work as hard as I could. But I always believed there would be a context for my writing, some place for it to go, something – or someone – to draw it out. I never believed I would have to convince anyone to pay attention to me. I wrote every day, as I had since childhood, yet my output so far had consisted of a few short stories, and I felt lucky to have an apology scribbled on the rejection slips that regularly arrived in my mailbox. I knew that this was perfectly normal, that most writers lived this way, yet I could not shake the feeling that I had failed.

I could see it was not good for me to spend time with this stuff. Whatever hours I spent in the library were going to take away from building a career, making a home. My energy already felt consumed by the needs of an earlier generation, and consenting to sort these things threatened to take away the tiny margin of self-determination that was left to me. It seemed a failure in itself, a capitulation, and yet another example of my inability to look after my own interests. But I had said yes, and no matter how grimly, I was look-ing forward to it. The task of sorting those boxes was mine. Mine, even if nothing else was mine.

⚜

My first day of sorting was scheduled for the Friday after Mona's death. I made my way to the Fisher Library, an annex of Robarts, the main University of Toronto Library (sometimes known as "Fort Book"). I knew as soon as I stepped into the lobby that the Fisher was different; it was private, unhurried, refined. The air was humid, and the lobby dimly lit. I checked my coat and bags at the door – "Special collections require special security" a sign warned – and I walked, free of winter's clumsy burdens, into the foyer. Glass cases displaying ancient maps lined this room, and all around, stretching up for several stories, were shelves and shelves of rare books. I thought: *Mona would love – would* have *loved – this place.*

I was greeted by Edna Hajnal, the manuscripts curator for the library. Mona would have loved Edna too. She was a miniature woman, dressed in a fine wool suit, seemingly ageless under her cap of impeccable hair. Edna showed me to the spot in one corner of the basement where seven boxes were piled, ready for sorting. The first seven. There were thirty-one more boxes. The library had already sent a truck to Barrie to pick them up. They were being stored in a remote corner of the library's basement, to be brought over in batches, replenishing the pile that now stood in front of me as I worked my way through it.

Edna went away to get a library truck, and I took a look around. There were many stacks of boxes in this room, one marked "Atwood," another, "Lee." Mona's didn't fit. Her papers were stuffed into great big toilet-paper boxes, or greasy cartons from the grocery store that didn't really close at the

top. They looked ungainly next to the tidy liquor store boxes everyone else
seemed to have used. They even smelled different. Into the library's respectable atmosphere crept Mona's trademark combination of sweet perfume
and dust, and something metallic underneath: perhaps old cat hair or silver
in want of polishing.

Edna was back. "This is what my grandmother smelled like," I told her,
then blushed. *What a stupid thing to say.* She signalled me to load the cart.
I picked up a box, fumbled, and Edna recovered it for me, her delicate wrists
and hands belying her strength, her authority over such unwieldy things.
"Most of the sorting is done in the basement," she told me, "But being down
here alone, sorting even a stranger's papers is enough to make you feel a little
depressed. And we don't want you to give up."

Edna installed me in a carrel on the main floor. She went away for a while,
returning with file folders in several sizes. I then received my five-minute
briefing on how to create an archive. Edna warned me that I should always
use legal-size folders for manuscripts. "You can be sorting through one pile
that you think are all letter-size, and you will need to put a legal-size paper
in with it. Then you'll have to start over again." Newspapers and posters
were to go in large, flat boxes and were to be listed as "OVS" (O-Ver-Size).
Metal paper clips were to be removed and replaced with plastic-coated ones.
Edna gave me some white corrugated plastic boxes to put the files in when
I finished, and turned to leave. "But how do I DO it?" I asked.

"Something will emerge," she replied, closing the door behind her.

⚓

The first thing I took out of the box was a scrapbook from 1942–43. Mona's
most famous poem, "This Was My Brother," had been written in 1942 after
her brother's death in the Canadian Army's raid on Dieppe. Eight months
later, her first book of poems, *Tasting the Earth,* appeared. The thick pages
of the album were yellowed. I picked gingerly at the corners of the clippings
and letters she had pasted there but found they could not be budged. There
were newspaper articles attached to a special kind of notepaper that Macmillan had printed for sending authors the reviews of their work. The notepaper read: "The Macmillan Company of Canada Limited beg to forward the
accompanying cutting from ..." and there was a space for the date and the
name of the newspaper.

"As lovely a book of Canadian poems as has ever been written," read a clipping from *The Globe and Mail.*[1] Another from *The Montrealer* proclaimed: "It is doubtful if this war has brought forth a more moving poem than 'This Was My Brother.'"[2] A reviewer at *The Hamilton Spectator* wrote, "While she is obviously attracted by Nature in her varied moods and seasons, Gould also exhibits a deep sympathy for human suffering and the tragedy of war strikes deeply into her consciousness. This little volume will appeal to all readers who can appreciate distinctive lyrical poetry."[3]

Flipping back-to-front through the album, I found a letter from E.J. Pratt in which he described *Tasting the Earth* as "a honey." The poems, he wrote, "strike at the solar plexus" and "tug the heart."[4] I found an invitation to Mona to address the University Women's Club, along with two other women who had distinguished themselves "penwise."[5] There was also some copy for a radio program called *Design for Women.* "Just how you may feel about reading poetry I don't know but to me it has always been a most satisfying way of escape from any upsetting emotional mood. There is something every [sic] comforting when one is off balance about things in general to pick up some poem and realise that the poet has expressed just HOW YOU are feeling ... someone else has lived YOUR experience and put it into words."[6]

Ellen Elliott at Macmillan of Canada asked Mona if she might have four copies of *Tasting the Earth* to submit to the Governor General's awards: Macmillan, it seemed, was out of stock. Finally, Marjorie Freeman Campbell of *The Hamilton Spectator* apologized for taking so long to forward a review. "I had expected to get into the office much earlier but last week was rather dreadful. I had to meet a deadline on one article and go out for a day and a half on material for another. As I had arranged for extra help for housecleaning which needed my supervision, and the family ate the same three meals per day and needed the same weekly wash done, you can draw your own picture. I worked so hard that I felt faintly ill all the time."[7]

Mingled with the delight of discovery, I felt a kind of vertigo – as if I'd prepared my body to step down two inches and found myself plunging four feet instead. I felt as if a dwarf or an elf or a mermaid had just come to life in the yellowing pages of this scrapbook. Mona's stories had been made real.

❧

Friday became my library day. Each week I took the elevator down to the second basement to pick up a cart full of Mona's papers. The cart bore the cardboard box I was currently sorting, along with a stack of partially completed files. I took the cart upstairs to "my" carrel and closed the door. From the box, I started taking out papers. I formed rough piles on the table. Prose: typed. Poetry: typed. Poetry: holographic (handwritten, in other words). Holographic notes and prose. Then there were Print Appearances, Business Correspondence, Personal Correspondence, Radio Scripts, Photographs. Before long, the piles overlapped. Sometimes, pure impatience caused me to grab a huge handful of pages, more than I knew what to do with, and I ended up shuffling them so roughly that the delicate paper threatened to crumble. Sometimes I sat with a single page in my hand, unable to decide where to set it down.

Sorting, I realised, is like editing. Sitting with all this paraphernalia, sifting it, piling it, reading it over again and again until you can feel the structure emerge, the skeleton beneath the skin. I was taking this inchoate pile of papers, everything that remained of my grandmother now that she was gone, and turning it into a story. Like editing, sorting is painful. There is so much activity in the mind while the body has to remain still. After a few hours in the study carrel, my attention dulled, wandered off, and had to be wrenched forcibly back again. Focus eluded me. I put something on a pile and instantly forgot where it was. I could not remember which pile was which. The room itself seemed to come alive in a mischievous and none-too-friendly way, and I imagined that papers were shuffling themselves, playing hide-and-seek. If I noticed a theme – say, correspondence with neighbours – I began a file on the top of the cart. Any attempt to put these files in order seemed fruitless, so I reconciled myself to remembering approximately where in the stack each file was, and leafing through it repeatedly until I found the right one. On Edna's advice, I also created some files which preserved the original arrangement of Mona's papers. Every so often, I would put a clump of papers into a file just as they were. I called this category, "Mona's Logic."

Sometimes I thought of all the boxes that remained in the basement and became so overwhelmed I lost my place. Then I had to put the day's papers back in the box and start again. I made rough notes as I went along, and tried to type them up in the form of a table on Friday evenings, but most of the time I didn't get the chance. My lists were maintained in scrawling handwriting, on the backs of drafts of essays for my courses at OISE. Sometimes

I forgot to take a pen or pencil, and had to scrounge one off the tables or borrow one from a weary librarian.

So many things had to be done over and over again. My first day, Edna gave me a package of the plastic envelopes called "sleeves" to store photographs in. I put all the pictures into short sleeves, but this left the longer pictures perilously sticking out at the ends. Then I discovered there were longer sleeves to be had, and transferred the larger photos into them. But I had already written names on the original sleeves. I had to cross them off, resulting in a mess of scribbling, and ink-stained hands. I now had room in the shorter sleeves for more photographs, but they were smudged with ink and crunchy with little flecks of dust.

Dust was everywhere. At the end of each day I ceremoniously gathered a pile of dust from the counter in the study carrel with a wet paper towel, swept it onto my hand and threw it in the garbage. The dust had sat in Mona's various apartments and gone into the boxes when she moved, settled on top of other dust from other apartments and traveled with her to her next place. The dust was, in fact, flecks of Mona's skin. Molecules of Mona surrounded me in the study carrel. Her familiar perfume was on my hands when I left the place. Sometimes, I found one of Mona's white hairs. Sometimes, I found one of my own white hairs.

⚜

That spring, *The Globe and Mail* printed an obituary of Mona. A few weeks later the paper called to let me know a Judge Ferguson had been trying to get hold of me. Judge Edra Ferguson. And she wanted to talk to me about my grandmother.

Judge Ferguson seemed to be expecting my call. "Oh yes," a deep voice boomed, when I identified myself. "At *The Globe* they refused to pass on your number to me. Ridiculous. But I played along. You will meet me next Thursday for lunch at my club."

Winter was supposedly over, but it was still very cold outside. I could not figure out how to dress. I ended up – though I wasn't sure why – in an old wool suit I'd bought at a rummage sale, ten years before. It was ill-fitting and out of style, and its tan colour made me look anaemic. In the freezing rain, I clumped along St George Street in my heavy, slush-resistant boots until I found the University Women's Club, a renovated mansion set back from the street. I felt awkward and downtrodden and wished I had found some excuse to stay home.

In the entranceway, I removed my boots and crammed my feet into a pair of pumps. They were flat, like all my shoes, but tighter than anything I usually wore. They hurt. I heard a commanding voice from the shadows, somewhere to the right of me: "In here!" I turned and saw Edra, seated in a deep chair in the lounge, surrounded by packages and paper bags. Her legs were solidly planted, hands on her knees – a cross between Lady Bracknell and Gertrude Stein. She looked me up and down. "We'll go upstairs in a minute," she said. "First, you may comb your hair."

I did my best to tame the frizzy mess, and returned to stand awkwardly by Edra's chair. Now what? Edra made her way with only a small amount of difficulty to her feet. Suddenly, I knew what to do. I gathered Edra's packages and arranged myself a little behind her, extending my arm but not quite committing to the gesture, in case she didn't need – or want – the help. "That's right," she said, "Just as if I was your grandmother." She slipped her arm into mine, and we walked up the grand staircase together. "We're going to understand each other very well, you and I," Edra pronounced.

The place was filled with couches and easy chairs in delicate shades of peach and pink. It smelled faintly – but only faintly – of cigarette smoke. The sound of soft conversation filled the air as the members met briefly on the stairways or settled with their coffee cups in small groups. Most of them seemed to be over sixty, and each wore a badge stating her university affiliation. Despite my merciless shoes, I felt soothed in this atmosphere. To Edra and her contemporaries, it was clear that we women need to gather in a room of our own, sometimes, and close the door.

Edra was a native of St Thomas, Ontario, a town just south of London. This was where Mona had moved when she left her parents' London home to become a newspaper reporter. Edra was a graduate of Alma College, an elegant finishing school on the edge of St Thomas. The school was designed to be an educational United Nations, where girls from all countries could receive their high school matriculation as well as a thorough grounding in the arts. An amphitheatre on the grounds provided the setting for plays and presentations of poetry. Edra went on to become an alderwoman in St Thomas, and later, a judge.

Edra told me she was ninety-three. At first, I raised my voice when speaking to her, but she immediately set me straight. "My dear," she said, "I may have let you carry my packages upstairs, but I'm not deaf." The considerable

volume of her speech was not a sign of failed hearing, but of a life-long habit
of taking charge. First things first: she handed me a form she had created,
with spaces for the names of my parents, grandparents, and my own education and religious affiliation. She inquired about my situation. I'd gone back
to school, I told her, to study philosophy. (She sighed.) I'd started my own
editing business. (She brightened.) I had a boyfriend, but we had no plans to
marry. (She nodded.)

"Older man?"

"Yes."

She looked me up and down. "Good. And your parents?"

"My dad had a stroke. He can't talk any more. And mother's in the hospital a lot. That's well ... it takes quite a bit of time."

Edra rolled her eyes. "Brothers? Sisters?"

"Well, my sister lives in Europe. She has a little boy, you know, and I don't
have children, so ..."

Edra cut in, "Family doormat, hm?"

"Well I wouldn't put it quite that -"

"Now listen." She leaned toward me confidentially. "Don't give up your
life for your mother. There are do-gooders in this world. Leave it to them.
And you need to get to know the right people. Join the University Women's
Club. We need young members."

Lunch was salmon, prepared without butter or breading, to accommodate my numerous allergies. Edra offered me a glass of wine too, but I
declined. "I don't drink much, and never in the afternoons," I told her.

"Hmph. Did Mona drink?"

"Oh yes. Yes, she drank. But she quit, finally."

"At what age?"

"Seventy-five or so."

"Ha! What did she drink?"

"Um ... whiskey and milk, mostly."

"What kind?"

"Of whiskey? Canadian Club. It was Canadian Club, as I remember."

"Well, it's no wonder she had to quit. I drank nothing but Irish whiskey
and I kept going until I was ninety."

Edra had invited a number of club members here to meet me. All were
natives of St Thomas, and all knew Mona when she was barely out of her
teens. I was stunned to learn that there were people still alive who remembered Mona in those days, and that they were within easy reach. In spite of

Mona's constant storytelling, I had always had a sense of being cut off, as if by an ocean, from her past. Mona's old friends began to appear at the door of the small room which Edra had booked for the afternoon. It was clear to me, now, that she had set up this meeting so that I could gather information. I had not even brought along a notebook. It was enough to fit all those hours of sorting into my life. Surely I could not be expected to write Mona's story, on top of everything else.

Edra looked at me with disapproval when I failed to take out a pen and paper. I sighed, and inwardly shrugged off the glance like a defiant teenager. Outwardly, I smiled sweetly at the roomful of women. They were well turned-out and trim, and seemed untroubled by their narrow, high-heeled shoes. I felt dowdy and rumpled in their presence. I felt I must be missing something. Some strength or vibrancy which they seemed to radiate, despite being so much older than me. *Maybe it's just the way life unfolds,* I comforted myself, *maybe they felt downtrodden in their forties, too.* I remembered an early morning conversation with my grandmother.

"How are you?" she had asked.

"Tired," was my inevitable reply.

"Me too," she said, "But not like you, not *streetcar* tired. I remember that feeling when I was your age."

The women remembered growing up with Graham, my grandfather, the nicest and best looking man in St Thomas. When Mona moved into town, she simply snatched him away. I probed for a hint of rivalry, but there was none. "Oh, Mona was a lovely person. Always so bright and full of fun." They remembered Catherine (or Cocky, as she was called), Graham's younger sister. When my grandparents married she was still a child. She was lonely, and self-conscious on account of her thick glasses. But Catherine was a beauty, with a great deal of musical talent. Mona instantly took her sister-in-law under her wing. "Mona was so kind. Everyone warmed to her immediately."

The group turned to reminiscing about people I had never met. I sat back in my chair and let the conversation waft by. My feet, I realised, had stopped bothering me. I felt invigorated yet relaxed, as if I'd accepted the glass of wine Edra had offered. I imagined the strength of these women seeping into me: whatever had allowed them to get through *their* forties, fifties, sixties – and beyond. That strength had something to do with their cheerfulness, their way of putting the best face on things. The self-doubt and agony of my work in the archives seemed unimportant, all of a sudden. Why was I always digging for hidden motives, unpleasant secrets? Why not live on the surface for a while? That afternoon, for twenty minutes or so, I did.

ৎৎ

Of course, I went on to write Mona's story. Maybe it was that afternoon with Edra and her friends that I decided to take it on. Maybe it was a year later, when I heard that my aunt Catherine was terminally ill. I ran into Edra on St George Street around that time, and told her the sad news I had just learned. Edra sniffed. "She may be sick," she said, "but she can still talk. Go and interview her. Go up there right away." I didn't. I called Catherine on impulse one day, just to say hello, and she died within the week, leaving my many questions unanswered. I realised then that there was no one else left to tell Mona's story, to me or to anyone else. It was up to me. And leaving the story untold was out of the question.

The Vicissitudes of Life

Mona's ancestors on both sides had immigrated from England and Scotland and settled in the area around London, Ontario. Mona was born in Saskatchewan, though, on the cold winter night of 25 January 1908. The third child of Alfred and Ellen McTavish and the only girl, the newborn Mona Helen was placed in the oven to keep her alive. According to Mona, her birth date determined her destiny. She came into the world on Robbie Burns' day, and her father declared then and there that she would become a poet.

The family had moved west in 1907, because Alfred had been having trouble with his lungs and the dry prairie air was thought to be good for respiratory illnesses. There were already two boys: Howard, born in 1903, and Douglas, two years younger. The first stop was Prince Albert, where Mona was born and spent the first two or three years of her life. Though it had been incorporated as a city in 1904, Prince Albert was still rural at that time. Mona's first home consisted of a two-story, four-bedroom house and a barn with a cow. Another small house with a lattice fence also stood on the property. There was a wooden sidewalk in front, and water was delivered by horse-drawn wagon.[1] By 1911, the family had moved to a homestead about eight miles south of Melfort. Alfred had been a dry-goods merchant all his working life, but listed himself as a farmer on that year's census. This was the first and only time he ever did so. Homesteading seems to have held a strong appeal for the McTavish family; Alfred's younger sister Nettie and her husband had already moved to Saskatchewan, and saw a lot of success as homesteaders. All told, they "proved up" six different homesteads in the province and eventually became successful land speculators.[2] Next came Alfred, and then his brother Will, along with his wife and five daughters. One of these, Ruby, ten years older than Mona, corresponded with her all her life.

Some work had already been done on the homestead when Mona's family arrived. Their lives were rugged nonetheless. This was a matter of some pride to Mona and her brother Douglas when they got older. Douglas's son – also named Douglas – recalled this in a letter to me.

My dad would often tell tales of himself and Howard encountering [a] bear on the way to or from school. The climax of the story always had Howard driving off the bear with a shot from Alf's rifle, which the boys religiously carried to and from school every day. To this Mona would always respond that nothing of the sort ever happened and that mother never would have allowed the boys to take the rifle to school in the first place. My dad's immediate retort was always: how would you (Mona) know, you were just a baby, mother never let you out of the house. This ended any discussion as they silently glared at each other across the room, self satisfied that each had popped the other's bubble but frustrated to have been exposed a fraud themselves.[3]

Ruby wrote a memoir of her experiences on her own family's homestead. Like Alfred's, it had been worked by one other set of residents before they took over. It gives a good sense of what Mona's parents would have felt the first time they saw their land. Ruby's family, with their possessions loaded onto a cavalcade of wagons, traveled to the new property. "We had a large lake to cross before reaching our destination. Before long we came to it, and were slightly apprehensive when we saw such an expanse of what looked to us rather thin ice, with water lying here and there. The trail across was built up high and looked as if it was still being used so we slowly proceeded. Half way over we could see Dad out on the hill waving us on so all was well. His helpers had assisted him in setting up the stove and cramming what had come out of a six-room house into a two-room log cabin. Of course there was the attic, minus partition and reached by a ladder nailed to the wall."[4] Mona herself remembered the frigid winters of her early years, the dusty, sweet-smelling barn, the animals whose fur she loved to bury her face in. She spent

An early snapshot of Mona on the homestead: holding
her own among a crop of unknown boys.

her days in the company of animals and growing things, the cycle of life playing out around her. The prairies stretched out in every direction, offering her
wide vistas to gaze at, and plenty of room to run.

In April 1913 Alfred was given the title to his homestead, but the family
soon left Saskatchewan. Alfred's father had been a farmer, and he may have
taken some pleasure in homesteading. Ellen, on the other hand, came from
an area of Ontario where towns were close together, easily reachable by both
rail and road. Shipping on nearby Lake Erie ensured a flow of commerce
and culture from the United States. Life on the farm must have seemed terribly harsh to her. She would have longed not only for her family but for
Southern Ontario itself, with its well-stocked main streets, its brick houses,
and the genteel parties where she could wear clothes made from fine, im-
ported fabrics. By 1915, when Mona was seven, the McTavishes were back
in London again, though they retained ownership of the Melfort property
until the 1960s.[5]

Their first home was on Pall Mall Street, in an old and stately district of
London. In 1920 they moved a few streets away, to 490 Princess Avenue.
This was the home of most of Mona's childhood memories. London has its

share of splendid mansions, and the McTavish houses were not of this caliber, but they were capacious and handsome, built from the yellow brick which is often used in the region. Both houses were designed and built by Ellen's father, James North Howard, who, along with his brother William, was responsible for many buildings in the Exeter and London area. In addition to being a stonemason and contractor, James North Howard was a captain in the reserves, part of a long tradition of military service in the family.[6]

The Howards were a prestigious family. James ran a stage-coach from London to Exeter, and owned a great deal of property. Mona remembered visiting his house in Exeter and standing on the staircase, enthralled by the beautiful colours shining through the stained glass window above. James was a severe man, well aware of his own importance, and he had little time for Mona. If she approached him quietly in his office, though, he would give her a sweet, take her on his knee, and show her the plans on his desk. For all his severity, James had a sense of humour and was a bit of a showman. Each time one of their building projects was completed, James and William would stand on their heads (one by one, not together!) on top of the chimney.[7]

Mona was surrounded by dashing and powerful male figures in her youth. Her grandfather was one, so was her father, and so, too, was her brother Howard, known as "Mook." Strong, athletic, and five years Mona's senior, Mook was her protector from school bullies. Douglas, the middle child in the family, did not inspire the same kind of hero-worship. Mona told stories of how she would defend Douglas when the other children teased him about wearing glasses. In pictures, he is reedy and tall, with an intellectual air. Glasses notwithstanding, Douglas was vigorous and healthy, and enjoyed a successful career in banking. This did not count for much as far as Mona was concerned. Mona's taste ran to hard-drinking, flamboyant men, with deep pockets and a willingness to indulge her every whim. A modest and careful man like Douglas was the butt of her ridicule.

Mona worshipped her father, Alfred. In her stories, he was kinder and more nurturing than her severe mother, though other accounts make him out to be a hard-driving businessman.[8] Although the McTavish family was established and respectable, they were farmers, and not of the Howards' class. Marrying Ellen was a social coup for Alfred, and no doubt he felt he had to make her life especially comfortable on account of this. I only heard one story from the early years of my great-grandparents' marriage. Before their move to Saskatchewan, The McTavishes lived in Galt, Ontario. According to Mona, their next-door neighbours were the Pearson family, and Ellen

often invited young Lester over to sample her baking. Mona claimed that
Canada's future prime minister got his lisp from politely trying to chew his
way through Mrs McTavish's rock-hard cookies.

Alfred and his brother worked together in the dry goods business. They
had their own stores in London and St Mary's, and would also buy up the
stock of stores that were going out of business and hold liquidation sales.[9]
For a time, Alfred was employed by Chapman and Sons in London as a fabric buyer. This meant he traveled to Europe by sea. He brought back lovely
fabrics, which Ellen had made into dresses. When he left the job, the "boys"
at Chapmans' bought him a gold-tipped cane inscribed with his name on
the handle.

The driven Alfred was a distant figure in Mona's life, and she romanticized
him. Her mother – safer and more dependable – was the receptacle for all her
negative feelings. She portrayed Ellen as judgmental, distant, and cold, though
unquestionably beautiful. But others had a different impression of Ellen.
Douglas's son said she was aristocratic and serious, but cold? Never. She
adored her children and grandchildren, and protected them fiercely.[10]

Ellen's history was dark, and she never fully left it behind. She had grown
up in material comfort, but her household was steeped in sadness. Her
mother, Esther Atkinson, had given birth to numerous children, of whom
only four survived into adulthood. This was a time when many children died
before the age of six and according to a macabre custom, their names were
often used again for subsequent offspring. Thus, Mona's mother was named
after another Ellen Jane Howard, who died only a year before she was born.
As a small child, she would have visited the cemetery and seen her own name
inscribed on the family tombstone!

Still more losses followed. Ellen's mother died at the age of forty while
giving birth to yet another child. Ellen was about ten years old at the time.
James North Howard married again, to Mary Ellen Brimacombe, in 1889,
but Ellen had to get through her early adolescence on her own. (She got along
well with Mary Ellen, and the siblings who came afterwards, but there may
have been a few awkward moments at first. Her new stepmother was only
six years older than herself!) Some twelve years later, Ellen's favourite sister,
Mary Emaline, died of cancer at the age of about twenty. Mona once wrote
to her brother Douglas about this, saying that Howard had been a baby at
the time. According to Mona, Ellen had been so grief-stricken by her sister's
death she had "lost her nurse," though the problem corrected itself soon af-
terward.[11] The weight on young Ellen must have been enormous.

Once they were settled in Ontario, Alfred bought a cottage in the smart resort town of Port Stanley, about twenty-five miles south of London and an easy commute on the local "L&PS" railway line. There is a photo of Mona in front of the cottage, flanked by her two brothers. A handmade sign nailed to the porch reads "Belvedere, 1919." With her hair piled on top of her head in a bow, the eleven-year-old Mona is lean, athletic, and unquestionably cute. Radiating mischief, she is the type of child who promises to offer her parents a wild ride when she gets into her teens.

Mona's stories of her teenage years were mostly set in Port Stanley. She spoke often of the halcyon summers the family spent there: days of swimming until her skin was as wrinkled as a prune, and nights where she snuck out to dances or sat on the beach with friends. Youthful summers were depicted as a time of heightened experience in Mona's stories, something like the war, except that these memories were carefree, full of possibilities and unmarred by loss. One of Mona's boxes contained a photograph album given to her by her brother Howard in 1925.[12] Titles had been scrolled at the bottom of each picture in Mona's handsome, extravagant backhand: "Hula Lu," "The Inseparables," "Sis." Her friends had nicknames like Ginger and Gibby and Tuck. Mona spent that summer at the centre of a pack of handsome and laughing youth.

Port Stanley was a fashionable destination in the twenties. Easily reached from both London and Cleveland, it boasted a dance hall, The Stork Club, as well as a casino. Bands like Guy Lombardo's Royal Canadians headlined at the Stork Club, which remained in business until the 1970s. Mona told of picking her way at night down the steep slope from the cottage with her dancing shoes in one hand. She was drawn, she told me, by jazz, a new and scandalous kind of music that was being played at the clubs. Her behaviour may have worried her mother, but in truth, Mona's wildness never got her into serious danger. After all, her big brothers were always at the dances with her.

Mona's shy friend Margaret Steven also appears in the photographs. Shoulders hunched, eyes downcast so that her curls fall in her face, Marg hides a little behind Mona in a line-up of bathing beauties, kneeling on the sand. Marg later became a writer herself, and the two remained friends until Marg's death in 1991. The Mona of these pictures is androgynous. Her hair is cropped short and she is athletic, narrow in the hips and broad in the shoulders. She is often surrounded by boys doing headstands and piling around her in different configurations. Unlike Marg, Mona proudly shows off her body, particularly her spectacular legs. There is a handsome boy with her in several pictures, but one image of the boy alone has an "X" marked across the face. "*C'est fini*," reads Mona's note on the back. "By my own hand."

By the time these photographs were taken, Mona was already thinking of herself as a writer. She was confident not only in her good looks but in her talent as well. From an early age, Mona had sent poetry to newspapers both locally and in the United States. She often told the story of how she had won ten dollars in a contest in *The Windsor Star*, and concluded at that point that she was a full-fledged professional. I have never been able to find the prize-winning poem, though she kept numerous clippings of her publications. Also during Mona's high school years, *The London Advertiser* published her English translation of Heine's "*Die Lorelei*."[13]

In the early decades of the century, *The Globe and Mail* ran a regular feature called "The Circle of Young Canada," which included drawings, verse, and music by youth between the ages of seven and twenty. Mona was an enthusiastic contributor. For her publications in *The Globe and Mail*, Mona took on the pseudonym "Garthe." (Sometimes she made it Garthé, adding an extra, exotic-sounding syllable.) The editors included comments after many of the poems, as if they were her teachers at school. After "Coquette," written when Mona was eighteen, one editor made public her faith in her gifts.

> Fair muse – would you forsake me heartlessly,
> Because I clip your wings to earn my food –
> And leave me mute and voiceless and afraid
> When phrases will not come to cloak a mood?
>
> Ah! Muse, if you but knew the pangs I feel
> When I am forced to check your shining flight –
> You would not starve my soul for lovely words
> And plunge my spirit starkly into night!

"We like this verse, Mona. Its originality and technical perfection are both admirable. You seldom send a verse nowadays that is not first-class, so we hope you will contribute with increasing frequency."[14] She also sent silhouettes of flowers and pixies, drawn with no small amount of skill.

In 1928, Dr Aletta Marty edited an anthology called *Creative Young Canada*, which was drawn from the past ten years of contributions to The Circle. Mona's work was featured, with seven poems and three drawings included. (This was more than any other contributor.)[15] In its review of the book, *The Chatelaine* magazine commended Mona's poem "Rain" as "disarmingly lovely."[16] The book's two introductions, one by The Circle's editor, Nancy Durham, and the other by Marty herself, give a good sense of the climate in which Mona launched her career. Durham wrote that the practice of taking pseudonyms was helpful to shy youngsters who "have breathed their literary ambitions to the editors and have asked protection against the withering scorn of family and friends who mistook the creative urge for foolish egotism."[17] Durham herself wrote under the pseudonym of Agnes Delamoure. Dr Marty wrote that The Circle was the outgrowth of a new educational philosophy in Canada, one which encouraged self-expression rather than rote learning. Her predictions about its outcome were cautious, however. "There is no intention of suggesting that those whose names appear are embryo poets and artists, or musical prodigies," she wrote. She did hope, however, that "those who try to thus express themselves, will eventually form the nucleus of an appreciative public."[18] Marty died a year after the book appeared, so she never got the chance to see Mona defy her expectations. Nor did she learn of the later success of "Circleites" Margaret Avison and Marjorie Pickthall, or of Charles Goldhamer (aka Ensign), who became a war artist.

Mona's expressiveness and her willingness to share her creative efforts set her apart from many of her classmates. She was – albeit modestly – in the vanguard, and she reveled in this image all her life. She was by no means alone, though. The Circle's pages were full of works by young women like Mona. She never mentioned her affiliation with The Circle, or the collection which had made so much of her early efforts. Instead, she spoke only of her relatively unimportant prize from *The Windsor Star*. Surely she did not make a conscious decision to conceal her affiliation with The Circle, but I could not help feeling I'd been thrown off the trail when I saw the exquisite anthology, containing page after page of Mona's poetry. This was an accomplishment to tell your grandchildren about. Yet Mona had not mentioned it.

She may have wanted to distance herself from The Circle, not only because it revealed she was just one of many promising poets, but also because of its nationalistic bent. Mona's idol was not a local girl. She saw herself as kin to Edna St Vincent Millay, whose work was well known by the late twenties. Like Millay, Mona cultivated the persona of a plucky gamin, beautiful, high strung and impulsive, but sensitive and compassionate as well. She believed her role as a poet was to throw herself upon the world and experience everything life had to offer, then respond in her own unique voice.

But Mona was a far cry from Millay. She might have cavorted openly in a bathing suit with other teenagers, but she was still a middle-class girl, growing up in wholesome southern Ontario. As a young woman, Millay explored various Sapphic love affairs, whereas Mona had an experience tame enough to be recorded in the local newspaper. She was out in the family car with her friend Marg one night. They stopped at a scenic and secluded place, where they sat with heads inclined, composing poetry together. A policeman thought they were a young couple "spooning," and gave them a stern warning. The incident was covered in *The London Advertiser* under the headline "But that Old Moon Kept on Shining Just the Same."[19]

Echoing Millay's "Renascence," Mona wrote of nature and its deep effect on her. Her work was very much in the style of its time, a style which literary scholar Munro Beattie has described in excoriating terms:

> [T]he versifiers of this arid period [the 1920s], having nothing to say, kept up a constant jejune chatter about infinity, licit love, devotion to the Empire, death, Beauty, God, and Nature. Sweet singers of the Canadian out-of-doors, they peered into flowers, reported on the flittings of the birds, discerned mystic voices in the wind, descried elves among the poplars. They insisted upon being seen and overheard in poetic postures: watching for the will-o'-the-wisp, eavesdropping on "the forest streamlet's noonday song," lying like a mermaid on a bed of coral, examining a bird's nest in winter, fluting for the fairies to dance or "wandering through some silent forest's aisles."[20]

Beattie might have had a poem of Mona's in front of him when he wrote those lines! His criticism shows just how radically poetic tastes changed in the course of the 20th century. But even though her style would later fall out of fashion, the young Mona was considered very promising in her own time.

It may be on account of this early success that Mona chose not to attend university. It was certainly not for lack of ability. She was a brilliant young woman, with high marks in all her subjects except math, and while her father was not at the top of the social ladder in well-heeled London, he could certainly have put Mona through university. I consulted Edra, who answered that at the time, university was considered a pathway to teaching, and Mona was not attracted to teaching. As well, if a girl lived in residence she would be subject to a lot of rules and regulations. This, Mona would have found intolerable.

Mona was not the only young woman of the time pursuing a career. Numerous girls who came of age in the twenties managed to go a long way in a man's world – including Edra herself. Nonetheless, there was a pre-scribed path, a rigid set of expectations which they had to resist in order to follow their dreams. Edra told me, "You were expected to be staying home, doing anything to amuse yourself until you got married. Then you had no say at all – and if you had money he got your money ... [The husband would] expect his wife to wait on him ... Girls would just get married when they were young to the first boy that came along. They were very stodgy, they didn't know anything. They played bridge. You didn't have bingo in those days but to socialize you probably went to church, and it was likely a church group that was raising money for something or other, and you would make cookies, and try to sell them."[21]

Mona wanted to escape this destiny. She also wanted financial independence, and was well aware that she would need to take on some kind of writing that offered immediate rewards. Mona spoke with contempt of her penny-pinching brother, Doug, and his obsession with money, but money was an important value in the McTavish household. To earn a living meant you were grown up – a "real" person. To earn a living from writing meant that you were a "real" writer. At eighteen, Mona probably did not think through the complexities of the issue, but she did know how to move in a direction that would make her feel strong.

She may also have sensed that to take the route of a university education would cause upheaval within her family, and within herself. No one else in the family had been to university. To this day, a difference in education can separate a person from her roots, even when the family remains on good terms. Going to university means initiation into a new culture, a new way of using language. For Mona, the stress of this division might have been too great, and not worth the dubious rewards. Mona finished her grade twelve matriculation at Central Collegiate in London. According to her, she was unpopular among her teachers, except for one or two who appreciated her talent and were willing to spend extra time with her. Her teachers' reaction does not surprise me, seeing her school pictures. She stares frankly at the camera, her eyes full of challenge. She's smart, and she knows it, and anyone who wants to tell her what to do is going to have to win her respect the hard way. She liked to tell the story of how she was asked to do a series of exercises in gym class. She found them ridiculous, so she sat down on the floor and flatly refused. The teacher approached, ready to reprimand her, but Mona simply gave the teacher "the Gould look" and the teacher retreated. (It was never clear to me how she managed to display the ancestral trait of a family she had not yet married into, but such details never stopped Mona from telling a good story.)

In an era when obedience and conformity were expected, especially from girls, Mona's attitude must have unnerved her teachers. In the compositions which she saved, the handwriting is tidy, the sentence structure, impeccable. She received marks in the eighties, but not a word of praise. On one composition the teacher wrote, "Notice how many unnecessary commas you have used," and docked her two marks.[22] Mona declared herself "allergic" to math, but her grade twelve education left her well prepared for the life of a writer. She could acquit herself in both French and German. She knew Canadian, European, and ancient history, and was familiar with all the plays of Shakespeare, even the ones rarely produced. Most importantly, she had an ability to tackle any text from the ancient to modern, comprehend it quickly, and write cogently on any subject.

The last year or two of formal education disappeared from Mona's history. She used to tell me that she dropped out of school at sixteen and begged her father for the chance to become a journalist. Like so many of the stories I grew up with, this proved to be untrue. Yet – as I would discover again and again as I worked my way through her papers – the reality was much more interesting. In her boxes I found evidence that she graduated from high school, and did not start trying to get a job until she was almost nineteen. A letter from Nancy Durham of *The Globe and Mail*, dated 1927, shows that Mona wrote to her mentor at The Circle inquiring about employment. In her reply, Durham apologized for a long delay. She sympathized with Mona's ambitions to be a journalist, saying Mona had "the germ," and conceding that "the late Dr Macdonald used to say, 'If one has the journalistic germ nothing but journalism satisfies.'" However, Durham counseled Mona to avoid a full-fledged journalistic career, at least for the time being. "I may say,

Garthe, that I think your talents point to more literary work than the daily newspaper affords. I would hate to see you get into the incessant grind of a big journal. You would not have nearly enough time for reading and at your age you should read, read, read. Then, too, your imagination would get so punctured that it would cease to function, and, – well, you would never make a name for yourself that way."[23] After reminding Mona of her youthfulness and literary sensitivity, Durham made an odd statement: "Death, marriage and all the other vicissitudes of life have to be taken into consideration ... I would not worry about getting on The Globe or any other big daily. Let Fate take its course and gradually you'll find yourself in the places where you can best develop."[24]

Was she predicting that Mona would get married soon, and that her journalistic ambitions would be short-lived? Mona was an attractive girl from a "good" family. If a career in journalism was only for those who could not find a husband, then Mona was not destined to enter the profession. But Durham may also have been suggesting that marriage might afford Mona the financial security – and thus the leisure – that a poet needs. She wrote, "I sincerely hope your financial position will always enable you to flee the journalistic ruts."[25] She recommended that Mona contact a Mr Rossie to see if she could find work on his small daily, *The London Advertiser*. This would afford Mona a range of experience without the long and irregular hours that she would have to cope with on *The Globe and Mail*. Mona followed Durham's advice, and got a job as a "stringer" for the social pages of *The London Advertiser*. Her job was to cover parties and dances, and write about businesses in nearby St Thomas. She would also travel south to Port Stanley on the L&PS to write about the boats that came in and out of the port. Illustrious people took those boats, and their presence in town had to be recorded: what they wore, where and with whom they were seen. On one occasion, Gloria Swanson was a passenger on one of the ships, and this gave rise to Mona's first front-page story.

Mona never mentioned Nancy Durham – either in stories of her early poetic development, or in connection with her journalistic career. In Mona's version, her father introduced her to Mr Rossie, who immediately hired her to work on *The London Advertiser*. She presented this job as a *fait accompli* arranged between two powerful men on her behalf. This was typical of a pattern I was to discern in all Mona's accounts of her professional life. She liked to present herself as a girl whose talent was noticed by powerful men,

*Nothing but journalism
satisfies.* The young
reporter in pursuit of
a story, about 1927.

who then simply offered her jobs. She never had to struggle to get attention,
nor was the influence of women upon her career ever taken into account.

Before long, Mona moved on to *The St Thomas Times-Journal* as editor
of the women's pages. Here again she was unusual, but not unique. Marjory
Lang, in *Women Who Made the News*, has written about the young women
who became editors and writers for the women's sections of various local
newspapers. These pages had numerous functions, one of which was to interpret the new world of consumer goods and household technology for the
homemaker, and to help her find her way amidst ever-changing expectations
of grooming and good looks.[26] The writers for this section often found them-

selves in the role of advisers. Mona took to this job immediately, and began dispensing advice like a matron.

To the Woman Who Would Be Smart We Say
"Beware of Furbelows."

This is going to be a plea for simplicity! Now that we have settled that, we will get down to business in earnest. Did you ever notice that the most artistic and stunning effects are always achieved through the spare use of garnishes, trimmings, "doo-dads," and general furbishing? Quality and not quantity always counts, to quote an old and frayed saying.[27]

Ironically, as Lang points out, the young women who did these jobs were mostly teenagers, who had never run households of their own.[28] Mona, at nineteen, was by no means skilled at traditionally feminine tasks. She was messy and scatterbrained, showed little interest in cooking, and none at all in sewing. Her father used to say that if it were not for the invention of the safety pin, she would go naked. So in essence, this early writing demanded that she adopt a fictional persona.

The women's pages also afforded Mona her first experience of writing advertising. Lang writes that the women's pages served as pseudo-advertising vehicles. Although newspapers were ostensibly free to say what they wanted, they still benefited from mentioning the services and goods of local businesses. This was the dawn of a kind of advertising/journalism fusion in which an informed consumer would tour the shops and report on what was available. These sections later grew into whole magazines, such as *Town Talk* and *Gossip*.[29] Mona was ideally suited to this role. She had a breathless excitability about life in general, combined with a natural eloquence. In her columns, she observed the latest trends in dressing and decorating, and rhapsodized over the wares that were available in local stores. "The modern home brags of kitchens that shout with gay colors," she wrote – flagrantly abandoning her dedication to simplicity – "bathrooms tiled in pastel greens or daffodil yellow or 'orchidacous' mauve."[30]

Lang also writes of the dilemma of a journalist on the social pages "the task of society reporting combined high prestige in one context with low status in another. It demanded the best social connections and involved daily contact with the leaders of local society, yet in terms of status in journalism, few departments ranked lower."[31] It must have been a rare prize to find someone like Mona, a smart, enthusiastic, single girl who would be able and will-

ing to work full-time. But Mona, being a newcomer, was out of touch with
the St Thomas social order. Edra told me she found an ingenious way of getting around the problem. She made the acquaintance of Gladys Elliot, the
spinster daughter of a family that was well regarded in the area. Gladys
would have liked to get out more, but was expected to stay home with her
aging parents. Mona would call Gladys with questions about which events
to focus on, whose cooking to praise, which dresses to describe in greater detail than others. Gladys would fill in the necessary tactical information, and
would vicariously enjoy accounts of the local goings-on. The arrangement
worked will for both of them.[32] Mona's own account of the relationship with
Gladys was different. According to some notes for a lecture which Mona
gave in 1946, Gladys was the editor of the social pages. When she took a trip
to Europe, Mona was asked to step into her job.[33]

Mona's stories of her initiation into the life of a journalist were full of
high drama. She told of her struggles to win respect among the tough journalists on the paper. They allotted her no desk space, she said, so she claimed
a counter in the entrance hall, and wrote her copy on a portable typewriter
there, standing up. (In Port Stanley, the chosen office was the ticket booth of
the railway station.) It is hard to imagine what sort of tough journalists
would be employed by The St. Thomas Times Journal in 1927, but I love to
picture them trying to get some work done alongside their headstrong and
vivacious new colleague. She said that they tried to frighten her off newspaper work. In one of her favourite stories, there was a murder in Cleveland,
and the male journalists invited her to travel there by boat in the middle of
the night to see "the stiff." She didn't back down from the challenge, but
kept her eyes closed the whole time she was in the room with the body.

⁂

Mona's early newspaper work required her to live in St Thomas, and her
father insisted that she board with a respectable family. This family was the
Goulds. Graham Gould and his much younger sister Catherine (Cocky)
lived with their widowed mother, Ethel. The family owned a department
store. When I asked Edra Ferguson about her impression of the Goulds she
answered, "They had a social position to maintain, but not much income."[34]
With Herbert Gould's death in 1926, the family had fallen on hard times.
A series of managers was hired for the store, but it was eventually sold
(though it is not clear when). In any case, finances in the household were

strained, and Ethel had to take in boarders to meet her expenses. She was also a drinker who left her daughter to fend for herself much of the time. Somehow, Catherine was able to attend Alma College, however. It could be that she received a scholarship, but perhaps her education was simply given a high priority in the house. Graham's life was not so sheltered. He was just eighteen when he became the man of the house. Within the next year, Mona arrived on the scene.

Mona told me that when she arrived in St Thomas, she took ten-year-old Catherine under her wing. Mona took her to dances in the evenings and even to work. And it was to Mona that Catherine turned when she needed frank information about growing up. Mona found the prudery of the time ridiculous, even cruel, and was determined to spare Catherine the doubts and fears that she herself had experienced because of her own mother's vague explanations. Mona continued in the role of surrogate mother to Catherine for many years to come. At Catherine's wartime wedding, Mona proudly presided as Matron of Honour.[35]

Years later, I visited my great-aunt Catherine in the house in north-western Ontario where she had settled with her husband, Frank McConachie. The house was small, like a winterized cottage, and scrupulously clean. Their two daughters worried about them, getting older and living so far from any town, but they loved the place. He had his spot at the window where he could look out at Eagle Lake; she, an electric keyboard that she played every day. I saw Catherine so seldom that I always forgot how comforted I felt in her company. In her seventies, she still had the wide-eyed prettiness I recognized from photographs taken in her youth. She and Uncle Frank spoke to each other gently and carefully, beaming like newlyweds.

On that visit, I discovered a side of Catherine's mother, Ethel, which had never been mentioned when I was growing up. I was impressed by two drawings of women which hung over the dining room table in their home. With heavy, piled-up hair, pale skin and idealized features, they resembled the Gibson Girl illustrations which were popular in the late 1800s. Their lines were confident and lyrical, the work of a practiced hand. "Who's the artist?" I asked, and learned that it had been Ethel. Mona often said that my father had inherited his artistic talent from James North Howard, who produced architectural drawings for his company. This was the first time I had heard there was a visual artist on Graham's side of the family.

Graham's musical talent was no secret, though. He played violin, and directed a band called The Collegians. Edra told me that The Collegians would play for dances at a local photography studio called Scott's. The place was frequently empty, so Scott and his wife made it available at no charge for local young people. Sometimes, if it were an important enough occasion, the band would even be paid.[36] A photograph in the local archives shows that the band also performed in the basement of Gould's store, which had a dance floor of its own.

By the time Mona met him, Graham was darkly handsome, sporting a shock of thick, black hair which stood back from his forehead like a matinée idol's. His ancestors had come from England, but Mona claimed he had Spanish blood, perhaps even Moorish. He was an enviable "catch" but Mona did not emphasize this. Nor did she speak at all of boarding with the Goulds. Instead, she told the story of meeting Graham at a dance. She is, of course, surrounded by admirers, and on this particular evening, is being pursued by a handsome and popular bore. She rests her head on the man's shoulder, mentally composing the article that she has to write for an early-morning deadline. Suddenly, she is startled to find that her partner has stopped dancing. Someone is cutting in! It is none other than the bandleader, Graham. He is barely taller than her, and clearly impecunious, but he is an artist, like her, and he captures her heart. She jettisons the bore, and Mona and Graham become inseparable for the next thirty years.

Mona often told me she had fought with her mother about her wedding plans. She said that she and Graham wanted to live together without getting married. But Ellen would not hear of this; her only daughter must have a church wedding, complete with a white dress, bridesmaids, and a fancy reception. Mona spoke bitterly of how her mother had forced her into a ceremony that meant little to her. This is how I heard that there had been disputes in the family about my grandparents' marriage. Mona never told the real story, but it was never a secret, either. Mona and Graham "had to get married." She became pregnant with Graham's child late in the fall of 1928.

She would have discovered her pregnancy a few months after *Creative Young Canada* appeared. At twenty years old, she had outgrown The Circle. It was time to leave Garthé behind.

Introducing Mona Gould

Mona and Graham married on 2 February 1929. Between their wedding and the birth of their son, the couple moved to Toronto, where Graham worked in the display department at Simpson's and took whatever musical gigs he could find. Their surroundings were shabby; their lives, probably unstable. They had at least two addresses in the course of those first few months. Yet Mona was still writing, and industriously sent her work to various publications. The results were encouraging. *Chatelaine*[1] published several of her poems, and she began a friendly correspondence with its editor, Byrne Hope Sanders, who invited her to send more work. This meant that Mona was making a significant contribution to the household income. In the 1930s, Mona's typical payment for a poem in *Chatelaine* was between five and ten dollars. During the same period, the average rental price in Canada was eighteen dollars a month, and a salesman's typical take-home pay, about twenty dollars a week.[2]

John was born in St Michael's hospital on 14 August 1929. Fifty-five years later, Mona wrote an account in her journal of the event.

Odd, feeling. Remembering back to Jon's <u>actual</u> <u>birth</u>, <u>day</u>! <u>So</u>, <u>long</u>, <u>ago</u>!

The leg cramps – the morning? <u>Waters</u> <u>break</u> – G, off to wk. Report to doc. He, saying – get <u>ready to come in, to-day</u> (Aug. 14th, 1929) Mom there, I washing blk. Long hair – sitting on bath towel on toilet

seat top – to sop up "waters" – feeling fine! Lacking, bag! Calling Simpson's to tell G to come (on the double!) Then cab down to St Mike's –
Pain every 5 min. By 5:30 or so, up elevator in wheel chair. Popt into
bed. Storm coming – very hot & humid! My hair wet as in rain – plas-
tered to my head. In labor til 2:30 a.m.! Taken down to Labor Room
to get me out of the thunder and lightening! Up on the narrow "Cru-
cifixion" steel table. Jesus on the cross – huge – at foot end – no pillow.
Feet, strapt down! Nurses in and out – crisp and totally sub-human –
One leant over & in false voice quipt "What are we hoping for" & I
shot back out of my agony. "I don't care if it's a doughnut, as long as
I get this over with." – Dr. Frank O'Leary (who had gone home for dinner –) came back – leaned over me & I literally rose up feet still in
straps – clutched the lapels of his suit & pleaded "Help me! Help me!
Do – something!"

Even then, he was stripping arm after arm out of his suit coat and
into the op. gown – nurse was holding and soon – mercifully – down
came the Ether cone & I went out on the dark tide –

Came TO in my bed – felt my girl-woman slim-ness (back!) Soon G.
was there & my son was laid in my arms! Blk hair – long fingers – long
narrow feet – blue, blue eyes & blk blk long long lashes – his wrists so
tiny his "Pa" could wear his birth identification round his thumb!)
"Gould, John, Male" – had arrived – I was filled with wonder & a joy
so deep it was to my toes! My son![3]

A few months later, the young family moved in with Mona's parents. It
is quite possible that this was planned all along, and that they spent the
winter in Toronto to stave off questions about Mona's "short" pregnancy.
Whatever the reason, the move to London was good for her writing. Despite
having an infant to look after, she remained as prolific as ever. In certain
ways this is not surprising. She was young and healthy, and had always had
plenty of energy. The excitement of having "arrived" – as a writer and as a
woman – probably carried her through whatever sleepless nights or dreary
days motherhood sent her way. More importantly, though, she had live-in
childcare. Mona's mother may have been stern, but she was always there,
looking after whatever practicalities Mona did not have time for. She was
also devoted to John. If Mona did not happen to be available, John always
had his grandmother to turn to for comfort.

Mona never expressed – in the stories she told, or in any of her writing – the kind of agony that Adrienne Rich describes in *Of Woman Born*: the conflict between a writer's need for solitude and silence, and the demands of her child. Either she hid these feelings masterfully or they did not arise. She seems to have had the ability to protect some central part of herself from the needs of others. Maybe she had this ability to begin with, or perhaps she developed it during that time. By the same token, Mona's relationship with writing did not demand that she withdraw from everyday activities. She was passionately committed to writing and took genuine pleasure in the process, but it did not pull her away from everyday life.

Mona wrote of romance and domestic happiness, of dusk and dawn and sunlight glinting on water. These poems were created and sent out in a rush of enthusiasm. They may not have been literary masterpieces, but she knew that a thriving market existed for the type of poetry she could readily produce. "To One Who Scoffed" is typical of what she wrote during this period.

If motherhood be bitter,
Then bitterness is sweet,
For where is there such loveliness
As little baby feet?

And where is there such winsomeness
As two small dimpled knees?
Ah, surely there is recompense
In treasures such as these![4]

❧

In pictures taken during John's first year, Mona appears to be thriving. Graham's expression in the pictures is more difficult to read. Though he smiles for the camera, his deep-set eyes are overshadowed by his brows. For all the maturity of his features, Graham's narrow chest is a reminder that he is only twenty-one years old. How did he feel about having a child? His own father had died early, leaving him with a tipsy mother and a sister barely entering her teens. He knew only too well the responsibilities of being head of a household. Where Mona found in motherhood an opportunity to be taken seriously, I suspect that Graham had been taken a little too seriously all his life.[5]

John's infancy over, the young family moved to St Thomas again, where Graham – unable to support his family playing violin for dances – found what work he could, in sales and in offices. He may have worked in the family business for a time, but whatever he did was not very profitable. These were the early years of the Depression. Mona was a housewife at this point. She never spoke of boredom or isolation, though they were hardly wealthy and life as a young mother in those days included such chores as washing cloth diapers, wringing them out one by one, and hanging them on the line. Mona's hatred of pettiness made her accept in silence what other women would have protested. She claimed years later that Graham was helpless around the house, but this was said with affection. She raised her son to be similarly impractical.

The role of adviser to homemakers was already familiar to Mona. Now that she was a homemaker herself, Mona wrote a short piece entitled, "Don't be TOO Good a Housekeeper!" "Far too many of you women, spend a whole lifetime absolutely immersed in housekeeping. From daylight till dark, you wend your busy way, scrubbing, washing, waxing and tidying ... and by the time your husband comes home in the evening, you're either too tired to be companionable ... or too cross. And no wonder! You haven't been able to relax ... to laugh about something trifling and amusing ... to feast your eyes on something beautiful and so you're faintly antagonistic and 'nervy' and anything but a helpmate. Don't you think it's a little too bad?"[6] Mona could never be accused of being too good a housekeeper. Her brother Doug used to tell the story of how – at one point during the Depression – he tried to supplement the diet of the young family. He thought they were all looking a little pale, so he purchased four steaks and presented them to Mona to cook for dinner. She boiled them.

Graham didn't mind. He had not chosen his wife for her domestic abilities. After all, he knew what he was getting into when they married. They had already lived together in Graham's family home for at least a year. In fact, they had only known each other that way, sharing their living quarters and – from their days of taking Catherine along on their dates – they had always had a younger person to take care of. In some ways, they were parents together from the start.

According to my father, Graham was the only one who could moderate Mona's extravagant storytelling. "Oh, come on Mona!" he'd say; "You made that up and you know it," and she would back down. By the time I got to know her, Graham was gone, and I remember her as being outrageously stubborn. She would stick to a story, no matter how inconsistent it was. She'd persist with utter determination and even bring the subject back into a conversation two or three weeks later, when you thought it had finally been laid to rest. Even concrete facts were not sacred to her. She had the idea, for instance, that I had grey eyes (they are brown). When I visited her, she would say that one of the reasons she loved me so much was that I had grey eyes. I was left tongue-tied by her complete self-assurance. What was there to say, if even physical evidence was not enough to convince her?

Graham was the only one with the force of personality to stand up to Mona's determination. Maybe he was the only one who loved her enough. Mona loved Graham, too. In those lean years, they prized each other and saw themselves as working together on a common project of learning. They would get stacks of books out of the library and read them together, or stay up late at night talking about literature and theatre, music and art. Mona used to say that she and Graham would not get any sleep at night, because they didn't want to miss any time together. In a fragment which was probably never published, she wrote: "To-day we are young. Life is a dare. Even sadness, has a drop of aching sweetness in its bitterness. Gaily we ride forth to try our glittering lances. Eagerly, we go, our faces bright with dreams ... with the music of the ages for a marching song."[7]

Mona wrote as much prose in her son's younger years as she did poetry. In addition to her numerous short newspaper pieces, she also wrote fiction. Her idol in this field was Katherine Mansfield. Mona emulated Mansfield's lyricism and attention to detail, as well as her clothing and hairstyle. Viola Pratt would later write to Mona, "You have always reminded me of [Katherine Mansfield] – both in looks – and in style. You have the same piquant poignancy and sharpness of images."[8] The resemblance between the two writers did not go very deep, however. Mona's worldview differed radically from that of her idol. In the plots of her longer stories, Mona's optimistic outlook shines through, as do her commercial ambitions. They are comic romances, with none of Mansfield's subtle melancholia, and their endings are happy, not hauntingly ambiguous. As far as I can tell, these stories were never published. They do, however, give a very good clue to Mona's fantasy life as a young woman.

Mona's stories are usually told from a male point of view. A man meets a beautiful and fascinating woman, becomes enchanted with her, makes some terrible gaffe, is rebuffed, and finally, through great trials, wins her heart. Their heroines are creative women: artists or singers. Much attention is given to describing each woman's charms in the voice of an outsider completely entranced with her. Only one story, entitled "Silver," takes a woman's point of view. Gay Gordon has found herself caught up in a scandalous situation. She is named as a co-respondent in a divorce case, for her innocent friendship with a married man. There is nothing inappropriate between them, but the man's jealous and grasping wife does not believe this. She divorces him and spoils Gay's reputation. Gay is trapped, living with her disapproving mother, whose guilt-inducing diatribes derive more from her own selfishness than from concern for her daughter. One night, Gay storms out of the house and goes for a long swim, dangerously far from home. While resting on a beach, she begins to sing, as a way of calming herself. Her singing attracts the attention of a young man who is walking in the area. He happens to be the leader of a band. "She finished on a high note that trailed off and shivered away into the dark. There was a long silence. Suddenly, she was jerked violently to her feet – and the young man was shaking both her hands and thumping her delightedly and recklessly across the shoulders, while he flung a perfect torrent of enthusiastic words at her. 'You're great! Simply great! Egad! To think that you can sing like that! Why they'll gobble you up – absolutely – swallow you whole! You're marvelous.'"[9] Was this the story Mona told herself about her home, her marriage? It seems she cast herself as the passionate artist, and Graham as an impresario, loving both the woman and her work, devoted to presenting her talents to the world.

If we think of all the characters in the story as representing people in Mona's own life, we have to wonder about the married man. The rejected youth in Mona's teenaged photograph album hardly seems the type. Unless she conducted some secret affair before the age of nineteen, there is no such figure in Mona's history. Except, of course, her father. The emotions expressed in her later poem "Sire" were a common refrain for Mona.

My mother often stopped me
From having fun
With the echo of her proper
"It isn't done!"

But I'd feel my father's hand
As he'd rough my hair
Saying "black ... and rebellious.
We're a bold, bad pair!"[10]

Time and time again, Mona talked about being a disappointment to her mother, who rejected her daughter, and loved her sons more. Mona was bold, passionate, and dreamy, and she lacked the propriety expected of a girl. She portrayed herself as a kindred spirit to her father, who was as oppressed as Mona by his wife's Victorian ways. Mona liked to be seen as spirited, a free-thinker, yet she never spoke of rebelling against her father. In her stories, she unquestioningly submitted to his authority, and was happy to give him credit for the writing ambition and business success she had every right to be proud of, herself.

Mona accorded her father special status, as children often do with a less-than-available parent, yet her stories and writings took this to an extreme. They had such an uncomfortably romantic flavour that I came to wonder whether Alfred had behaved in some way inappropriately with her. I doubt very much that he crossed any lines, physically, but he may have called upon her to meet emotional needs his wife did not. And rather than diffusing her childish attempts at flirtation, he may have – however unconsciously – encouraged them. In that case, Mona's anger at her mother would have stemmed, not only from rivalry, but from a sense of abandonment. Mona seemed to "protest too much" when she characterized her mother as a severe and prudish killjoy. Perhaps she wanted more and not less discipline, more and not less protection from her father's attention.

Returning to Mona's "Silver," no matter how we choose to interpret the story's sources, one thing is clear: none of the relationships in Gay's past are good. The bandleader rescues her. He takes her in the direction of a fresh new future. Graham certainly did this for Mona. He was no impresario, though. Either Mona did not realise this, or it did not bother her. She was ambitious enough for both of them.

❧

Marriage was good for Mona's writing. At some point in John's early years her poetic voice ceased to be so derivative. She began exploring what was called "free verse" – setting aside fixed rhyme and metre for cadences more closely resembling speech. Mona continued to write rhyming poems all her life, but in free verse, she found a more mature voice. Her cloying sentimentality dwindled (allowing for the fashion of the time). Her unpublished poem "Coronation Day," shows this change starting to happen. The poem begins with a faintly ironic description of a Coronation Day parade, then focuses on a veteran of the First World War who experiences a breakdown, triggered by the sound of the twenty-one gun salute. (Like many of the writers of her time, Mona was a staunch pacifist in the early 1930s.)

His face a mask of twisted horror ...
Arms flailing ...
Mouth agape ...
His knees buckling beneath him ... (It takes 3 or 4 men to hold him!)
And meantime
The guns boom on!
God save the King![11]

Though her short stories remained unpublished, Mona's poetry and journalism became increasingly visible in magazines. In 1931, *Every Boy's Own*, a Cleveland-based quarterly, ran a feature story she had written about a cartoon character called Squegee, and his creator, Tommie Crawford Hill. One of the authors also listed on the masthead was Edna Ferber. Tommie Hill had been a purser on one of the ships Mona wrote about during her newspaper days. Later, he moved to Hollywood, where he made good as a cartoonist. The author's description reads:

Introducing Mona Gould
Without a doubt Mona Gould is one of the outstanding young writers in Canada. Young – very pretty – very clever – and the mother of a young son who would make a fitting playmate of Jack Dempsey.

Living in London, Canada with a splendid young Canadian husband, this young lady spends her time (when not hunting for a husband's lost collar button and attending to the diet of her young son) in writing splendid verse. We are grateful for this splendid story of "Squegee" – and feel proud that we are publishing the early work of a young woman who in a short while will add new colors to the maple leaf. The Editor.[12]

The article shows that the "product tie-in" which we see in toy stores these days is nothing new: "Because he's such a great little personage, he's going to be glorified in a great many ways. Big manufacturing concerns have already set the wheels to turning, and Squegee Nursery Furniture ... can you imagine anything more Ideal? ... Squegee Dolls ... Squegee Soap ('that'll float' ... a small Pirate, to glorify the Littlest One's bath). Squegee Lamps ... Picture Books ... Tinker Toy Squegees ... Squegee Lollypops ... and Chocolate Bars ... an endless chain of Squegees to spread the legend of happiness, and a laugh a minute."[13]

Around this time, Mona developed a relationship with a magazine called *The Montrealer*. In his history of Canadian magazines, Fraser Sutherland describes it as "a pale approximation of *The New Yorker*."[14] Pale or not, it appealed to Mona. She corresponded in a friendly way with Alvah Beattie, *The Montrealer's* editor, who encouraged her to send both poetry and prose. Their correspondence reveals some of the struggles of a fledgling magazine in Canada in the 1930s. It also shows that a female writer was expected to put more than just her work on display when applying for freelance assignments. In response to an initial query from Mona, Beattie wrote, in January 1931, that he would like "a few particulars" about her: "age, appearance, etc."[15] He went on to ask Mona to try to convince some local newsstands to carry *The Montrealer*. A month later, he thanked her for sending her photograph, saying she was "quite nice looking." He added that the letter which accompanied the photograph was "by way of being a classic, and you have a great deal of personality. Keep on sending your stuff."[16] Mona did.

The impression one gets from these letters is that work on the magazine was an endless lark. Every aspect of production and budgeting had to be improvised. The staff were having fun, even as they barely kept ahead of their creditors. Beattie pioneered a section called "Around the Town" which, he said, would contain the type of short "breezy" pieces to be found in *The New Yorker* and *Reader's Digest*. Mona sent a lot of such pieces, but she sent others, too, which did not fit within the magazine's categories. Beattie accepted them anyway, but did not commit himself on the question of payment. "Frankly, Miss Gould, we know what rate we are paying for 'Around the Town' but we have no definite rate outside of that and we send cheques as the spirit moves us!"[17]

The magazine continued to grow. In April of 1932 came the announcement that they were planning to "branch out" nationally.[18] A few months later, however, they found themselves behind in their payments. Mona wrote to them inquiring about a payment she was expecting. This time, the reply did not come from Beattie but from Irene Kon, citing the Depression as the reason for not sending Mona's cheque. "I really feel like a piker, although it is not my company or my obligation ... but being in the same boat as you are I can sympathize very readily."[19] Kon wrote that financial matters had been handed over to a Mr Walker to manage. Mr Walker was not so friendly in his letter of 4 August 1933. He scolded Mona, "You may have your troubles as a writer, but you ought to be in the publishing business to really know how hard the lucre is to find ... If you pray hard the possibilities are that next week there may be a fiver, and if you pray very hard, it may be a tenner."[20] In the midst of all this, Beattie wrote Mona a letter encouraging her to move to Montreal, and hinting that there might be some work for her there with the magazine.[21] This never came to fruition. For all its apparent troubles, *The Montrealer* was a surprisingly long-lived publication. It continued to appear until 1970, when *Saturday Night* took over its subscription list. Over the years, it numbered Hugh MacLennan, Mordecai Richler, and Peter C. Newman among its contributors.[22]

Mona continued to write for *Chatelaine*. Byrne Hope Sanders – also a young mother – had a lot in common with Mona. She wrote, "Did you know that I have a very beautiful daughter of my own? She is three months old now and is utterly bewildering in her loveliness. But then you know what it's like!"[23] Through *Chatelaine*, Mona's poetry was published in England. At that time, the Curtis Brown literary agency circulated "American" magazines (*Chatelaine* among them) to editors in England. This was how Mona's work came to appear in *Woman's Illustrated* and *Woman's Journal*. Sometimes the agency contacted Mona regarding interest expressed by an editor, and at other times, she took the initiative of sending her poetry to them. In response to these queries the agents did not offer much hope, but they agreed to circulate one or two pieces. Mona tried to sell her short stories through Curtis Brown as well, but without success.[24]

Closer to home, a pair of sisters named Hilda and Laura Ridley launched a magazine called *The Crucible, a Quarterly Dedicated to Canadian Literature in the Making,* in 1932. The magazine was an outgrowth of a newsletter circulated among members of their Writers' Craft Club. The Ridleys had started this group in 1925, with about twenty members from around the country.[25] Mona was eager to be part of the new publication. In a letter dated 21 July 1932, Hilda accepted a group of poems Mona had submitted. She praised the poems but regretted being unable to pay, noting that, "So many good things in Canada have gone under just through lack of support ... we should like to be in a position to take a generous and broad attitude, instead of a cautious and circumscribed one."[26] Mona had mentioned she might move to Toronto, a possibility which Hilda greeted with enthusiasm. "We have several poets here that I'm sure you would like to meet."[27]

Hilda Ridley is best known for her 1956 biography of L.M. Montgomery, but her career was long and varied. Beginning in the 1920s, she contributed to several commercial and scholarly publications in Canada. She also read manuscripts for the *Canadian* magazine before starting *The Crucible*. *Canadian*, which published from 1893 to 1939, was a mass-market periodical with a nationalistic bent.[28] Its letterhead in 1931 described it as "A Monthly Magazine Read by ALL the Family."[29] *Canadian* published several of Mona's poems during the 1930s. Hilda Ridley showed a strong commitment to nationalism in her work, as well as a dedication to bringing women's writing – and their life stories – into the public eye. Together with her sister Laura, a poet, she was active in the literary community for three decades. In *Editing Modernity: Women and Little-Magazine Cultures in Canada*, Dean Irvine seeks to restore the sisters to their rightful place in history. Of Hilda, he writes, "Given her writings as a historian of modern women in Canada, it is fitting that Hilda Ridley should now be recognized (albeit belatedly) as one of the first woman editors of a modern literary magazine in Canada."[30]

P.K. Page and Anne Marriott published a few early poems in *The Crucible*, but no others. Nor did these poems ever appear their collections.[31] Mona's contributions followed a similar pattern. She published only three poems in *The Crucible*, and these did not go on to be printed in her books.[32] This may well be because *The Crucible* provided a niche for the type of poetry that did not have an outlet elsewhere and was – even then – falling out of favour with publishers. These were rhyming lyrics, often about love and nature, and very much in the style that Munro Beattie deplored. Irvine notes that the disappearance of the Ridleys from literary history is part of a trend which became stronger throughout the century. Critics attacked women poets by disparaging their sensibility, and that of the publications which featured them. This attitude persists, in the view of Irvine, into the present day, and has led to the "invisibility" of *The Crucible* in historical records.[33]

Hilda Ridley mentioned her concern about monetary constraints in her letter to Mona. Having a financially viable magazine was important to its editors. In correspondence with potential members of the editorial board in 1932, the editors made it clear that business acumen and willingness to generate income were part of the job.[34] Irvine comments, "the border between commercial and non-commercial periodicals was often highly permeable in

the early period of Canadian little magazines (1916–1947)."[35] Mona strad-
dled these two modes of writing all her life ... or at least, tried to. In later
years, publishing was to polarize into two distinct camps. When she was
starting out, though, her commercial leanings were not seen as contradic-
tory to her literary ones.

꿋

As the decade continued, it became clear the Goulds would have to leave St
Thomas if they hoped to prosper. When John was about six years old, they
moved to Owen Sound, a city of about thirteen thousand people.[36] The
1930s brought hard times to Owen Sound, as they did to every part of the
country, but it had been, until then, a boomtown, with a tradition of resili-
ency. With its history as a port and shipbuilding centre, its railway service
and grain elevators, it must have seemed an attractive spot for a young
family looking for a better life. After so many years of successful trade, the
city was now home to a thriving financial services industry. This is where
Graham hoped to build a career. He soon got a job with the brokerage firm
of Goulding, Rose and Company.

Another tradition in Owen Sound was its devotion to temperance. In its
first three decades, the city had become known as "The Corkscrew Town"
because of it lax drinking laws. Gambling, counterfeiting, and all the vices
typical of any port city were also rampant. So in 1906, the city imposed strict
prohibition laws, which did not relax until 1961 and were not fully lifted
until 1973.[37] Living in a "dry" town would not have sat well with the
Goulds. Graham and Mona loved drinking. What made the situation tolerable was the image they cultivated of being rebels. This, of course, meant
seeking out other rebels. They read avidly about the group of writers, artists,
and radicals who gathered in Provincetown, Massachusetts, around the time
of the First World War, sharing their writing, their ideas, and sometimes their
partners as well. Edna St Vincent Millay was among them. So were Eugene
O'Neill, Susan Glaspell, and for a while, John Reed and Louise Bryant. The
Goulds may have hoped to establish a similar community when they set up
their household in Owen Sound.

They became active in local theatre. The mid-1930s saw a flowering of
regional theatre in Canada; The Dominion Drama Festival, formed in 1931,
created a focal point for theatrical activities around the country. Graham
had already been involved in productions in both London and St Thomas.

Mona and Graham had tried working together on these projects, but their collaboration was a disaster. In a production of J.B. Priestley's *Dangerous Corner*, Mona played the role of Freda Chadfield. Graham was the director. It was her first and last role. They argued, and Mona stormed out of the rehearsal hall more than once.

Mona was more comfortable writing about theatre than she was performing. She wrote articles for *Curtain Call*, the Dominion Drama Festival's publication. In 1935, *Curtain Call* published Mona's comic poem "Drama Festival," which takes "sacred and profane peeps" into the minds of various participants in an amateur production. An actor begins:

> "I wish by all the gods of war
> I'd put my foot down long before.
> Why, even Barrymore himself
> Would make a rather silly elf!"

The poem then takes the point of view of an audience member, who happens to be married to the woman playing the lead role.

> "I hope when this thing's past and gone
> That Martha won't be so … so … weird …
> She hasn't baked a single pie
> Since getting in the public eye,
> And every time I speak to her
> She strikes a tragic attitude
> It's just like living with the Duse
> I sometimes think I'll blow a fuse …!"

The last word is given the adjudicator:

> "I make my entrance last of all,
> I play my part, and take my bow,
> And if they don't agree with me …
> I live in England, anyhow!"[38]

A program saved from the 1936 Dominion Drama Festival in Ottawa is full of Mona's pencil marks.[39] Graham and Mona attended the festival together,

Graham performing the role of Prince Rudolf in *Candle-Light* and Mona covering the festival for various publications.

Graham became the producer and director of a theatre company called The Sydenham Players. In 1937, the company presented an evening of four one-act comedies. The program for the show was printed on heavy, cream-coloured paper and contained ads from local businesses. Mona was given a credit for publicity. Graham succeeded in motivating a large segment of Owen Sound's population to support his group, or to perform in his plays. He would simply walk into shops on the main street and inform people what their roles were to be. The group became increasingly ambitious, and in February 1940, mounted a production of *The White Oaks of Jalna* at the local Savoy Theatre with a cast of a dozen people and a full set. John made his theatrical debut as young Wakefield.[40]

Meanwhile, Mona was getting more and more attention for her writing. In October 1938, she was invited by B.K. Sandwell of *Saturday Night* to contribute to their women's column, "The Distaff Side," on a rotating basis with three other women. Sandwell wrote, "I should like your monthly column to be definitely characterized as that of a small town woman (of fair culture) as distinguished from the large-city approach which will characterize the other contributors." The fee was to be ten dollars per column of at least eight hundred words.[41]

In addition to her column, Mona regularly contributed poems and features to *Chatelaine* and the *Canadian Home Journal*. Her papers from this period display an uncharacteristic tidiness. She kept hardbound books of her drafts, handwritten in ink or pencil, with a note at the top of the page when a poem was accepted for publication. She even used a contrasting colour for her marginal notes. One book includes poems by T.S. Eliot, Louis Untermeyer, and Dorothy Parker, transcribed in Mona's own handwriting.[42] This labour of love would be tedious to anyone but a devoted apprentice writer. On the flip side of one of these pages, Mona transcribed John's first report card. The report mentions a few academic subjects: reading, writing, arithmetic, and spelling. There follows a long list of expected standards of behaviour: cleanliness, posture, neatness in work, honesty, application and effort, politeness, obedience, co-operation, regularity, and punctuality. He scored very well in obedience and cleanliness.[43] Mona was not merely saving paper when she combined these two important parts of her life in one notebook. Years later, she inscribed a quotation from Thomas Randolph in

the front of one of her own books: "If I a poem leave, that poem is my son."
This same quotation appeared many times in her journals and on spare sheets
of paper. Mona considered her son to be her greatest work of art. (Ironically
enough, Randolph's words have the opposite meaning when read in the context of the whole poem.)

Mona juggled motherhood and writing with aplomb, but her poetry shows
that the romance of domestic life was beginning to wear thin. She wrote:

Throw Back?

It's really funny I can't but think
As I loiter over the kitchen sink;
The beautiful places I'd like to go
And the interesting people I'd like to know.
But here I stay and putter and grouse,
The typical wife … in the typical house.

Back in the shades of my family tree
There must have been dozens like dutiful me.

With only a Gypsy here and there
Who wouldn't stay put; and couldn't wear
Aprons and s[m]ocks like a uniform
A Gypsy who hungered for strife and storm,
And took to the road when she felt the urge,
Whose mate was a stranger to neat blue serge
Who made her bed on a bough or two
And slept far sweeter than housed things do.

Did I inherit this will to roam?
Or am I content with this small snug home? …
I would have been happier spared the strain
Of Gipsy blood that fires my brain
So on nights when the wind gets out of hand
I wouldn't be fey … and stare and stand
Athirst for a miracle wild and sweet
To shake the tradition out of my feet.

And suddenly you're at the door, my dear
And I'm quite contented to stay right here![44]

She had once seen Graham as an exotic and passionate Moor, an impresario who would take her out of her repressive home and show her a brilliant future. Now he had become the comfortable husband, solid and unassuming, while Mona herself had gone from headstrong genius to contented – if somewhat impractical – housewife. Yet her restlessness could not be denied. On the surface of things, the Goulds' life in Owen Sound hardly promised to offer the mystery and adventure that Mona longed for. But "strife and storm" can happen anywhere, and the right kind of intrigue can bring enchantment to any place.

Full Circle

This is what I knew.

That Mona had an affair in the late 1930s in Owen Sound.

That her lover's name was Jim.

That Graham and Mona fought about the affair.

That Mona ran away from home one winter night, and Graham went out in the car to find her and bring her back.

That both Jim and Graham went away to war.

That only Graham came home.

Mona said: "What happened with Jim ... that was nothing. That was really nothing. Just – you know ... a passing thing. My real love was Graham. He was the love of my life."

My father said, before his stroke: "That perfect love my mom talks about all the time, between her and my father. Pure fiction. Stories. She's making it up. They fought all the time. And she had an affair. They split up over it. When my father joined the army it was really a cover-up for their separation. He fell in love with a girl in Belgium. He almost stayed in Belgium. But he came back."

My father said, after his stroke: "She's there and the thing goes 'ring' and she takes the thing and she says, 'Yes,' and the guy goes, 'I'm sorry. I'm sorry.'"

He pointed to a picture of Graham.

"And that was your father on the phone?"

"That's right."

"Your *father*?"

"That's right. He calls the guy and he says, "I'm sorry. I'm sorry.""

"Your father was the one who told your mother about Jim's death."

"That's right."

"Are you sure it's not her brother you're talking about? Are you sure you're not talking about Nanna getting a phone call when her brother Mook died?"

"No, it was the guy! It was the guy!"

"*Graham* told Mona about Jim's death."

"That's right."

◈

The final few poetry books in Mona's collection ended up with me. She had kept everything written by Edna St Vincent Millay. In the flyleaf of *Fatal Interview* she had written, "January 25, 1932 From Graham," in pencil, and then her own signature, Mona Gould. Then (years later), "Birthday! Mona Gould from Graham, 1932," in blue magic marker.

Make Bright the Arrows had, in almost girlishly tidy script, the words: "To Mona with love Jamie, Xmas 1940," written in the front. There was also another book, *Aphrodite,* by Pierre Loüys, recounting the amorous exploits of Chrysis, a powerful and hedonistic courtesan in ancient Greece. It begins with a scene in which the heroine prepares to go out for the evening, bathing and dressing with the help of her slave girl: "The hour of the bath was that where Chrysis commenced to adore herself,"[1] it remarks. The book was illustrated with drawings of scantily draped women, and the flyleaf bore the inscription – in recognizable, tidy handwriting: "Jas Henderson Owen Sound 1939 takes pleasure in presenting this book to Mona, in recognition of her many unique services."

Jas was Jim, and Jim was Jamie, and Jamie was the lost pilot to whom Mona dedicated a poem in her first book, *Tasting the Earth.*

"Toujours Gai"
For Jamie, of the R.A.F.
"He has outsoared the shadow of our night."

Bravely he kept his tryst with Death –
Who somehow knew it would come to pass –
But he tipped his cap at a rakish slant,
And he gave himself a smile, in the glass.

If his hand was clenched there was none to see,
If his heart was sore for the home he missed,
And the eager face of his dearest love
And her flying hair … and the lips he'd kissed.

He had made for himself, from a little phrase
A shield and a buckler to save the day –
And the little phrase was a bit of himself,
And he laughed when he said it, – "Toujours gai!"[2]

In person, Mona liked to allude to her affair in ways that would invite specu-
lation, then shut her lips in a firm line. As widowhood slipped twenty and
thirty years into Mona's past, she spoke more and more often of having had,
and lost, a lover. Still, she never said anything specific. Often Mona would
itemize all her losses, and casually drop in a mention of him: "I lost my brother,
my babies, my parents, my lover, my husband" and quickly go on with the
story so that you had no time to ask about the "lover" part. In Mona's last
weeks, a nurse who was looking after her asked, "How many children do you
have?" Mona answered, "By my husband, only one." Her voice closed the
topic off definitively. Did she mean only one child lived? (She had three preg-
nancies.) Surely she could not have meant she had a child with someone else,
other than Graham. Maybe she meant that there was more than one man who
could have made her pregnant.

⬱

The manuscript was alone in an envelope, one of the few envelopes that contained uniformly sized, uniformly coloured pieces of paper.[3] Its pages were
graying, the print faded by mold and time, and there were four holes down
the left side, as if, at one point, someone had stitched the manuscript together
then later removed the thread. On the first page were handwritten the words:

Full circle.
Being the complete cycle of a love
By Mona Gould

And then the first poem, carefully typed:

And if some day in after years, you look
Between the pages of this little book,
And find some bit of me you did not know
And feel delight to know that this is so,
Say to yourself "here she was light and gay,
Here she was moody ... sad ... perhaps, alone ...
And here, when she went begging after bread
Some stupid mortal answered with a stone".

Small portraits ... bits of days ... and little songs ...
Strung to a tune, I lay them in your hand;
Treasure them; disregard them if you will.
Only I charge you ... read and understand!

At last, a document of Mona's love affair – a chance to find out what really happened! Mona never told me about *Full Circle*, but I always knew – or hoped so hard I thought I knew – that there was something written down, some concrete document of the affair I had heard about from an early age. This hope may have unconsciously encouraged me to take on the task of sorting her archives in the first place. "And if some day in after years you look ..." I felt as if Mona were speaking to me directly, from beyond the grave, inviting me to discover the true story. Eagerly, I began to read.

The Splendid Moments.

The splendid moments are so very few
Flame-spent they go quite quickly down to death,
Only a fragmentary dream remains,
A breath of hidden flowers on the wind –

I found my attention straying almost at once. Hard as I tried to concentrate, my eyes slid all over the page, unable to settle. "So very few," "quite quickly," indeed! I felt disappointed. I wanted something more resounding, more dramatic, more sexy or ironic or intellectually brilliant. The manuscript seemed faded and prim, lacking the vividness I associated with Mona. The whole thing reminded me of the journals I kept as a teenager, when I wrote in the lightest pencil, in the vaguest of terms, so that no one would ever be able to figure out what was going on. Increasingly impatient, I continued to read.

For One Who Rode On

"I should like to climb and climb" she said.
"To the topmost crest of this quiet hill.
And sit with your head against my knees
And shadows of trees
Across your face,
And I could lean above and trace
With the variest points of my fingertips
The curve of your lids
And the curve of your brow,
And the twist of your unbelieving lips" –

I was filled with irritation. From the tone of *Full Circle*, I found it hard to believe Mona ever really desired Jim, much less slept with him. I got the feeling that the whole love affair was something Mona created in her imagination and never consummated at all.

Why should that bother me?

Because if she never really had an affair, then all her stories, and my father's, and all my beliefs about my grandparents' marriage were thrown into doubt. And, it seemed, these beliefs were as important to me as they were to Mona herself. I needed to see Mona as a strong, unconventional, even brutal woman; needed to see her as a winner, even at the expense of others. I didn't *like* my version of Mona, but it was part of my internal balance to see her that way. This manuscript showed Mona losing at love, then clinging, pining, and refusing to accept the affair's inevitable end. It showed her as a woman with a secret infatuation, which, hemmed in by convention, she hid from everyone, penning her gushing verses in secret.

The poems seemed so arch to me; so overworked. I tried to read with an open mind, but could not prevent myself from finding fault with every word.

Why was I being such a tough critic? Wasn't she allowed to write some bad poems in an eighty-year career? What constituted a bad poem, anyway? And how could I possibly judge Mona's writing? I had listened to her stories year after year and now, steeped as I was in her history, her work had come to seem like my own. Not like my own writing, but like a part of myself: a voice I heard in my head. It was impossible to be objective. Why did it matter so much to me? Why did I not just place the manuscript in a file marked "Unpublished poems: typed," and move on? Yet I lingered, as if worrying a half-healed scab. At last, found a poem I didn't mind.

Awe

Let me distinguish light from dark.
Let me distinguish blaze from spark.
But when your kiss is on my mouth
Let me believe that north is south.

At least there was some ease here; some playfulness with language to remind me Mona was a skilled writer, not a love-struck girl. Yet it nagged me. It did not seem to fit with the rest of the manuscript, and I begin to think I must have seen it in print, somewhere. This possibility irritated me too. Even though Mona hid a whole manuscript, she was clearly on the lookout for what might be saleable. Why was that a problem? What writer wouldn't have done the same?

It was a problem for the reason this whole manuscript was a problem: because it challenged the roles I had set out for the various people in my life. I wanted to believe Mona had buried this manuscript, telling herself it was her greatest work, never to be seen in her lifetime, and that she was hiding it to protect her husband and son. I wanted her not to know it was bad.

But maybe she hid the manuscript *because* it wasn't up to her standards. This was a possibility I could hardly bear to think about because I had to be the discerning editor in this relationship; Mona, the one who could barely control her pen. Complain as I might about the burden of sorting her papers, I held on to my territory jealously.

The manuscript ended with:

I find the circle now at last complete
With wide discerning eyes, accept defeat

And if I find this brew a bitter potion
You shall not be aware of it; emotion
As sharp as this, were better hidden deep
This Sleeping Beauty, safer left asleep ...

It didn't fit. The "defeat" in this poem did not fit with my understanding that war had ended Mona's love affair with Jim. The manuscript told the story of losing at love. Either Jim rejected Mona before going away, or she took his signing up as a rejection. Or the manuscript was about another love affair entirely. But why would she hide one and talk willingly – if somewhat coyly – about the other? This new manuscript raised more questions than it answered. The fact that the poems were undated made it even harder to understand the story behind them.

I had privately decided that her affair with Jim held the clue to Mona's core: the hidden self behind the stories she was always so eager to tell. Now I began to wonder if she had been trying to throw me off the trail with her enticing hints about it. "Full Circle" disappointed me because it did not help me know my grandmother. I began to wonder if I ever would.

❦

Not knowing where else to look, I returned to the information that had been in front of me all along. I read *Tasting the Earth,* Mona's first book, interpreting the familiar poems in a new way. There were poems about motherhood, poems about nature, poems about peace. But there were many – not just *"Toujours Gai"* – about lost love. Some could be interpreted as the longing for a husband who was away at the front. In others, it was quite clear the beloved person was dead. This theme permeated the book, and yet to anyone who read the author's biography on the jacket-flap, it would be obvious that Mona's husband was still alive. There was no attempt to hide anything.

According to a story I heard many times from my father, Mona's affair almost ended his parents' marriage. I do not remember how old I was when I first heard this story, but certainly, it was part of my basic knowledge about my family. I also felt from an early age that there was some deep hurt in my father, an insecurity and disillusionment that sprang from his mother's affair. My father had to be treated carefully on account of it. There is no doubt that the Gould household was turbulent, and that this was traumatic for my father, but as I spent more time with Mona's archives, I found myself wondering about the true state of my grandparents' marriage.

Tasting the Earth came out in 1943 while Graham was in Europe. Mona used to say that when the book first appeared, she gave it to Judge Gordon, the commissioner of the Red Cross, who was flying to England by bomber that very night. He was able to transport it for her, and put it in Graham's hands long before the mail could have done so.[4] This story is less far-fetched than it might seem. As a paymaster, Graham was in a better position than most to receive a parcel. In Mona's archives, I found confirmation that he must have at least known about the publication, because she kept his telegram, dated March 25. "Congratulations dear best of reviews Graham Gould."[5] In a medium where every word had to be carefully chosen, Graham made a point of expressing his affection and support. What must he have felt? What must have passed between them? Of course is a mistake to interpret poetry as literal, autobiographical information. Mona, like any writer, allowed her imagination to play on the events of her life. No doubt Graham knew this, and accepted Mona's poetic license. Is it possible his acceptance went further than that?

As an old man, my father told me the improbable story that Graham had called to tell Mona about the death of Jim. Maybe it was a simple memory lapse: my father had confused Mona's lover with her brother and conflated two times during the war when she received bad news. Maybe he was trying to connect Graham and Jim, revising the story to make Jim less of an outsider, a friendlier figure. Or maybe he was trying – with what little language he could muster – to convey that the whole thing had been much more out in the open than he had once led me to believe?

It is not out of the question. Mona and Graham were children of the jazz age. They saw themselves as rebels against the prudery which had made earlier generations miserable. "Free love" was known and accepted in the 1930s, especially among the writers the Goulds admired. Edna St Vincent Millay and her husband, Eugen Boissevain, were notable examples, but there were many others as well. Anything unconventional appealed to Mona, and having an open marriage would have been no exception. Graham, too, may have told himself they were casting off outworn inhibitions in giving each other freedom to explore their separate attractions. This did not prevent hurt feelings, and certainly did not preclude fighting in the house. One thing is certain, though; if my grandparents and Jim had an "understanding," it was treated with much more secrecy than Mona's affair.

Whatever explorations my grandparents enjoyed were short-lived. In 1940, the two men left Mona alone, and life became deadly serious for all of them.

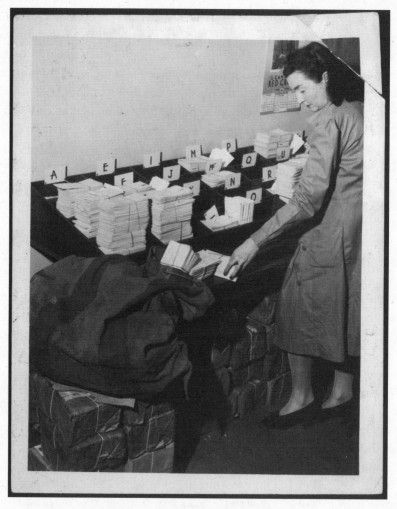

... *there was none to see.* On the back of this wartime photograph, Mona wrote may years later, "Searching for news of Jim. H."

A Grand Surprise

Graham entered active duty on 17 June 1940, as a sergeant in the infantry. This ended a four-year period of living in Owen Sound, and the Goulds' life as a Bohemian couple. Within months, Mona and John moved to Toronto, to an apartment at 464 Spadina Avenue in Forest Hill. Mona had written to Eric Rechnitzer, a contact at the MacLaren advertising agency, asking him if he knew of any work. At the end of August 1940, he wrote that there was nothing available for the time being. Then three weeks later he offered her a job starting at a salary of thirty dollars a week, on a trial basis, until the end of the year.[1]

It was through her work in advertising that Mona made the acquaintance of Dodi Robb, who later became a well-known television writer and producer, as well as Mona's dear friend. Dodi told me that Rechnitzer thought highly of Mona. He was attracted to her – not sexually, Dodi hastened to add – but professionally.[2] But Mona never mentioned the name of Eric Rechnitzer in her stories of the war years. Nor did Mona ever speak of looking for work. She said in so many words that this advertising job – like every opportunity in her life – had come to *her*, without her having to seek it out. It did not happen that way. Although the process of getting a job at MacLaren was quick, Mona had definitely been the one to initiate it.

Her first priority when war started was to get herself and John out of Owen Sound. Employment, of course, was the main reason for going to

Toronto, but it was not the only one. Mona had, at last, the opportunity to be in a major centre for Canadian poetry. Since the mid-thirties, Mona had been developing as a poet, partly through the help of B.K. Sandwell of *Saturday Night*. Their correspondence – at least, what she kept of it – began late in 1936, when Sandwell scolded her for a gaffe that might have ruined her chances with a less forgiving editor. He discovered "with some grief" that Mona's poem "Stillness" had been published in *Gossip* magazine, and that *Gossip*, in turn, had reprinted it from the *Montrealer*. But the same poem had also been accepted by *Saturday Night*. In his letter, Sandwell went on to say that if Mona was in a hurry for a response, she could give him a date beyond which she would send her work elsewhere.³ Since *Gossip*, *The Montrealer*, and *Saturday Night* were well-known magazines, Mona might have caused all the parties in involved a lot of embarrassment. This letter – reproving, but under the circumstances, very indulgent – set the tone for a correspondence which went on for twelve more years.

A few months after his first letter, Sandwell lectured Mona on her slapdash approach: "May I point out that while it is perfectly all right for you to 'write for the thrill of it,' it is absolutely immoral for you to expect the public, or even editors as agents of the public, to spend their time reading what you produce from that motive. Literature is an art, and no important work of art was ever produced merely for the thrill that the writer got out of producing it – a thrill which is exactly like the one that a small child gets out of whistling when it first discovers it can do it." Finally, he threatened to "Give [her] up." "I am a very busy man and cannot be bothered trying to improve the work of contributors who do not want to do their own improving."⁴ In the same vein, he lamented, in early 1938, that she was using him as little more than a free editorial service: "I suppose you send these to me just to get my idea as to how they could be improved," he wrote.⁵

Some of his influence must have filtered through, however. Throughout the late thirties and early forties, Mona's poetry became more substantial in its subject matter, and more and more authentically her own. About his bugbears – punctuation, variation in rhyme, simple carefulness in writing – Mona continued to get a curmudgeonly earful, but Sandwell accepted a lot of her work. On 4 April 1944 he wrote,

Dear Miss Gould, I have just finished retyping eight excellent poems of yours. I always have to retype them, because that is easier than fixing up your fantastic punctuation. A properly written poem shouldn't need flocks and flocks of dots to denote pauses ... Damn it, I was going to return SPRING TWILIGHT. It will be a horrible nuisance, because I shall have to keep chasing it for four weeks to make sure that it doesn't get left out until it is too definitely summer. But when I have knocked those infernal rows of dots out of it it will be a darned good poem. (Believe me, this is not just a personal prejudice; I am the Universal Reader, and I know what we readers want, and we hate meaningless punctuation!) All right, that makes nine.[6]

Mona continued to shower him with poems. By July 1944, he had received another large batch. "Dear Mrs. Gould, If you were to send me a lot less stuff, just only the stuff that you know in your heart of hearts you really want printed with your name over it (or under it) in *Saturday Night*, and if you sent it in the form of impeccable copy, all ready to go to the printers, I could, (damn it, I'm catching the italics habit myself) edit it when it comes in, and if it were very topical, which yours often is, it would have a better chance of getting it in while it was fresh. And could you, could you be induced to sign your name 'Mona Gould' in the bourgeois manner and thus save me the trouble of indicating to the printer where the large caps go and where the small caps?" He went on to accept eight of her poems.[7]

Four years later, he was still berating her: "For an other wise good writer you are the laziest and most careless I have anything to do with – and Canada is full of lazy and careless writers! ... Why do I have to give you these lessons in elementary verse-and story-writing? You probably know them anyhow but just won't bother with them." Towards the end of this letter, he added ominously, "Let me assure you that any arid place you may come to in writing is entirely due to this lack of attention to important details."[8]

Mona saved these letters with uncharacteristic care, and sold them to the Toronto Central library in 1977 for fifty dollars.[9] Sandwell implied that she sent him sloppy work because she knew she could rely on his editorial skills. I began to wonder whether she had deliberately provoked him in order to amass a valuable collection of his correspondence. Whatever the reason, he was a willing participant in the game.

&

Mona always said that the publication of "This Was My Brother" catapulted her to recognition as a poet. But the flowering of her career was by no means that sudden. The acknowledgments page of her first book shows that Mona had paid her dues. *Saturday Night, Chatelaine, Montreal* CAA *Year Books, Canadian Forum, Gossip, The Montrealer, Canadian Magazine,* are all listed, along with *Woman's Illustrated* and *Woman's Journal* from England. The appearance of *Tasting the Earth* rested on a firm foundation.

Mona was an active member of the Canadian Author's Association and contributed frequently to its journal, *Canadian Poetry Magazine.* This placed her in the company of such poets as P.K. Page, Dorothy Livesay, Raymond Souster, Miriam Waddington, and Louis Dudek, among many others. The publication did not pay its contributors, but awarded a few cash prizes with each number, and Mona's were often among the winning poems. The 1920s and 1930s were a time of foment in poetry, in Canada and elsewhere. A variety of groundbreaking styles were starting to receive respect, while traditional forms still flourished. With the rise of socialism and pacifism, political themes began to appear as well. People defended their tastes in style and subject matter with considerable heat. The CAA was the subject of contemptuous attack in such publications as *Canadian Mercury, McGill Fortnightly Review,* and *Canadian Forum.* The so-called "Montreal Group" of poets, concerned with creating poetry of social value, considered the CAA to be stodgy and self-congratulatory.[10] This position is perhaps best articulated in F.R. Scott's poem, "The Canadian Authors Meet," in which its members – "virgins of sixty who still write of passion" – are likened to ladies who congregate in church basements for tea and edifying conversation.[11]

Despite so much conflict, *Canadian Poetry Magazine* under E.J. Pratt strove to find a middle way. Its attitude was open-minded, welcoming a variety of styles. The first poem of the first issue was Dorothy Livesay's "Day and Night," which Pratt praised because he was "delighted to find a poem written by a Canadian that was not concerned with the colour of maple leaves, but with the social and industrial scene in the cities."[12] In the same issue, however, a prize was given to Audrey Brown's romantic "Penelophon."[13] This eclecticism may have drawn criticism from various factions, but looking back at the issues now provides a marvelous cross-section of poetic voices during that formative period in Canadian literary history. When he took over the editorship from Pratt in December 1943, Nathaniel Benson wrote:

A word to contributors: Will all Canadian poets please regard this as an invitation to send in their poems *now*, whether their Muses follow the inevitable sonorities of Lord Tennyson or the more cryptic utterances of Mr Eliot. To mention two distinguished poetesses, we welcome the privilege of publishing the poetry of both Audrey Alexandra Brown and Dorothy Livesay, whose works, all will admit, have almost nothing in common. We want the poems of both Leo Cox and his fellow-Montrealer A.M. Klein, of Watson Kirkconnell and Louis Dudek, and that legion of young unknown poets who are just coming over the horizon – the poets of to-morrow who usually begin by smiling at our great poets of yesterday and end up by following them. Come one and all – the door is wide open.[14]

In our present literary climate, Mona's work does not seem particularly groundbreaking, and it has been frequently passed over in anthologies and books of literary history. In the CAA of the 1930s, however, her poetry leaned towards the cutting edge with its strong use of images, its simplicity, and its lack of rhyme. It steered clear of the political, though, and concentrated on human relationships and shades of emotion.

E.J. Pratt had for years been an enthusiastic supporter of Mona's work. (His wife, Viola, was also an admiring reader.) He was in the process of retiring as editor of *Canadian Poetry* at the time when Mona's work began to appear regularly in the magazine's pages. However, he did write her an acceptance letter on 25 May 1943, which contained generous words of praise. "You have the real touch and I am proud of you. There's a long road ahead of you, with places to go. I have been 'boosting' your stuff here in the University amongst my friends."[15] It was Pratt who reviewed *Tasting the Earth* in 1943 for *Canadian Poetry Magazine*. He emphasized the lyric qualities of the poems: "The songs seem to come not so much out of the air as out of the ground with a low rich timbre which recalls us to our physical origins, and at the same time suggest germination and the struggle for life. The poems look exceedingly simple and may appear easy to write, but only a deeply stored nature, furnished with a gift for communication, could reveal those intimacies and make impressive what we so often take for granted."[16]

Ellen Elliott, Mona's editor at Macmillan, was also Pratt's editor, and Pratt and his wife Viola hosted the launch party for Mona's book. Mona was to write, on Pratt's death in 1964, a letter to Lotta Dempsey's column "Private Line."

I was a very young, green, unpublished, trying-to-be poet ... Ned Pratt

was a famous professor and a many-published one. I had read him.
I stood in awe.

He said I could come and see him at Victoria College one spring
noon. It rained buckets. I arrived draggy and sad.

He surveyed me from a vast sea of books like a benevolent merman
and said, "Here is the girl with the pretty name." He said I looked as
if I needed a good steak. He took me to lunch.

When I had my first book of verse published it was wartime. My
husband, Graham, was overseas. It could have been ... doleful.

But Ned and Vi Pratt threw a vast author-studded party that spilled
over into the garden. Sir Charles G.D. Roberts sat down on my squashy
summer handbag. I couldn't disturb this venerable raconteur. I had
to stay on ... and on ... Ned Pratt roared with laughter and said:
"Sir Charles did it on purpose, you know."

And now he has gone away. But he stayed as long as he could ...
which was like him.[17]

Pratt wrote a song in 1943 to be sung to the tune of "God Save the King"
which commended the talents of a number of Canadian writers: Sir Charles
G.D. Roberts, Elsie Pomeroy, Mona Gould, and Amabel King (whose book
Crusaders appeared at the same time as Mona's). It was sung at a party at
the Pratts' house at 21 Cortleigh Blvd. The last verse reads:

Mona and Amabel!
May your two volumes sell:
We hail their birth.
May new <u>Crusaders</u> rise
To cheer the poet's eyes,
And find a grand surprise
<u>Tasting the Earth</u>.[18]

Viola was a regular correspondent of Mona's. After Pratt's death, Viola and
their daughter Claire continued to send Mona Christmas cards with Claire's
line drawings on the front. A note on one of these cards from Viola reads:
"I treasure my memories of you."[19]

The correspondence from Pratt was much more encouraging than Sandwell's, but Mona almost never spoke of him. This is strange because Pratt's
is a prestigious name in Canadian literature – and Mona was not shy of

name-dropping. I had no idea that such an extensive correspondence existed between them, and no idea that they saw each other so regularly. Mona scattered Pratt's letters among phone bills and newspaper clippings, sometimes leaving them perilously close to discarded food, broken glass, open jars of hand cream and Vaseline. The encouragement of the Pratts must have been vital for Mona, but its very tender, nurturing quality may have led her to discount it. And there were many times later in her life when Mona had no wish to be reminded of the promise she had shown as a young poet.

However, the single most important influence on Mona's poetry career was not Sandwell or Pratt. Rather, it was Ellen Elliott of Macmillan. In Mona's favourite story, Elliott received an order from B.K. Sandwell to produce Mona's first book of poetry. In reality, Elliott was a person of influence in the literary community, and the pecking order may well have been the other way around. Elliott had worked at Macmillan for a number of years as the highly valued secretary to president Hugh Eayrs, and later became secretary to the company. When Eayrs died of a heart attack in 1940, Robert Huckvale became president, but he primarily took care of financial matters, while Elliott was in charge of the artistic aspects of the publishing house. She remained in charge until 1946. With a discerning eye for both literary merit and salability, Elliott championed not only Mona's work, but that of W.O. Mitchell and P.K. Page, among many others.

Elliott worked with Mona extensively, steering *Tasting the Earth* past wartime delays and shortages not only of staff, but of materials as well. Mona always claimed that her poetry was simply "discovered" and that she was swept off her feet by a strong man who insisted on publishing it. This could not have been further from the truth. Like many poets of the time, including Dorothy Livesay, Mona covered the production costs of her first book herself.[20] Her contribution was merely a jump-start, however, since both this book and the next sold out. It was clear that Elliott's faith in Mona was justified.

The climate of the day also played a part in Mona's success. Despite the logistical challenges it created, the Second World War was a good time for Canadian books. Ruth Panofsky, who has done an extensive study of the Macmillan Company of Canada, notes that Canadian books were enjoying unprecedented sales, both at home and in the United States. There was less competition from British publishing as well, since England was not able to export as many books during wartime.[21]

❧

Mona also never mentioned that she was let go from MacLaren advertising
in January 1942. She had worked on the Helena Rubenstein and Dack's Shoes
accounts, as well as on a number of accounts that were probably only assigned to a woman because it was wartime.[22] These included General Motors
of Canada and the Hydro Electric Commission. I cannot say whether the ads
she kept contained her own copy, because they are unsigned and the originals
are nowhere to be found. The style is characteristic of Mona, however. She
kept a calendar issued by General Motors which featured a different dog each
month, each dog being identified with a car. She also wrote ads for munitions,
and it was here she earned the reputation that she could "write like a man."
The inside front cover of *Liberty* magazine, 18 November 1944, carried a
General Motors ad in verse form entitled "Going Our Way." Mona was no
longer employed by MacLaren at that time, but the heavy use of exclamation
points and italics makes me think it must be Mona's. She could well have
written it on a freelance basis, because her relationship with MacLaren remained cordial.

> The time is ... now! A widening steel wave is
> – going our way – rolling toward Berlin.
> The very earth shakes under the crushing Force
> Of Victory on Wheels! Men in Armour –
> Men, living in the little tight world –
> that is a tank. It takes skill and precision –
> Craftsmanship and good salt sweat to build a tank.
> Take the M-4 – for instance –
> *Huge* and *deadly* – General Motors
> Workers are *proud* to build the
> Hulls – of these war worthy giants –
> "Victory is Their Business, too!"[23]

Mona's contract with MacLaren was terminated amicably; in a letter
of recommendation, 3 January 1942, Rechnitzer wrote that she was let go
because of financial constraints, and he praised her as a "brilliant and very
versatile writer." Thereafter Mona wrote to a number of publications looking for steady work. One of these was *Saturday Night*. The response from
Sandwell was clipped: "I am very sorry to hear of your unfortunate experi-

ence with the advertising profession. But I cannot hold out any hope of regular employment in connection with *Saturday Night*."[24] No one can blame him for discouraging her, given the scatterbrained image she had cultivated with the magazine so far!

Mona said she left MacLaren because she was "borrowed" by the Red Cross to be the Girl Friday of J.N. ("Pat") Kelly, the national director of publicity. In fact, her position was much more prestigious than that. She was hired not simply a representative of the Red Cross, but as a public figure in her own right, bringing her personal contacts and cachet to the job. It was seen as an accomplishment to have her on staff. The annual report of the Red Cross in 1943 stated that they had hired an "outstanding poet and writer" to represent them.[25] Mona downplayed her own importance, choosing once again to emphasize her relationship with a powerful man.

Her job for Red Cross involved a lot of writing: prose, poetry, and even her first scripts. She was out in the world, making speeches, attending functions, seeing and being seen. She was, in short, a professional celebrity. Nothing could have suited her better. Mona loved attention, and this job placed her not only at the centre of attention but in the mainstream, as few poets have the opportunity to be. Mona made a good public figure. She was attractive and knew it, but did not overemphasize her sex appeal. She was comfortable being seen as a woman at the height of her maturity – as a wife, and the mother of a teenage son. She was a respectable everywoman, with something special about her: flair, charisma, and a gift for self-expression. She could find something to say for any occasion, and even when faced with a completely unexpected subject could sound as if she had been thinking about it for weeks. She also had a quality of warmth and compassion which, to those who knew her tough core, might have rung false. But broadcast large, it worked, and worked well. People felt as if Mona understood them.

With the Red Cross, she was in the business of compassion: of eliciting compassion for wounded soldiers and their families, and of expressing compassion for the men she met in hospital, those who had lost family members to war, those whose sons and husbands were missing in action. Mona's job was to get people to donate both blood and money. The fundraising campaign in 1942 raised nine million dollars, and she was commended in a letter from Pat Kelly in June of that year for her excellent efforts. Despite the admiring tone, the letter made it clear that Mona's position at the Red Cross was not guaranteed. Kelly wrote that he *hoped* she would be working with him on the next campaign.[26]

Mona's background as a journalist was helpful in her position, but she was also employed to write verse as a kind of company poet laureate. The Red Cross published its own periodical, entitled *Despatch*, including pictures of its activities, letters from prisoners of war and stories of those helped by the Red Cross's various projects. In October/November 1942, Mona wrote "The Preferred List," a plea for contributions for war-torn countries:

> We're Canadians ...
> So we're still on the Preferred List;
> The Preferred List is getting short;
> The names on it
> Are the names of the countries
> That haven't been blitzed –
> Yet! ...[27]

The voice was tough, straight shooting, and spare, with an ironic, understated way of approaching the most painful points. Mona clearly drew on the work of another of her idols, Ernest Hemingway, when writing these ads. She also wrote articles which the Red Cross placed in various publications.

The poetry she wrote on behalf of the Red Cross hints at what was to become a late-blooming talent (or perhaps a talent that was there all along waiting for an outlet). This was the writing that she did for radio. Any poem is different when it is read out loud; some would even say that poetry is an essentially oral art and that giving a poem voice, in a sense, brings it into being. This is true in a particular way of Mona's poems. They may seem trite on the page, but read out loud they carry surprising emotional power. The liberal use of capitals and the extravagant punctuation which Sandwell deplored are more suited to a radio script than to a page of text.

In 1944, Mona did have the opportunity to write a script. This was for a short film called *The Quality of Mercy*. Produced by Associated Screen News, it was a tribute to the "Red Cross Girls" traveling overseas, and to the volunteers at home, including regular citizens who gave blood. It also gave information on the activities of the Red Cross, solicited donations, and encouraged others to volunteer. In the background is a clergyman's voice reading the Portia's "Quality of Mercy" soliloquy from *The Merchant of Venice*, while the narrator says: "In time of war, the sky is the limit of letting blood ... that's what some writer has said ... and it's terribly true! So, for the wounded and dying ... the living come ... gladly ... to give their blood to save men fighting to keep us free!"[28]

Mona used her skills as well as her connections in the literary community to put the Red Cross in the public eye. She also did her best to parlay her position with the Red Cross into freelance work. She was in contact with Margaret Christie, a literary agent in New York. Christie turned down Mona's offer to submit verse. ("Verse is something that I shy away from as fast and as far as possible," she wrote.) However, Christie encouraged Mona to write a story in serial form, "filled with romance and effort" and set in the context of the Red Cross. This, Christie wrote, she could sell "without half trying."[29] Mona never produced the series. When she wrote to Herbert Hodgkins, editor of *Mayfair* magazine, about various Red Cross efforts, she also took the opportunity to promote her own book. Hodgkins congratulated her, and wrote that he would run a review of the book along with a photograph of its author.[30]

For Mona, all kinds of writing – advertising, poetry, and prose – came from the same source. Her writing assignments were carried out with deep sincerity. She flung her whole self into whatever cause she was espousing, and this made her a brilliant copywriter. By the same token, her poetry often had a clear idea to put across, a message to sell. Her poem "Blood Donor Clinic 10 a.m.," for instance, ends with the lines: "It only takes a few minutes/ But it lets *you* in on a miracle!"[31] This facile couplet may seem a harmless aesthetic misstep, but it takes on an ominous quality when I think of the way Mona let her fantasy life run away with her, in later years. To me, it seems important boundaries were already being blurred, that Mona was losing not only the distinction between verse and slogan, but between who she was, and the persona she felt she must project.

This Was My Brother

Gordon Howard ("Mook") McTavish was adored by his whole family. He was strong, tough, warmhearted, and loyal. With his powerful neck, round belly, and stout thighs, Mook would be considered a fat man today, but in the 1930s he was seen as healthy, his bulk a reassuring sign that he knew how to enjoy himself. He loved football, hockey, and golf, and was a member of the London Flying Club. For a time he worked as a traveling salesman, and at one point owned a dry goods store in Seaforth, Ontario. He was also a leader in the youth group of the local Metropolitan United Church.

But his true calling was the military. Army life gave Mook everything that was important to him: outdoor activity and lots of it, companionship with other men, and an opportunity to develop his talents as a leader. He was a member of the District Engineers of London for the fifteen years leading up to the war, eventually becoming the unit's commanding officer. For Mook, the outbreak of fighting meant that his hobby could become his life's work. A letter to Mona from basic training in Camp Petawawa, 15 June 1940, said that his training was "progressing merrily" and went on at length about his fishing exploits, listing all his best catches with their exact weights.[1] *The London Free Press* printed a letter from Mook during this period.

"These days of waiting are hard to endure, but we are sure as soon as you good friends at home put in our hands the guns and planes and equipment required to take up the war against the Hun, victory will be ours. God willing that day may soon come when our task over here will be done and we

Eagerness: Mook (centre) flanked by fellow soldiers.

may return to Canada and our loved ones once again. Please give my kindest regards to all the good friends at the Curling Club, Athletic Association, Golf Club, etc. 'Thumbs up and Cheerio.'"[2]

Mook was not the type of person that others worried about – if anything, they looked to him to allay their fears about the war. (Graham, who missed his beloved Owen Sound and his activities in local theatre, his reading and music, seemed much more likely to become a casualty.) The army provided Mook a context where he could thrive. It seemed – by whatever crazy logic we allow ourselves to feel safe – that the war itself would leave him unscathed. If anything, it would be good for him.

That logic so often fails. Early in the morning of 18 August 1942, five thousand Canadian soldiers set out from the shore of England and landed at various locations on the French coast around Dieppe. They had known for some weeks that an attack on a French beach was imminent, but were given little information, for security reasons. Their force was spotted by the enemy and almost a thousand men died in the space of nine hours. Mook was among them. Two signallers on his ship survived to tell the story. As the landing craft he was on approached the shore, the captain was shot down from the bridge. Mook took over command, but soon the bridge itself detached and he was carried away with it. Two sappers on a nearby ship saw a shell pierce the funnel and explode the craft's magazine.[3]

Mona kept many newspaper clippings from the days and weeks following the raid. A vein of them ran through one of the larger boxes, so that I sorted them all in one grim afternoon. I felt chillingly aware of *Mona's* awareness that history was being made, and of the pain she must have been feeling when she clipped and folded these papers. I had to go outside, walk around briskly in the sunshine to dispel a feeling of being haunted. The hands that touched these newspapers long ago must have been shaking. Everyone who handled them – even the seller at the newsstand – must have read the stories with thudding heart, combing them for familiar names, trying to gather information about the last few moments of a father or a cousin or a brother or friend. The pictures showed Mook very much alive, radiantly happy in his uniform, yet they were looked at through eyes that held knowledge of his death.

The sentiments expressed in this newspaper item were typical of the attitudes I found in many articles on the raid: "with ... grief there is a pride that comforts and heals. The pride that all of us have in being of the breed; the pride that we can take in holding up our heads in that great company of free men when the toast is 'Canada too.'"[4] Reading this story, I could not help but think of Mona's early poem, "Coronation Day," which implied that the true pain caused by war is camouflaged by patriotic pageantry. Were these thoughts on Mona's mind when she read the newspaper coverage about Dieppe?[5]

Pacifism was advocated by many writers and artists, both before the First World War and after. In the mid-thirties, the Montreal branch of the Canadian Authors' Association Poetry Group even offered a prize for peace poetry; a prize Mona won in 1936 for her poem, "Peace! Peace!"[6] But as news emerged of the threat of European fascism, and Prime Minister Mackenzie King stated that if the Nazis were threatening Great Britain, they were – by extension – threatening Canada,[7] many pacifists modified their position, seeing war as an unfortunate necessity. Mona was among them.

In this context, I would have thought it perfectly reasonable for Mona to express dismay at war and its attendant suffering. Someone else had started it, after all. Yet, as I learned looking through Mona's correspondence, a different kind of logic prevailed at the time. As early as 1939, Mona was under editorial pressure to keep the full extent of her feelings under wraps. Among Mona's letters was one from Alvah Beattie, rejecting Mona's poem entitled "A Woman Looks on War." He wrote, "I would have liked to publish it. Unfortunately, we are banded together in a common cause and the newspapers and the magazines of Canada must do everything they can to 'sell' the war to Canadians." Beattie went on to suggest that she try an American magazine. "Over there, they are trying to keep out of war and your effort would help to sell that idea ... I agree with the sentiments expressed 100% and would like to broadcast them, but I must not."[8] The poem begins:

A Woman Looks on War

I am a woman,
And I am being perfectly honest about this calamitous war,
I resent it!
I know that's taking the small view,
Not the wide ... or as it is sometimes called, the long view,
But that is because I was born a woman
The very fact that I was born a woman
Makes me naturally a possessive person.
The fruit of my womb, for instance,
Is pretty much mine.
And I'm not altogether anxious
To have it become cannon fodder.[9]

As I read these lines, and the correspondence with Beattie, I thought back to an incident that happened in 1996, the week my father suffered his first major stroke. He had been rushed to Toronto for brain surgery and the prognosis was not good. After a harrowing day, I phoned to tell Mona about his progress. I dialed her number in trepidation – concerned, I admit, for myself as much as for her. I was emotionally exhausted, and not ready to cope with the theatrics that came to the fore when Mona felt someone else was becoming the centre of attention. Yet I was stunned to see a different side of her emerge when the stakes were really high.

"Hi, Baby," she said, matter-of-factly. "Thanks for calling me. I know you're busy." Her voice was firm, completely in control. "Tell me everything, Dear. I don't want you to spare me, okay?"

"Okay," I answered, and told her it was not known whether her son would live out the week.

"Now, listen, Kid, don't worry about me. Just keep me posted, will you? Just tell me what you know, as soon as you know."

The whole scene felt like something out of an old movie. A war movie. Her stoicism in the face of anxiety and grief had clicked in automatically: a long-practiced response that was still available to her fifty years later, just waiting to be called forth.

There has been much discussion since the war about whether the Dieppe raid was necessary, whether the men *had* been used as cannon fodder. As I learned, there were hints of this debate even at the time. Among the articles Mona saved was a clipping from 28 September 1942, an interview with Wallace Reyburn in Montreal. The interviewer asked whether Dieppe had been worth the heavy casualties. Reyburn answered that it certainly had, because the information gained at Dieppe would be invaluable in launching a second front. Later in the interview, an uncomfortable question came out: "What of the part of the English in the raid?" The reply: "Mr. Reyburn said he had been 'disgusted and shocked' to hear statements that the Canadians had been used unnecessarily and that English troops had been saved."

I wished Mona had annotated this article, given some clue as to how she felt about it. Despite all her talk about Dieppe, she never mentioned that there had been controversy about the raid, and she certainly never criticized it herself. At the time, she must have felt pulled in two directions: one, the poetic – and indeed human – need to express her feelings, the other, the pressure – both from within and without – to support the stoical patriotism that was associated with winning the war. That patriotism meant focusing on brave sacrifice rather than on grief.

In the fall of 1943, "This Was My Brother," was taken up by General Motors, and run as part of a full-page ad in newspapers throughout the country. The ad was for the sale of Victory Bonds, and was printed with this commentary: "If all of us in our work at home pause and reflect on the heroism and sacrifices of our forces on every fighting front we surely cannot do less than make our own humble sacrifices, enabling us to buy more Bonds for Victory."[10] Here is the poem.

This Was My Brother
(For Lt.-Col. Howard McTavish, killed in action at Dieppe)

This was my brother
At Dieppe,
Quietly a hero
Who gave his life
Like a gift,
Withholding nothing.

His youth ... his love ...
His enjoyment of being alive ...
His future, like a book
With half the pages still uncut –

This was my brother
At Dieppe –
The one who built me a doll house
When I was seven,
Complete to the last small picture frame,
Nothing forgotten.

He was awfully good at fixing things,
At stepping into the breach when he was needed.

That's what he did at Dieppe;
He was needed.
And even death must have been a little shamed
At his eagerness.

"This Was My Brother" was part of my verbal landscape when I was growing up: as familiar as a nursery rhyme. I thought I knew the poem and all the nuances it contained. Years after Mona's death, though, I discovered a whole new layer of meaning in the poem, one she never spoke about directly. While researching the Dieppe raid I found "This Was My Brother" on a web site from the department of Veterans' Affairs. They had printed the poem without its last two lines. Thus, it ended "That's what he did at Dieppe, he was needed." The department corrected the error as soon as I let them know about it, but seeing the poem truncated made me realise that Mona had, in fact, written something quite subversive. Up until the end, the poem is a tribute to a brother's brave sacrifice, and a rallying cry for others to do the same. But behind the emotional clout of the final two lines lies the suggestion that she felt these men had been robbed of their lives.

❧

Mona told so many stories about Mook that I thought I knew all about him. I was wrong. Among her photographs were some tiny snapshots of a wedding, taken on 19 June 1939. The delighted groom is Mook and the unidentified bride resembles Mae West. She wears a wide-brimmed hat and carried an enormous bouquet dripping with ribbons and bows. Mona smiles pleasantly from the photographs. Her dress is a floor-length, floral print, on what seems to be a white background. Mook's bride does not look especially young, and there is nothing timid or bashful about the way she carries herself on her wedding day. The hearty, fun-loving Mook has met his match. Another photo taken a year later shows the couple about to take off in a small plane. Mrs McTavish is dressed in vertiginous heels with a jaunty hat. This time, Mook is in uniform.[11]

Mona never mentioned that Mook was married. I saw the woman's name for the first time when I sorted Mona's papers – in the articles which announced his death. She was Dorothy Margaret McTavish (née Hammond) of Wingham, Ontario, and she lived at 917 St Clair Avenue West in Toronto. This was only a few blocks from Mona's wartime apartment, so I asked my father if he could remember visiting his aunt. "I'm sorry," he said.

"You mean Nanna didn't visit her?"

"That's right."

"Even after your uncle was killed, did Nanna go and see her? Did Nanna help her out at all?"

"I'm sorry. It's not."

And he had no idea that his aunt had lived that close.

Mona's favourite story had always struck me as improbable (with the war office phoning Mona to announce his death). Still, I put this down to her in-

Mook's wedding, 1939. From right: Graham Gould, Mona Gould, Dorothy McTavish, Howard McTavish, Douglas McTavish, John Gould (small boy in front), Ellen McTavish, Alfred McTavish, unknown wedding guests.

flated sense of her own importance. It was not out of character for her to depict herself as getting preferential treatment or being privy to inside information. I also knew she was capable of downplaying someone else's role in a story in order to emphasize her own. In this case, though, she changed the cast of characters entirely.

Why would Mona hide the fact that she had a sister-in-law? The first reason that comes to mind is her fierce possessiveness. When it came to certain men – her father, her son, and no doubt, her brother – any other woman was a rival. It was also important to Mona to be the chief mourner, for Mook's death to be *her* loss over anyone else's. After all, it had given rise to the poem which made her famous. The heady rush of fame she experienced in the 1940s returned annually on Remembrance Day. From mid-October through mid-November, Mona would be invited to give speeches and read "This Was My Brother." There were requests to print it or use it in memorial services. It was the one time of the year when she was at the centre of things again. Mook's death was so integral to Mona's own story that she needed to feel like the most important person in his life.

And then there was her lover, Jim. He was shot down in 1941 in an aerial battle in the Near East. The date was 11 November, then known as Armistice Day. As I later learned, he was classified as missing in action for over a year before being confirmed dead. Another man on his mission was known to have survived, and been taken prisoner. Thus, newspaper accounts at first offered hope, and then dashed it. The announcement of Jim's death was made in the spring of 1942, a few months before the raid on Dieppe and a year before the publication of *Tasting the Earth*.[12] Mona was not a relative of Jim's, nor was she his wife or his fiancée. She might write poems in his memory but her day-to-day life offered no context for expressing her grief. She was married to someone else. It could not have been easy to see Dorothy's Hammond's name in newspaper accounts of Mook's death; to see her accorded the respect due to a widow when Mona had no formal status when it came to her own recent loss.

Mona's losses during the war were fraught with less-than-acceptable feelings. Whatever doubts she might have entertained about the Dieppe raid carried the stigma of being unpatriotic. Her relationship with Jim may have been tolerated in some circles, but most people would have condemned her for betraying a man who was now risking his life at the front. It is possible that for a while, she loved both men, and believed she did not have to choose between them. The war had chosen for her. How did she react in the face of all this? Did she cover up her feelings, or even fully experience them? Perhaps one secret led to another, and it was only a short step from denying her emotions to cutting a person out of her history.

ॐ

"This Was My Brother" brought Mona instant recognition, and by the following spring *Tasting the Earth* was published. The book was hailed by E.J. Pratt and the CAA. It was also praised in the newspapers for its emotional power and accessibility. Mona was truly a popular poet. Not only did her poems achieve sales and critical acclaim, they were loved, and Mona was loved for writing them. She gave voice to the feelings of a nation, particularly its women, who found themselves alone without their men, surrounded by loss and the threat of loss, having to explain war to their children or living with the constant anxiety that if the war went on long enough, their sons, too, might enlist.

In one case, reading Mona's poetry inspired a fan to attempt some verse of her own, in tribute. Grace A. Reinhardt wrote:

I long, like you, for distant hills
Yet know perhaps some handy skills
And with my hands I knit or weave
While you, with words and mind achieve
A poem, for the songless ones
Who bake meringues or sugar buns.[13]

"Clara M." wrote from Vancouver, in April 1943, "'The Book' is here at last and has been read and re-read a dozen times since Steve brought it home on Friday night. I must confess I wept over it on Saturday morning and was consequently a half-hour late at the Bank incurring the displeasure of all and sundry. I am not given to weeping at any time, I might say, but your poems have always had the effect of touching me in some way. Perhaps it is because they have the feeling of fitting the 'secret' places in one's life and give the impression that I often get in church (the Anglican Church, of course) of having it all especially for me, in some way."[14] Women were not the only fans, by any means. Everyone was subject to the feelings Mona expressed. Clara M.'s response was typical of fan letters and reviews of the book, in which the most common sentiment was, "She has said what I would say, if I could."

Mona's mother, Ellen, was also unreservedly encouraging. The disapproving mother of Mona's stories showed nothing but pride when it came to her daughter's literary triumph. Ellen's loss of her favourite son may have softened her, or it may have been that Mona had finally gained her mother's respect ... unless, of course, that respect had been there all along. "Tuesday a.m. Doug brought your book home last night. I have just been looking at it again. I as you know cannot express as you can just what is in my heart or mind. But to say it is lovely is not enough. There is such a warmth about the colour scheme. Then B.K. Sandwell has said the [illegible] It is all so different and the simple sincere and lovely expresses it. Tasting the Earth at this time seems to mean more than ever before."[15] At one point, Ellen copied out a tribute to Mona which was published in the *London Free Press* following the GM Victory Loan ad. Mona did not keep the newspaper clipping, only the slip of paper with her mother's almost unreadable script.[16]

Mona also kept a letter from her brother Doug (on letterhead from the

Detroit Trust company). "Dear Mona, Just haven't had time to thank you for your book. Have enjoyed it very much. I hope it will sell. Can see no reason why it shouldn't. They are the sort of poems that should have an appeal to a great many people. [The letter is cut off with scissors at this point.]"[17] Doug was not given to extravagant praise, but in his own way he showed how impressed he was by his sister's achievement.

&

The war went on for six years. To many people, it must have seemed that it had always been with them, and that wartime conditions would go on forever. Mona examines the new order that had entered in the workplace in an article in *Chatelaine* called "They used to say 'Never work for a Woman' ... but now?" She begins the article with the assumption that full equality for women has already been achieved, and that the changes will be permanent. "Maybe in the beginning, when women were new to the downtown world of offices and stores, there was friction among the gals. Biggest reason for this was the fierce competition. A woman had to surmount and survive the prejudice existing in the male mind that 'a woman's place was in the home.' That made for strain, and too much trying. Once she'd made a job for herself, a woman had to clutch hard to hold it, and that naturally tended to make her thorny and abrupt and none too charitable in her dealings with other women. There was always the shadow of fear that another woman *might* worm her way in and kick the props out."

After acknowledging that women haven't had an easy time integrating into the workforce, she goes on to extol the advantages of the woman-led workplace. Women bosses, she writes, are fairer than their male counterparts, and their female employees feel that they are being judged on merits rather than appearance. Woman bosses are more compassionate, thus enhancing productivity. Moreover with women in charge, class distinctions are downplayed: "War work is doing something to job snobbery, too. In a second big plant I visited, the candid young woman in charge of female employment said right out that one of the things she had insisted on was that there should be no demarcation between the girls on the factory machines and the office workers. When that was firmly fixed in everybody's mind, a war plant became a first class place to work." Mona interviewed women in war plants, advertising agencies, and department stores – though no places or names are cited in the article. She concludes that a balance between the sexes makes for a better working environment, and that the ideal situation is to have both male and female supervisors.[18]

Mona's efforts during the war were largely directed at cheering people up. She wrote amusing anecdotes of her everyday life, not denying how lonely and anxious she felt, but rather, making the best of a tough situation. She also wrote about good things that were happening on the home front. The Red Cross remained her primary client, but she also wrote a story about the Salvation Army Appeal, which was printed in *Saturday Night* in September, 1942.[19] A letter from H.D. Burns at the Bank of Nova Scotia to *Saturday Night* remarked, "There is no doubt that this publicity in The Saturday Night has greatly aided in making the Appeal successful."[20]

꙳

Mona's increasing success as a writer during the war years meant that there were many demands on her time. But my father, John, insisted that he didn't mind his mother working such long hours. On the contrary: he was proud of her.[21] With so many women in the workforce, it was not unusual to be a latchkey child in Toronto at the time. Still, amidst all the fan mail, newspaper clippings, and articles, there are some photographs showing mother and son enjoying a trip to Centre Island one summer day. They rented bicycles, and took photographs of each other trick riding around the flowerbeds. In one or two close-ups, fatigue is evident on Mona's pale face, but from a distance, all you notice is her athleticism, her youthfulness, and her sense of fun.[22] And reading her correspondence I realise that, busy as her life seemed, there were still long (and boozy) lunches with friends, and sacred holiday time in the summers to enjoy with her son.

About this, she corresponded affectionately with E.J. Pratt, who always left the pressures of the city behind for delicious summers in Muskoka.[23] Every summer, Mona and John spent the entire month of July in various rented cottages in Muskoka: at Rossclair and Browning Island. These cottages were only accessible by boat, and they would spend every possible moment swimming and canoeing. Mona was a strong swimmer and accomplished outdoorswoman, and she taught these skills to John.

A short piece Mona wrote entitled "This Ever Happen to You?" recounts the trip home after one of their summer jaunts to the island. "We were tired. The sort of tiredness that succeeds terrific pedaling … riding 'no hands' … and playing a sort of devil-may-care, mad game of follow-the-leader in which you circle trees, ride around drinking fountains and be as much of a ninny as you please and to heck with what people think. Anyway we were both fairly subdued. Not much fight left in us." The story goes on to tell how a large and very sweaty lady sat down on Mona's lap for the duration of the journey.[24] In another story, her son insists on taking his two white mice, Margaret and Loo-ey, up to Muskoka with them, only to have them get loose in the cottage.[25]

"We" was the pronoun Mona used to refer to herself in all her prose, dating from the time she worked for *The St Thomas Times Journal*. By the sixties and seventies, this affectation was probably outdated enough to have cost her some work, but it was common in the early part of the century, especially in the type of personal pieces that Mona became known for. It lent the stories a chatty tone and diffused the attention, saving her from having to use the self-aggrandizing "I." In later years, the writerly "we" took on more associations. At times, the "we" Mona talked about was her household as a whole. It was never a large household, but the pronoun gave the impression that there was a constant, merry buzz of activity – so much activity that Mona would have been at pains to list who was actually there. Being forever surrounded by people was an important part of the image Mona cultivated for herself.

At times, the "we" refers to Mona and John as a unit. There is the disturbing sense that no distinction at all is being made between them. They are gathered under the umbrella of the same pronoun. He walks in step with her except for the odd occasion when he helps her carry something or chimes in with a witty line. He is treated as an extension of Mona herself. When I read these stories I feel claustrophobic, on my father's behalf.

If being an only child was difficult for John in those days, though, he soon found relief. He met a boy by the name of John Aylesworth, who lived in one of the larger Forest Hill houses. At twelve years old, John Aylesworth was almost exactly a year older than my father (both had birthdays in August). The two shared similar interests, and a wacky sense of humour. They became instant friends, known as "The Two Johns" or – for some long-lost reason – "T-Zone and T-Zonie." John Aylesworth called Mona "Mammy," and all but moved in with the Goulds.

Despite hearing many stories about him, I only met John Aylesworth once, when I was about ten years old. When he visited us at our cottage that summer, it was an occasion for much excitement. At that time, he was the producer of the comedy show *Hee Haw*, and I looked forward to his visit as if we were going to enjoy a live performance in our own home. As it turned out, the two men spent the day outdoors in the blazing sun, laughing and talking in loud voices. It seemed as if their intended audience was each other, and that everyone else was in the way. I spent the rest of the visit trailing after my mother as she stamped back and forth to the cottage with trays of beer and snacks, cursing under her breath about being treated as a servant.

For years I delayed interviewing John Aylesworth, though I knew he would have vivid memories of Mona in the forties. I knew, from Mona's stories, that he had become a happier and more settled man since his fourth marriage, in 1985. Still, it took me a long time to work myself up to making the call. His voice was not what I remembered; it was gentler, cracking a little with age, and his encouragement of my project was disarmingly warm. So, too, were the feelings he expressed for Mona. He considered her his surrogate mother. They had, according to John, "hardly a serious moment," but his affection for her ran deep. Mona offered him an escape route from his unhappy home life. She made a point of introducing him to great comic literature, especially to the works of Perelman and Thurber. He credited those years as decisive in his choice of career. He spoke matter-of-factly of his own mother's alcoholism, and of his isolation until he met the Goulds. This was different from the complicated dance I had to do with my own family, interpreting veiled layers of meaning, negotiating conflicting version of the truth. I found myself drawing a long, relieved breath, not just because he put me at ease with his own frankness, but because he *was*, to all intents and purposes, a member of my family: as close to an uncle as I'd ever had.

John Aylesworth also told me that before he ever met my father, he had noticed Mona from his usual perch in a local malt shop. She cut a striking figure in Forest Hill back in the 1940s. He told me, "I would see this lady with her hair flying walking with high heels and a real click-click up from St Clair towards her apartment on Spadina. And she was always just sort of charging along and I never knew who she was and then of course as soon as I met her with John and I said, 'Aha! Now I know who you are.'"[26]

Mona and the two Johns made a zany trio, the young men falling over themselves – sometimes literally – to impress Mona and make her laugh. Their pranks included terrorizing local merchants, crawling on their knees along the floor of a Toronto streetcar on their way home from seeing *The Emperor Jones*, and even hanging an orange suspended in a jockstrap on the light fixture which hung over the elderly Mrs McTavish's bed one summer in Muskoka. Mona would do nothing to reprimand them when she found out about their exploits, but would say with a wry expression, "Oh, you lit-tle bas-tards!" She was clearly enjoying every minute of it.

Finally, I asked John a question that had loomed large in my own mind.

"Do you feel you really *knew* Mona?"

His answer surprised me. "Oh yeah. I don't think Mona was ever particularly deep. She was just one of those forces of nature who just had a wonderful life and had fun doing it and never complained about anything. And I guess that was her. People always wonder what's going on inside. And often there isn't anything going on inside. What you see is what you get. And I think that was true of Mona."[27]

Two days later, though, he sent me an email. A memory had come to him, of a summer visit to Browning Island some time during the war. "We were all standing in the lake, and John and I started splashing water on Mona. She joined in our laughter at first, but then suddenly broke down crying uncontrollably. We were amazed. We tried to console her, but she just marched back up to the cottage without a word. When we finally sheepishly went up to join her, it was as if nothing had happened. She was Mona again. We never did figure out what happened, and I've never forgotten it because it had never happened before, and nothing like it ever happened again. Maybe it was triggered by a memory of being splashed years before by her brother. We'll never know."[28]

Demobilization

Among Mona's papers was a photograph taken by a street photographer the weekend the Goulds spent in Toronto just before my grandfather, Graham, went overseas. I wanted to know about the day that picture was taken, and travelled to Barrie for the weekend to ask my father about it. We sat in their kitchen, my father, Ingi and I, pulling closer around the table as darkness gathered outside.

First, I asked about my grandparents' years in Owen Sound, about the Sydenham Club, about the move to Toronto when the war began. Ingi's eyes were watchful on her husband's face. I asked questions, and for the most part, she initiated the answers. This was something she could do based on the understanding she had evolved, over the past few years, of all his gestures and inflections, based on her knowledge of the stories he used to tell before the stroke. Like Mona, my father had been a storyteller. I was amazed by how much Ingi knew, and saw that over the years she had absorbed everything he'd said, as if to make their histories one.

I placed the photograph in front of my father. "Can you tell me about that day?"

He pointed to each of the figures in the picture: Mona first. "She is marvelous. Marvelous," he said. "Will you look at that!" He demonstrated the movements of Mona's shoulders as she strutted down the street: "Bang! Bang! Bang!" he said, as each shoulder punched forward. My father pointed to Graham's picture. "But he ... Look at the thing!" My father set his jaw and clenched his fists, grim and resigned.

"He wasn't happy about going to war."

"No."

"And how did you feel that day, can you remember?"

He pointed to himself in the picture, but spoke in the third person. "He said, 'Alright. Alright, then.'"

My father got up and stood in the middle of the room. He demonstrated the way he lifted his chest, ready to meet whatever might be coming his way. A manly pose, or a boy's interpretation of what a man should look like, the chest upheld and stiffened, a solid shield of ribs, clavicle, and sternum, leading the way. What did his father tell him? *Be good. Look out for your mother. Study every day.* And what had his mother told him about getting through this last weekend with his father? *We mustn't make it hard for Daddy. We mustn't cry and make a scene.*

"This is what he does," my father said, traversing the kitchen in two determined strides, demonstrating the posture he adopted at the age of twelve, and had maintained all his life.

❧

My father told me many stories about his past, but I was into my thirties before I heard the one about the day Graham came home from the war. And I heard it only once.

Dressed in a new tweed suit, John went with his mother to the exhibition grounds, where the men returning from duty were to arrive by train. Mother and son stood behind a high, chain-link fence with all the other women and children, gripping the wire with their fingers, trying to catch a glimpse of Graham. A huge stretch of asphalt separated them from the place where the trains stopped and the men poured out into the brilliant sunshine of that winter day. Is that him? Is that him? No.

And at last, there is Graham, unmistakably Graham, his small but solid figure, the strong angle of his chin. He grasps the bar that flanks the train's door and swings himself down to the pavement. He scans the crowd pressed against the fence. Then he sees them, Mona and his tall son. He waves to them, and with slow deliberation drops his bag on the ground. He squats beside the bag, digs inside. Finally, he takes out a flask. He drinks, the harsh swallow resounding through his body, and puts the flask away again.

John is sixteen, and has been in the cadets for two years. If the war had not ended when it did, he would have been called up. He has his own uniform, knows how to make a bed so you can bounce a penny off the covers, and keeps his locker at school as tidy as if he were already a soldier. He has prepared a speech, gone over it again and again in the weeks they've known Graham was on his way home. Among other things, he has decided to stop calling his father "Daddy," and switch to the more mature "Dad." When Graham goes upstairs to unpack, John rises from the table. He is taller than his father now, almost six feet and still growing.

"I'll go with you, Dad," he says in his rich new baritone. He glances toward his mother in a way that says: leave the two of us alone.

"Okay," she answers, smiling.

John helps his father unpack the duffel bag: awkward now, with this important speech inside him, and not knowing how to begin. He takes each piece of clothing which Graham hands him. An army-issue shirt, three pairs of socks. He has to start somehow. Drawing himself up to his full height, he snaps his elbows to his sides in the pose he's learned in cadets.

"Dad?" he says.

"Yes, John."

"There's something I want to tell you."

"What is it, Son?"

"I wish I could have gone with you. I wish I was just a couple of months older. I wish I could have fought beside you, Dad."

Graham balls up the socks and dashes them on the bed. He takes John by the arms and sits him severely down. Sitting down beside him, so their eyes are level he says: "Don't you ever ... *ever* let me hear you say you want to fight in a God-damned war."

⌁

As the war drew to a close, Mona had become a spokesperson for a national clothing drive sponsored by UNRRA, the United Nations Relief and Rehabilitation Administration, which was formed in 1943 to assist refugees. For this campaign she coined the slogan: "What can you spare that they can wear?" Mona's contribution to this campaign was highly valued; still, there were disputes with her employers. J.E. Chandler, director of publicity, wrote to her on 29 October 1945 complimenting her on her excellent job; however, he requested an invoice.[1] A second letter from Chandler has the top cut off, but it makes clear that there was some angry correspondence from Mona. She had been anxious for a payment to arrive, and had accused him of trying to make her a "sucker." He wrote that he was grateful for her work, but added caustically that he had no wish to be made a "sucker" himself and that she should wait until the drive was over before rendering an invoice for a reasonable amount.[2]

Mona's relationship with the Red Cross remained unclouded by the bad feeling that crept into many of her other business dealings. She left the organization gracefully. In a letter to Dr F.W. Routley on 31 March 1945 she wrote: "Mr. Kelly brought me in to write wartime publicity for Red Cross, and with his leaving I feel that my job automatically comes to a finish." She added that she was not planning to go on to other employment, and left the door open for future work by saying she would be freelancing from home.[3]

Mona's letter made it clear that her leaving the Red Cross was a given. The war was over, and she was going to let her husband take over as breadwinner. Routley, appreciative though he was, did not try to hold her back.[4] Mona gave the impression she had accepted the status quo when it came to household roles after the war, but I learned from her papers that she actually had other plans. In the fall of 1945, she made a query to Sydney Morrell of UNRRA about the possibility of employment overseas. He replied that they were looking for staff in Czechoslovakia, Poland, and Italy, and suggested that public information might be a good department for her.[5] She wrote to him again, this time about the possibility of employing Graham as well. He declined, saying that the organization had a rule against employing spouses in the same mission. But he invited Graham to apply on his own behalf through the personnel office.[6]

I wonder whether she and Graham were in touch about the inquiries that she made for him at UNRRA. Did Graham want to stay in Europe, or was this Mona's initiative? Was she doing everything possible to avoid a return to Owen Sound? Or was she driven by a knowledge – conscious, visceral, or both – that Graham would return irrevocably changed?

Mona kept three telegrams charting his progress home.

November 26, 1945
Should arrive ninth or tenth written regularly call you on arrival
Graham Gould.

December 2 1945
Arriving New York Elizabeth home eighth meet me Love Graham.

December 7 1945
Arrived on Queen Elizabeth leaving on special army train today.[7]

These telegrams give precious little sense of how Graham felt about returning. My father's memory of his needing a stiff drink before greeting his wife suggests all was not well. He also told me Graham had "fallen in love" with a woman in Belgium during the war. At the time, I accepted what he said unquestioningly. Later – even though I had begun to think more deeply about my grandparents' relationship – I did not press him for more information.

The topic made me uncomfortable, or rather, I sensed it would make *him* uncomfortable. I still don't know whether he was using the word "love" to spare my sensibilities, or to elevate the importance of his father's affair so that it would be on par with Mona's. Mona mentioned nothing to me about the woman in Belgium, but her papers suggest she had to rise above feelings of hurt and humiliation in order to resume her marriage. Among the souvenirs of Graham's army service was a poem entitled "Promise." The ribbon was running out when Mona typed it, so that the letters are half in black, half in red.

It's far too late ...
It's far too late for "kissing ... and making it better" ... you see
It's far too late for kissing and making it well
And I know now if you love ... and it's a good LONG love ...
The perimeter ... is ... hell!

Fill my hands with flowers ... speak to me tenderly
Have every consideration under the sun
And I shall thank you ... and appreciate and duly write you
But ... I am ... done.

I can manage to smile in the marketplace
Display my courage
My medals are obvious pinned on my breast
By midnight ... I am ... nothing in my own house
Cry I for rest!

Who was it said "time is a great healer?"
Ah ... but can I WAIT?
Easy ... and sweet and simple and quick
To slip the latch of the gate

So tho' I feed on ashes, taste clay
I shall see it out to the long night
I shall stay ... I shall stay.

Something keeps me ... something whispers "Not now"
Once there was a marriage that WAS marriage
A long vow![8]

In later years, Mona was happy to add to her mystique by suggesting that her own history was tinged with a little scandal. She never mentioned that the roles had once been reversed. In the event, she showed a profound adherence to tradition. She "looked the other way," welcomed her husband home, and never spoke of the matter again.

꒜

Graham's formal release from the army was sent to Mona's address in Forest Hill. It was issued to officers and nursing sisters, and outlined the regulations for his return to civilian clothes. The certificate said that he had served in the United Kingdom and Continental Europe and was "struck off the strength" on 19 January 1946.[9] Mona kept this and other records of his army service, including his badges,[10] a letter of thanks from Major General E.G. Weeks, and a souvenir of a farewell dinner given to members of his transit camp.[11] She kept a few photos of his basic training as well. In one, he carries an enormous shell. In another, he is loaded down with a canteen and heavy clothing, and sits on a log with two other soldiers. He grins at the camera. The rigors of training have trimmed any excess weight from his frame, and the narrowness of his chest makes him look little more than a boy. There is also a photograph of Graham in uniform with his mother and sister. It must have been taken just before he left for Europe, and the weight of the occasion shows on all of their apprehensive faces.

Graham had initially served as sergeant in the tank corps. He became a captain in May 1943, and was given the job of paymaster. This meant that he traveled with his unit from England, through Belgium, and into France. He was responsible for paying the soldiers, and keeping financial records. He did this from a tent or from the back of a truck. The job was grueling, particularly in the last year of the war, when the paymasters in his campaign were responsible for transporting local currency in small denominations to where the troops were stationed, all the while monitoring for possible abuses. The paymasters worked with little respite, since the demands on them only increased when the troops went on leave. The pay corps was not immune from attack, and some paymasters were killed and injured. At one point, a bomb fell directly on Graham's mobile office, injuring two men and destroying most of his documentation. He happened to be outside the tent at the time and received nothing but "a slight shaking up."[12]

For Graham, though, it was the chilling quality of war's bureaucracy that left lingering memories. Years later, he wrote a story about his experiences.

It opens in a military hospital where he is working on the repatriation of a group of soldiers. He visits one who is gravely wounded. "[The nurse] warned me that the boy was dying and would never live to see the boat. He was not suffering too much and didn't realise his condition. I knew his name would be struck from my Draft list." Graham refers to the character as a boy and not a man, though the story deals with a baby the young soldier has fathered. The soldier dies the next day. Even those who get to go home are in a terrible state, however. "I watched them leave in the morning. I checked the names once more on my Draft list. A long line [of] ambulances stood waiting in the driveway. Then they came out ... on crutches ... on stretchers ... walking (the lucky ones). Repatriation Draft #1043."[13] In the knowledge that he himself was "one of the lucky ones," Graham returned to civilian life.

Immediately, Goulding Rose and Company, the investment firm where he worked in the 1930s, offered Graham a position as head of their Owen Sound offices. Housing was in short supply, and he traveled there as soon as possible to find his family a home. After her exciting and fulfilling years in Toronto, it is hard to imagine Mona was eager to return to Owen Sound. Moreover, the only way to get a house in those years was to buy one, and this prospect made her uncomfortable. In a story she wrote a story for *Saturday Night* about the experience, she confesses that: "I've always wanted to be so unencumbered that at the drop of a very small hat we could pack our bags and light out for far places. To own a house would mean to have strings attached." But she claims to have been captivated by Graham's description of the house, which has "possibilities." She reverses her position and enjoins Graham to buy it at once. She moves out of her apartment in Toronto (thus, burning her bridges) and goes to join him, though the house needs a lot of work, and they have to stay in a hotel. They eventually decorate the house to their liking, only to have the oil heater explode just before they move in. Mona's story concludes:

> My husband and I stood bleakly on the sooty lawn. We cursed. This is a churchly town but we were way past caring.
>
> "We'll sell it," my husband growled. "We'll sell the whole shebang first thing in the morning."
>
> "Oh no we won't." I said stubbornly. "We'll tear out that damned oil burner and live in that little house yet."
>
> "Well ... I know where there's a boot legger," my husband asserted.

"And when we get back to the hotel I'm going to phone him."

"Do," I said.

And he did.[14]

In this and all her stories, Mona presented her marriage as companionable, seasoned – never soured – by the odd bit of cheeky, verbal sparring. Like Nick and Nora Charles in the *Thin Man* movies, the Goulds were portrayed as a smart, attractive couple who never took anything too seriously, and like the characters in the films, they always had a drink in their hands. They never seemed to get drunk – at least, not to the point of losing control. If anything, the drinking rendered them wittier, more on top of their game.

Drinking also set them apart from their less sophisticated neighbours. In the "churchly" town of Owen Sound, they were buoyed up by a youthful sense of rebellion every time they obtained a forbidden bottle of booze. In her more caustic moments, Mona described Owen Sound as a narrow-minded backwater. "Small Town!" a poem which she never published, hints that Mona experienced some disapproval in Owen Sound, perhaps on account of her affair with Jim, perhaps on account of her flamboyant nature.

I only wanted to try my hand
At being like Dorothy Parker.
It wasn't a month ... it wasn't a WEEK ...
Till this small town had my "marker".
...
I only wanted to try my hand
At being what was intended –
I only wanted to laugh and sing
And wear my youth like a shining ring
But O, in this town the sin unforgivable,
Is daring to make your life more livable.[15]

In Owen Sound, the Goulds returned to a traditional family structure, the man going out to work and the woman staying home, but because of their different areas of interest, their household was quite egalitarian. As a returning soldier, Graham was given a position of some respect in the investment business. Mona was a celebrated author, in demand for speeches throughout the area, and she was free to devote herself to writing as never before. John was old enough to pursue his own interests, and was used to having a mother who was busy outside the home. For the first time in many years, Mona could look forward to a clear stretch of time to work on her literary projects.

In fact, Mona had established enough of a reputation for herself in Toronto that her career could be maintained from a distance. She had also been careful to keep up her connections in London, St Thomas, and Owen Sound. The Goulds' move to Owen Sound was deemed newsworthy enough by the *St Thomas Times-Journal* that the paper ran a feature article with a photograph of Mona. "The only difficulty now seems to be that Mona is liable to become so engrossed in housekeeping in her attractive home on 9th St East and so fascinated with the joys of digging in her garden that she may forget to jot down the lovely lines that every scene, every person and every daily happening inspire in her. The garden, the housekeeping, the black Persian kitten 'Bunk' and the black cocker spaniel 'Ming' will not, her public hope, pin back her wings."[16]

Mona showed no signs of abandoning her public. *Tasting the Earth* had sold out very soon after publication. Macmillan hoped to issue a second edition, but wartime paper shortages delayed the project, and by the time publication became possible, Mona had more than enough material for a second collection. Copy for *I Run with the Fox* was finalized early in 1946, but there were many hoops to be got through before the book appeared. Ellen Elliott selected, arranged, and edited the poems herself, since Mona was living so far away. She wrote frequently to Mona, keeping her up to date on every stage of the publishing process. Her letters always contained a bit of personal news, and closed with the promise of a visit (her sister lived in Shelburne, which is close to Owen Sound). A budding artist, John used the backs of these letters for his sketches.

Elliott's correspondence with Mona shows just how challenging it must have been for a publisher to function in the context of war and its aftermath. She wrote to Mona once in February, and then again a week later, about the shortage of supplies that she was facing: "When I think of what is likely to happen with manufacturing this coming year, I shudder. Paper is scarcer than hen's teeth. But even so I refuse to be beaten on my beautiful books of poetry, and I shall move heaven and earth to get them out ... particularly your book because of its timeliness."[17]

The following week, Elliott wrote that they would use "This Was My Brother" as the frontispiece for the new book. It had been previously published in *Tasting the Earth*, but had already become a kind of signature piece for Mona. The plan was to reprint the graphic that appeared in many Canadian newspapers. This resembled a brass plaque, with the words of the poem seeming to appear in relief. This presented so many technical challenges that the press finally decided to set the poem in a typeface which resembled a graphic.[18] Mona and Elliott continued to reconnoiter about the book's design. Elliott was trying to find scarlet cloth for the binding, along with endpapers in the same shade. However, she concluded, "A red jacket as well would be rather too much – so let us think this over a bit."[19] A month later, the struggle to obtain materials was still on. It was a challenge to find red cloth for the binding; indeed, to find any cloth at all.[20] The book ultimately appeared with a red jacket and cover, and white end papers. As summer approached, the book was still not out, and the company was racing to publish it in time for the anniversary of the Dieppe raid in August.

The interim period was eventful. Helen O'Reilly, Macmillan's publicist, wrote to Mona with the news that she would soon be in the public eye. Tying in with the twenty-fifth annual convention of the Canadian Authors' Association, Macmillan ran an advertisement in *The Globe and Mail* with thumbnail photographs of fifty-one of its authors. Mona was among them, along with Phyllis Argall, Claire Bice, Grey Owl, Frederick Philip Grove, Leo Cox, Byrne Hope Sanders, Sir Charles G.D. Roberts. Mazo de la Roche, and E.J. Pratt.[21] Approbation was coming from all sides. During the same week, Mona received a note from B.K. Sandwell inviting her to be part of a collection of "some of the best verse that has appeared in Saturday Night in the last three or four years."[22] The result was a simple and elegant chapbook called *Poems for the Interim.*

As it turned out, Mona's second book did not appear in time for the anniversary of the Dieppe raid, but it did come out for Christmas. Like its predecessor, it sold well. Mona was a brilliant public relations person, and did her share in helping to promote the book. She corresponded frequently with Helen O'Reilly, providing lists of people who should receive complimentary copies.[23] She also studiously built contacts in various community organizations. She may have derided Owen Sound as a small town, but it offered a substantial population of readers. Mona had a wide base of support in Southern Ontario, not only in Owen Sound and its surrounding communities, but in the London/St Thomas area where she had grown up.

Women bought Mona's books, and Mona knew how to get in touch with her readership. As a married woman, she was expected to attend meetings of local ladies' groups. F.R. Scott had heaped contempt upon such meetings, as did Mona, on occasion. But this did not prevent her from taking advantage of them as an opportunity to promote her work. In the late 1940s, her name appeared frequently in the women's sections of various newspapers. One story from Owen Sound announces that Mona (Mrs Graham Gould) has become a member of the Ladies' Garrison club. With Mrs George Clark, she has been elected social convener. The same story notes that "Mrs. A.A. Kennedy poured tea at a table centred with yellow roses in a green pottery vase."[24] Mona also read from her poetry at a meeting of the U.R. Welcome Club of Owen Sound. The newspaper account of the event remarks that Mrs Olive Ibbett played a piano solo, "To the Sunrise."[25]

Another story reported on a talk Mona gave to the Tuesday afternoon meeting of the Lyceum Club of Owen Sound. She spoke on what it was like to publish a book. The report commented on Mona's popular appeal: "She doesn't write her poems for posterity, but for here and now, she sings simply and clearly for people like herself, Mona Gould told the Lyceum Club and Women's Art Association at the January meeting on Tuesday afternoon at the Community Y. Mrs. J.M. Thomson presided in the absence of the president, Mrs. Charles Rogers."[26]

Mona kept the script of this speech.

I hadn't the foggiest idea of what it would be like to have a book ... I only knew I wanted one! – So you'll bear with me if I'll tell you this from experience ... and if sometimes I appear to be swelling unbearably with pride and conceit ... do forgive it, because actually I feel very humble in my heart to have had even one book – and equally fortunate, to have this November seen my second one roll off the presses.

... There is nothing to compare with the thrill of a first book. It is just a little less than when the nurse says "here is your son" and you look upon the face of your child for the first time. It is "Next best!" –You tremble. Your throat goes dry. – Tears, fill you [sic] eyes. If they don't, then you are a harder man, than I am, "Gunga Din!"[27]

She also made frequent trips to Toronto where Arleigh Junor of the Granite Club was active in establishing readings and cultural events. Helen O'Reilly wrote that "Mrs. William Junor is frightfully anxious to have you speak this season at one of her Granite Club teas – she says you were a mad success last time!"[28] She noted, though, that there was no funding available to reimburse Mona for her trip. The reading at the Granite Club went over well, though bad weather may have discouraged some people from attending. Mrs Junor thanked her for "looking so charmingly and reading so charmingly from your poems."[29] Another letter from Junor mentioned a possible guest appearance on her Sunday Broadcasts on CHUM.[30] This, of course, would have thrilled Mona, since Edna St Vincent Millay did readings of her poetry on radio. Mona also did at least one poetry broadcast at the local Owen Sound radio station, CFOS, on a program called "Melody Time."[31]

Along with numerous other public figures of the time, Mona was interviewed for a story in *Chatelaine* entitled "War Memorials, What Form?" Mona is the first person quoted, and she is quoted at the greatest length. She says that we should try to imagine what the fallen soldiers themselves would want to see. As far as she is concerned, they would want to see a society in which public services such as hospitals, playgrounds, and swimming pools would be more liberally funded. The arts would be given special focus. "This may sound idealistic," Mona says. "It isn't. It's very realistic." Mona's preoccupation, from that time on, was with commemorating World War Two. It happened informally in her stories, and publicly as part of Remembrance Day observances. She did not consider these to be a glorification of war. She felt that the purpose of Remembrance Day – indeed, of any kind of memorial – was to acknowledge the pain of war so as to avoid it in future. She was not alone in this. The same *Chatelaine* article contains a statement by Air Marshal W.A. (Billy) Bishop: "Let us form foundations to teach the youth of Canada that war is a grim business, not a thing of glory. Let us teach them that what is needed in the world of tomorrow is not people to die for their country, but people to live for their country."[32]

Mona continued to contribute to *Chatelaine*, but her efforts to create a section dedicated to books and poetry were rebuffed – albeit pleasantly – by Byrne Hope Sanders. "There is always the feeling that there are so many publications which deal with book reviews very thoroughly that it is questionable whether they belong in a general woman's magazine. But quite apart from that the big problem is one of space."[33] Two years later, she tried again, and again was refused; again, kindly. The difficulty was still space. Although she had established a reputation and continued to publish regularly, editors did not instantly leap upon anything Mona suggested. She was still a freelancer, and had to pitch new ideas constantly in order to stay afloat.

I Run with the Fox was favourably received. Although it did not garner as much attention as *Tasting the Earth*, the consensus was that Mona's second book built on the strengths of her first – with a more mature voice and

technical proficiency. "J'O'C" of *The Halifax Chronicle* wrote, "In the welter of today's juggling with words and abstract ideas that goes under the
name of poetry, it is a delight to run across anything as poignant and appealing as 'I Run With the Fox', replete with ideas and emotions which the
author has evidently felt deeply and expresses with words as sharp, telling
and bright as a rapier."[34] An April 1943 review in *Saturday Night* praised the
simplicity and honesty of the poems: "A poem may be perfect in traditional
form and do nothing more than emphasize the cleverness of the writer. But
if the thought has truth and beauty in full measure, both the writer and the
form sink into the background.[35] And from Sally Townsend of *The Globe
and Mail*: "Now she offers her second volume I Run With the Fox, in which
the promise of the first book is sustained and deepened with a maturity and
an assurance. She seems to have more confidence in herself and in the authen-
ticity of her talent. The quality of her work is impassioned and sincere. Her
lines never fail to move the reader."[36]

The only negative note I could find was in *The Vancouver News-Herald*,
printed under the headline of "Faux Pas."

In an uneven little volume of fragmentary verse – I Run With the Fox
(Macmillan, $1.50) Mona Gould proves that she can avoid hackneyed
approaches to less-original themes, but (start running Mrs. Gould, here
come the hounds!) her work is often ineffective because of limited poetic feeling and a narrow range of verse form and subject matter.

In fact, this Torontonian deserves to have her poetic license for 1946
revoked, for she has abused it more than once. Verse like Prayer in a
Hospital is lame and prose-like. At times, as in the title poem, Mrs.
Gould proves she has something to contribute to Canadian Literature,
but her sense of music and rhythm often fails her.[37]

Colleagues who had become friends wrote to Mona warmly, speaking of
how touched they were by her work. Bertha James, a colleague from the
CAA, wrote: "[your poetry] has completely cast its spell over me. Your gift
of expressing thoughts so exquisitely fills a depth in my soul. Darling you are
simply wonderful."[38] A letter from Lettie Ann Hill concealed within its praise
an ominous note. She wrote, "There is a pervading quality in Tasting the
earth, a quality of heightened experience, imaginatively brewed that I don't
feel in the second book so-much or is it that I always have a nostalgia for my
first love?" She mentioned a number of books she had recently read and con-

cluded, "Your book, Mona, has a finish and an originality that tops them all." Words of caution followed, however: "Watch your poetry that you do not type yourself with a certain style and form." She wrote that Mona could "outdo Pat Page and her kind," and warned her not to become purely a journalist but to continue to attend to her poetry. "If you think I am all wet please say so in good round numbers if you can find the time to answer me."[39] Hill's letter, diplomatic and careful as it was, cast the most critical – although ultimately sympathetic – eye upon Mona's second book. As a friend and reader, Hill must have sensed that Mona was becoming overly attached to a certain period of her development, the one when she thought she was at her most attractive. The youthful quality of *Tasting the Earth* was what many responded to, including Hill herself; however, it could only take Mona so far, and the question remained: where to go from here?

⁂

Another event took centre stage in Mona's life at this time. She made no secret of it – but its true impact was not acknowledged for many years. In the winter of 1946, just as *I Run with the Fox* was being launched, Mona discovered that she was pregnant. She lost no time in spreading the news – not even waiting the customary three months before letting her friends and relatives know. A letter from Douglas congratulated her on both happy events, though of course, his "big brother" tone was always there to temper Mona's enthusiasm. "Hope you haven't forgotten how to look after a baby. Sure keeps you busy."[40] Like the one complimenting her on *Tasting the Earth*, this letter was cut off at the bottom.

Mona was overjoyed. She wrote a poem during her second pregnancy which was never published. It began:

My body has become a place of dreams, again
Roof, to a child
What strange, enchanted creature
Sleeps in my flesh?
Host, am I now, to all my deepest longings
Kin, to the earth, where spring green wind will blow
Let the wind rise, let the sun shine
The seed is stirring
As in my kin, before me, long ago!

Notes were made in pencil – perhaps years later – on the upper margin of the poem:

> From the sperm to the worm
> From the womb to the tomb
> = security = so called.[41]

Mona was thirty-eight – and her experience of pregnancy was more sober the second time around. She had just come through a war, and could never completely erase her awareness of the fragility of life. Her big brother Mook had died, and so had her father. Her mother had moved to Michigan to stay for a time with Douglas, who had experienced his own crushing loss. Douglas's wife, Sadie, had recently died giving birth to the couple's first child, a son. The baby had also died. Mona wrote about her simultaneous awareness of the beginning and ending of life in "Visit," a poem published October 1949, in *Chatelaine*.

> How strange it was
> To stand above your bones
> My father!
> To read your name carved in Scotch granite
> The date of birth
> Of death.
> To feel the awful rush of loneliness
> Like a salt tide
> Taking the breath
> To lay my little flowers in the grass
> Daisies, you loved,
> And wish – oh wish so much
> You knew it!
>
> Thither I brought my unborn child
> To stand above your grave
> As if to tell you
> How it was, with me![42]

Though the tone of the poem is sad, Mona ends by saying she feels the "essence" of her father in the child she is carrying. Whatever comfort this provided was short lived. The child was born prematurely, in July, and died within the week. By this time, John was eighteen years old, and making forays away from home. He was away working for the summer when the sad event happened. Graham wrote to him, saying the baby was "just too tiny to survive."[43] Mona's friend Margaret wrote a letter full of compassion and tact (all the more so perhaps because she herself was childless). "I'm just sorry that this wasn't to be dear, for another child would certainly have filled your cup of happiness. But it's pretty nearly brimful as it is, and maybe you'll find it complete after all."[44]

Doctors these days would have cautioned Mona against drinking and smoking during her pregnancy. They might have saved the baby's life. But at the time, it was considered "for the best" if some children did not live past infancy. Mona reacted as she was expected to, counting her blessings and hastening to put the whole thing behind her, but she felt divided. Her daily life was fun, prosperous, and fulfilling; on the surface, she had little reason to grieve. Yet her spirit had suffered an indelible blow, and no one wanted to talk about it – at least, not for very long. Mona wrote a poem about her loss called "For a Very Small Wayfarer." It was never published. In abstract and high-flown language the poem deplores the injustice of her son's early death, "What happened, O capricious gods of Chance/Why did you frown on one small Unborn's dream?"[45] Mona never directly addressed her own feelings in the poem, and she remained silent on the loss of her child for another twenty years.

During the late forties, Mona began to suffer from what she called "nerves," and these only grew worse when she got pregnant again, and miscarried. She became restless and wanted to get away from everything she knew. It was out of this need that Mona and Graham began to speak of traveling. They decided to go to Mexico for a total change of scene. Graham was no doubt ripe for an adventure after three years of sitting behind a desk. He took a leave from his job, and they set off in their car. They discussed moving to Mexico with members of their circle, and in later years, Mona's stories sometimes gave the impression they had actually lived there. In fact, they only stayed a month.[46]

The trip was to be funded by the freelance work that Mona would generate. In August of 1947, Mona wrote to *Chatelaine* pitching a story on her trip, which was planned for the fall. Winifred Huff, secretary to the editor, Lotta Dempsey, replied that no commitment was possible, but that Miss Dempsey would have a look at the article when it was finished. In October of the same year, Mona received a letter from Lotta Dempsey herself, saying the same thing. Either her original letter was mistakenly answered twice, or she wrote to *Chatelaine* twice, hoping for a different answer if she reached Dempsey personally.[47]

In the end, Mona left Canada without a commission, but she used the material from that trip for years. A feature story in *Saturday Night*, entitled "Like Going to the Moon and Just as Exciting," shows her skills as a feature writer in their full maturity. It recounts the full story of the journey, beginning with a drive along the Pan-American Highway.

> The guard rails are low. You go up over eight thousand feet before you reach Mexico City. You see fields of clouds far below, acres of bright flowers, rushing strangely coloured rivers and always the Indians walking gravely along the highway wrapped in their bright serapes and rebozos, the women with the babies on their back and the men wearing the vast mushroom-like sombreros.
>
> You don't expect to come upon living things in the silence of these mountains, but always there are the little burros asleep on the thin edge of a gorge, the low palm thatched huts exuding smoke at every pore.

After a stay in Mexico City, Mona and Graham made their way to San Miguel to visit painter Leonard Brooks, and his wife Reva, a photographer. The Brooks had traveled to Mexico so that Leonard could study painting on a grant following his release from the Canadian army. Mona wrote of their visit to the so-called GI Art School, where veterans were studying. San Miguel was an exciting place, the site of a burgeoning artistic scene. Mona concluded her story with this description of the last night of their stay.

> It rains beautifully in San Miguel de Allende ... softly and comfortably like happy tears. Quite late we borrowed a flashlight and made our way slipping and plunging down the steep cobbles. The little town was asleep. Behind the adobe walls poverty and plenty slept side by side. A single light burned in the little Sanatoria started by a refugee Spanish doctor near our hotel. We were leaving San Miguel in the morning, now more certain that at any time since we had come.
>
> "Once the dust of Mexico settles on your heart, you can find rest in no other land."[48]

The article was illustrated with photographs by Reva. She had taken up photography – more or less as a hobby – at the time of their move to Mexico, but soon began creating haunting studies of the life of the indigenous people there. Eventually, her work became internationally known.[49] From Reva's letters, it is clear she felt that the photographs Mona had used for the *Saturday Night* article had helped put her work forward in Canada. A letter dated 29 November 1948 is effusive in its thanks: "It is practically impossible to convey to you my surprise, happiness and gratefulness for the article which you sent today. I can hardly believe it yet, and am actually close to tears of joy about it." She offered to let Mona keep whatever prints she did not use for the *Saturday Night* article and concluded, "many thanks for the wonderful break, and hope we will hear from you very soon."[50] Reva's popularity increased. A letter about a year later spoke of invitations to exhibit her photographs in the London Art Gallery and also at Eaton's College Street, in Toronto. In the same letter, Reva recounted how she and Leonard were settling in to life in San Miguel, which was to become their lifelong home.[51]

After years of drudgery and grieving, Mona and Graham could now drench themselves in an exotic, sensual world. It was a world, furthermore, that did not deny death. The miniature skeletons for sale everywhere, the open coffin shops and public funeral processions gave a matter-of-fact quality to what, in Canada, we tend to shroud in mystery. With so many deaths in their recent past, Mona and Graham found it refreshing to be in this environment. This was the Mexico of *Under the Volcano*, a book they both loved. And like the book's hero, their senses were heightened by copious amounts of alcohol.

It was during this trip that Mona bought the enormous silver pin which became her trademark. She had it custom-made in Taxco by Antonio and Salvador, two handsome and courtly silversmiths working for a company called Los Castillo. Mona herself chose the design, which is in the shape of a heraldic crest. It measures about two inches across and three inches down, and weighs down anything but the sturdiest jacket or sweater. One of Mona's favourite stories was of smuggling the pin across the American border. (It was never clear why she felt she could not take it openly through customs, but this definitely made the story more exciting.) After wrapping the pin in wax paper, she sank it into a jar of cold cream. Her charming smile and the illicit aura of a lady's cosmetics bag were enough to throw the customs officers off the trail.

Mona presented the pin to me as a gift on my thirteenth birthday. At the time, I was very thin, my shoulders not much wider than a typical ten-year-old's. The pin was too big for me, and its extravagance could not have been less suited to my character. All I wanted at that age was to make myself as inconspicuous as possible, especially in the region of the chest. As soon as I received it, and for the next twenty-five years, I fluctuated wildly between guilt and anger over that pin. My effusive thanks to Mona went completely against how I was feeling. I didn't want to wear it – *couldn't* wear it. At the same time, I was haunted by the knowledge my grandmother had given me her prized possession. It meant I was the most important person in her life, while her importance in mine was dwindling. Her giving it away also intimated that she was on her way toward death, and was casting off her material possessions. Though I could not have articulated it then, I resented the play for sympathy this gift represented.

For years I kept the pin in the beautiful wooden box – the watch box belonging to my great grandfather – that Mona had given me to house it. I did my best to forget about it, but it weighed on me, inwardly, as much as if I had been wearing it. Then one day in my thirties, for no reason I understood, I simply opened the box and put on the pin. I wore it that day and have worn it many days since. I liked the way it looked. What is more, I enjoyed the attention it brought me. Now, I think that the pin was the best gift Mona could have given me during that time in my life. It presented me with a vision of myself as a flamboyant, charismatic person. The image seemed alien to me then, yet on some level, I knew that I could – was even obliged to – grow into it.

I was wearing the pin the day I came across a letter from Antonio and Salvador among Mona's papers. Dated March 1949, it affectionately recalled Mona's and Graham's visit, and concluded with Christmas greetings. The letterhead was in the shape of a banner which read: "A woman without jewels is like a night without stars."[52]

9

Daily-ness

Mona's stuff took up so much space. I needed so many supplies, so many paper clips and file folders and photographic sleeves. I was always asking for more. The people who worked in the library were modest, understated. Everything about Mona – and by extension, about me – seemed "too much." Her saccharine prose embarrassed me. So did her extravagant punctuation, and all that *stuff*. There were photographs by the hundreds, overexposed, underexposed, double exposed. Who were all these children? I'd never seen them before. And so many cats, squirrels, racoons, and views of the back porch in every kind of weather. There were empty picture frames, dried-out wads of gum, open jars of Vaseline. There were chains of Christmas lights, broken glasses, seashells, half-eaten lollipops, ripped stockings. There were old TV guides, bills (never paid), ads for psychics and astrologers, fund-raising materials for a home for retired donkeys to which Mona evidently donated money in the 1960s. Papers were shoved into envelopes, rolled, crumpled, folded, in no order at all. Things were stuck together with Band-aids, masking tape and duct tape, layers and layers of it. Valuable papers emerged from the boxes in irredeemable clumps. I closed my eyes, some-times, and tossed a bunch of them in the recycling bin. "Sorry, Mona, I just can't," I said aloud.

At one point, I found an album of valuable correspondence with an empty colostomy bag adhering to the back. After consultation with a librarian I was sent to see the conservator, Emrys Evans, who examined the album, picked

```
                                                appy
                                            's is GE
                                            ---Music Box
                                         u:
                                            Attend:
----------------------------------------------------------------
Ann: Snap Judgment! So says a man (name of Sheed) in the New York Times lately!
     "Whatver people DO with old snapshots: they DON'T throw them AWAY" says
     Sheed. WE agree. So, must YOU?-You KNOW you've spent EVENING after EVENING,
     staring glassy-eyed at friends in Motor Boats: friends on shore: friends at a
     picnic: progeny: bathing: barbecuing: being married: hoisting the first petard-
     (we mean) progeny: camp (pix) of same: college (pix) of same: Graduation (pix) of
     same; and finally Marriage (pix of same. The cycle is now, COMPLETE: but IS
     it? 20 % of people put old snaps in chests and boxes: a few actually paste
     'em into albums. Most stuff EXTRAS IN loosely; so they fall OUT onto the
     floor when you're the LOOKER: Most adults put (pix) into drawers and hope SOME
     thing will happen TO them: One small boy given a camera for Xmas took his only
     1 roll of film and threw the camera away. He didn't know what to DO with it
     NEXT! Do YOU bury unwanted snaps under old sox? Or do you 'edge' em into al-
     bums sos's they fall into unaware visitor's laps? Or, are YOURS simply left on
     the floor of the Attic ? Well, NO matter. But we must do something about our
     old snapshots! Musn't we? YOU doing anything..to-night .hmmm ?-
      MUSIC BOX HERE ----------------------- Music ----------------------
```

Advice on what to do with old photos. This relatively
unblemished fragment from a radio script was easier
to file than most.

at the bag's adhesive with his fingernail, and, at length, said gravely: "I think
we'll just leave that." It was then I realised that the little round stickers Mona
used for years to put things up on her walls and seal letters were supplies for
the colostomy she had undergone in 1974. It was a very expensive method,
given that the stickers cost nearly a hundred dollars a box, and Mona could
barely pay her rent. I did not take the conservator's advice, but removed the
covers of the scrapbook and put the contents in a file.

❧

Isolated in my carrel, I was ashamed of my need to talk to someone … anyone. I made transparent excuses for trips to the reference desk and lingered
there long after my questions had been answered. In the washroom, I burst
into confessions with women I had never met. One particularly sympathetic
librarian seemed to meet me in front of the sink at the same time every Friday
afternoon. I wondered if I were unconsciously choosing her coffee breaks to

relieve my bladder, or whether she made for the washroom whenever she saw me go in.

I dreamed one night that when I got to the library there were pictures of me all over the walls. I ran around – terribly embarrassed – pulling them down, until I realised that the head librarian was the one responsible for displaying them in the first place, that the staff here enjoyed my flamboyance. Asleep, I reveled in their attention like a child at a birthday party. Awake, I continued to be ashamed.

I wanted to know what to keep, what to throw away. I wanted to know how to *do* it. One day, I sat with a crumbling address book in my hands for what seemed an hour. Should it go into a file? An envelope? A photographic sleeve? Should it be kept at all? Finally, the burden of decision forced me out of the carrel. I went to the reference desk. "What should I do with *this*?" I asked. The librarian looked away as if I had asked for instructions on how to perform the most intimate of tasks. "I'm sure you'll figure it out," she murmured.

Another day a librarian caught up with me in the hallway. "I just wanted to tell you that this is *your* collection," she said. "You're taking a meaningless pile of papers and creating a collection from them. When people a hundred years from now want to know who Mona Gould was, they're going to find what you have made. Don't rush. Enjoy it. Take your time."

ৰ্ষ

I had no time. The sorting added days and days of work to a schedule which was already packed with finishing my degree, trying to run a business, and looking after my mother, who had gone from very sick, to sicker, to sicker still. The years went by: 1999, 2000, 2001. Still the collection was not finished. Away from the library, I worried about how I was going to squeeze in another day of sorting, and even more, how I would fit in the time I needed to recover. Certain days at the library weakened me – not just emotionally, but physically. I felt as if I'd been moving stones around instead of sheets of paper.

On any given day, I might find what I had privately come to call "hot" letters. These were usually from my parents, and seemed to radiate anxiety and pain. After thirty years of separation my parents were still a unit in my mind, an embattled unit, their two voices still fighting. His word against hers, her needs against his. Being here in the library felt like a betrayal of my mother.

I knew I could not cure her, but I could make her feel better just by being there. In that sense, I was acting as *her* mother now. But here in the library, I was unavailable. She could not even reach me by phone. She was alive, and needed me; these papers were "just things." Painful things: everywhere in Mona's journals and notes, the letters she kept from friends and from my father, I saw just how terribly she had treated my mother. I knew that she had not made Hetty sick – that would be going too far – but the stress of that difficult relationship certainly had not helped my mother's condition. I was cleaning up Mona's mess in more ways than one.

I taught myself to recognize the pens and papers used in certain difficult periods of our lives. I quickly filed these letters, taking in as little as possible of their contents. Still, a word or phrase would always sneak through, and I'd be instantly submerged in the conflicts of the past. I left the library headachy and nauseous, as if I'd been exposed to poison gas. Except that getting away didn't help. The poison was inside me and took days to wear off. I resented my task to a point where I'd catch myself muttering angrily as I took a shower or prepared a meal.

Yet I might just as easily find a letter that would make my life more tolerable. I remembered my mother telling me that if you come in contact with a nettle leaf and get stung, you immediately rub the spot with the juice of the dock plant, which grows beside it. The antidote is found right next to the source of the pain. In Mona's archive, this antidote came in the form of hundreds of unremarkable, chatty letters from her friends, which Mona saved as carefully – sometimes more carefully – than the most valuable archives. When I left home for university Mona used to beg me, in letters: "Tell me your daily-ness." She wrote her daily-ness to her friends and they wrote back. These "daily-ness" letters did not have literary merit, nor were their writers, writers, yet these were my favourite things in the archive. I felt guilty for cherishing them, poring over them when other things should take more of my time, but they seemed like poetry to me. I lost whole afternoons in reading them. On those days, the library became a place of refuge.

Sunday
Darling;
I somehow seem to be <u>with</u> you today in my mind, a clear indication I should get down to this increasingly arduous task. Once I start I seem to ramble on – but I do an awful lot of pencil sharpening first – breakfast, dishes (mostly yesterday's) garbage, bed making, etc. etc. etc.

This is just really to reassure you that I really am quite recovered from my recent dentistry and my mouth is pretty much back to normal.

My neighbour G- ... came in about 5:30 last night for a glass of sherry and we decided to have a game of scrabble. She put me down by 75 points – had all the Qs and Xs and I had all the Us and Is. I kept having to put things back so I could hope for better luck but it continued to evade me. She puts me properly to shame I can tell you!

...

I make out your letters beautifully with my magnifier – it's your curlicues that sometimes conflict. Please keep writing. Do I understand you're writing an autobiography – you should. Cheers!

Lovingly, Marty.[1]

1/12/92

Dear Mona,

...

Hope you are all over your flu by now.

I am well but Lori is back and cleaned my house up Wednesday and Friday so it sparkles again. She took a Christmas vacation so my house hadn't been cleaned since Thanksgiving.

Talked with Doug [junior] on the phone this afternoon and they are all well. The children found out what snow looks like. They never had any in Palo Alto. Quite a change to move to Wisconsin in December.

Love, Doug

I liked your poem.[2]

Hi Mona –

The Jay's beat Kansas City 1-0 it's 2 A.M. & raining!!!

Love, Dora[3]

In these boxes, there was a whole lifetime's effort to preserve daily-ness. I loved that these letters were written decades ago. I love that Mona had a half-century's worth of correspondence from some people, filled with nothing but quotidian details.

Best of all, the Mona who coined the phrase "streetcar tired" was also in these boxes, and she was possibly the only person in my life who understood what I was going through. At one point, I found a photocopied clipping of an interview with an eighty-year-old woman. She had been expected, from an early age, to look after her parents, and had played her role without questioning it. She was forty years old when her mother died, and from that day onward, lived for herself. The second half of her life had been the happiest. What had possessed Mona to keep this particular clipping? I didn't know, but I took it home.

I understood Mona better, too. Everywhere, I saw evidence that her stories of being sought after had not been true. In her papers, I found a daily life not much different from my own: a feat of organization. My grandmother's constant task, as a freelancer, was to send out letters of inquiry, write articles on spec, come up with proposals and ideas. Many were accepted, but most were turned down, if they were acknowledged at all. My grandmother did well, but could never rest on her achievements because she knew that poverty and obscurity were just one step away. Eventually, they claimed her. Maybe this was a source of shame to Mona – and maybe this is why she exaggerated her stories of success – but discovering the details of her daily life, I felt proud of her. I didn't care about the outcome. It was her tenacity that impressed me. She never gave up.

10

A Good, Wide Wonderful Business

In May, 1949, Mona got a letter from the director of Radio programs at CKEY.[1] Monica Mugan, the host of a program called *Listen Ladies,* was moving to England, and the station was holding an audition for her replacement. The show ran six days a week at 12:20 pm on both CKEY, Toronto, and CHML, Hamilton. Mona was chosen for the job amid fierce competition. That week, her name was seen for the first of many times in "Kesten's Corner," a chatty column on media happenings which Bob Kesten wrote for *The Toronto Telegram.* Kesten wrote, "Replacement on the show has been a matter of some conjecture and just about every feminine miker in town angled for the assignment." He went on to call Mona "the gal who has carried off one of the more choice female jobs in local radio."[2]

Mona had already made some forays into broadcasting with readings on CHUM and CKOS (an Owen Sound station), and her byline appeared regularly in many newspapers and magazines. She was a dark horse, though. She had, after all, been out of Toronto for four years, and many seasoned broadcasters were in line for the position. But the station's officials must have known talent when they saw it. Mona had an ebullient personality, an ability to talk to anyone about anything and to sell anything to anyone. Most of all, she was a consummate improviser. She was the perfect candidate to host a daily program where she had to generate all her own ideas and write all her own material, including the ads. At the age of forty-one, Mona had found the perfect job.

Though it meant relocating to Toronto, the move made sense in more ways than one. John had begun his studies at the Ontario College of Art in the fall of 1948. After the war, the enrolment of OCA had expanded suddenly. The graduating class nearly quadrupled in size after 1945.[3] As John later told me, a number of his classmates were attending OCA on veterans' grants, and a weekly pay parade was held right in the school building. This meant that students like my father, straight out of high school, attended both classes (and parties) with a crop of sophisticated, war-hardened men. The effect was intimidating. In his first year, John wrote to his parents, who were still in Owen Sound:

> By next week the assignments will be pouring in. Believe me, I've never worked so damned hard in my life. – Got my first lesson in sculpture yest. Aft. – Teacher had a long beard. – Our first lesson consisted of building a 6″ cube with tiny pieces of clay – built on one at a time. – Hard, hard, tedious work. The object of the entire first year is discipline. – Just about like training an officer, Dad. And to make things stiffer, all the teachers are Imperial army types with mustaches or beards who stand over you and say, 'tear it up and make a fresh start you see'? No "arty" types. They seem to be made of iron. I eat lunches outdoors on the Grange campus, as there is seldom room for lowly 1st year shmos in the cafeteria. The meals there, however, are wonderful. A big meal for 30 cents. Must go now.[4]

Graham had a good job in Owen Sound, but it was not a particularly unique or fulfilling one. It seemed likely he would be able to find similar work anywhere. Macho pride would have been the only thing stopping him from moving, and Graham – unlike many men of his time – was not one to let his pride stand in the way of his wife's success. The move could not have been easy for him, though. Graham must have accused himself of weakness on occasion, even if the charge never came from the outside. Mona, who had a strong competitive streak, knew that in many people's eyes her status as a woman was based on how dominant a man she was able to attract. Yet in many ways, she was the dominant one in her household. This may be why she spoke of Graham's position in the army with such exaggerated pride. Whatever inner turmoil they were feeling, my grandparents moved, as a unit, into this new phase of their lives.

Mona started work in Toronto, and Graham followed a few weeks later. They found an apartment at 26 College Street, a Tudor-style building just opposite what was then the Eaton's College Street store. On the first floor was the Ward-Price Antique Gallery. The apartment itself was a radical choice in those days of suburban development. It consisted of one enormous room at the top of a building which was also used for businesses. It was, in other words, a loft. In earlier days, the building had been a private house, and the Goulds' apartment had been the billiard room. After their bucolic years in Owen Sound, the Goulds embraced life in Toronto's urban core. Eaton's and Simpson's – both close by – were not only major department stores, but also centres for Toronto's cultural and commercial life. Simpson's had an active book department and hosted special events such as The Homemakers' Show. Eaton's was home to an art gallery and a library, as well as an auditorium. Within a short radius of their apartment was Mona's old stomping ground, the Red Cross, and the studios of CKEY as well as the offices of MacLaren Advertising and of *Gossip* Magazine. The Royal Alexandra Theatre and Massey Hall were a few blocks to the south.

Mona called her neighbourhood "Toronto's Greenwich Village" in her broadcasts, forever identifying herself with Millay. The Toronto of the 1950s is sometimes portrayed as provincial, hopelessly bereft of culture, but this is a misconception. Immigrants were moving in from all over the world, particularly from Europe, and bringing with them new food and music, attitudes and customs. The city's cultural community at that time was compact. Limiting as this might have felt to some, it was invigorating to others. It was big enough to allow for diversity, but small enough that people from all disciplines and sensibilities had the chance to intermingle. In her radio work, for instance, Mona no doubt crossed paths with the young Harold Town, who took part in Howard Milsom's radio drama workshop for CKEY.[5] Iris Nowell describes Mona's and Graham's neighbourhood, based on the reminiscences of artists Walter Yarwood and Harold Town (who was Nowell's lover for many years). Yorkville, Nowell writes, was not Toronto's original Bohemia, "but the title rightly belongs to the Gerrard Street Village ... Artists lived and worked in turn-of-the-century three-storey houses on Gerrard Street and its annexing Grenville Street, cheek by jowl with a collection of certified eccentrics – musicians, poets, jewelry makers, writers, actors, a tea-leaf reader, and the live-ins of a well-known 'house not a home.' The noted Grenville Street restaurant, Mary Johns Village Inn, was a cheap and cheerful

life-saver for nearby interns, nurses, and artists. At Mary Johns, sixty cents
bought an adequate lunch of soup and meat loaf; a dollar rated an epicurean
chicken pot pie."[6]

According to Nowell, artists Albert Franck and Florence Vale ran what
amounted to an open house in the 1950s.[7] So did Mona and Graham. There
was an endless party in their apartment. John would make his way to his
parents' home almost every night, bringing a bevy of friends including artist
Paul MacDonald and actress Joy LaFleur. John Aylesworth – with a recommendation from Mona – had been hired by MacLaren advertising. Starting
out in the radio department, he shared an office with another young writer
named Frank Peppiatt, and the two joined forces to form a successful comedy
writing team. Aylesworth soon married, and his wife, Jean, was magnetically
drawn into the atmosphere of the Goulds' home. Jean spoke to me about
her impressions of the household.

> There were a lot of people. It was a place where you were always wel-
> come and the door was always open. It felt very Bohemian. Mona was
> so laid back and so relaxed. It was always interesting. You could talk
> about anything you wanted to talk about … The atmosphere with the
> raised hearth and the benches on each side and candle light and books
> and drawings all over the walls. The two huge brown corduroy-covered
> beds that were flat on the floor without any legs on them … As you
> went down towards the front of the apartment there were leaded glass
> bay windows that were raised off the floor like a little stage. There were
> books all the way around this bay window, below the window. Tiers of
> books. Mona would be given the books after interviews. There would
> be masses of books around, and of course your dad's drawings. And
> there was always something new to look at.[8]

This raised area, as John Aylesworth recalled, became a stage for impromptu
comedy routines as well as for music performed by John Gould and his
friends. John had been studying clarinet since childhood, and – like his parents – had a passion for jazz.

Mona and Graham had all the necessities for daily life right on their
doorstep. A sidewalk café outside the building and a flower shop down the
street provided two essentials. An establishment called "Malloney's" on
nearby Grenville Street took care of the third. Drinking was strictly regu-
lated in Ontario in the late 1940s, though conditions were gradually loos-

ening. A change to the province's liquor laws in 1947 had meant that hard liquor could be served in public for the first time in thirty-one years. Four hotels, two restaurants, and one nightclub in Toronto were now given the right to serve cocktails.⁹ Malloney's was not, strictly speaking, a bar, but rather an art gallery, which – according to John Aylesworth – functioned as a private club to get around the liquor laws. He remembered Malloney's as one of the only places in town where you could drink without also ordering a meal. For the most part, drinking for its own sake had to be done in an unadorned and ill-smelling "beer parlour." Malloney's patrons were primarily media and entertainment people.¹⁰ In those days, it was not uncommon for Mona to buy a round of drinks for everyone in the place.

Mona's questionable cooking skills did not present a problem with so many restaurants in the area. Most evenings, Mona and Graham ate at Old Angelo's on Chestnut Street, where they might also meet up with friends. And drink some more. The artist Fred Varley was a familiar face at Old Angelo's at that time. John Aylesworth told me, "we used to go there [to Old Angelo's] an awful lot and have spaghetti and meat balls and a lot of wine and Fred Varley used to come in with a couple of women one on each arm."¹¹

An important addition to the Gould household was Chi Chi Bu, the first in a series of cherished Siamese cats. All three Goulds doted on Chi Chi. While he was away from home, John would write and exhort his parents to "take care of my brother."¹² And when they traveled, Mona and Graham would remind John in letters to keep the cat well supplied with fresh liver, and pipe cleaners to play with.¹³ John, in turn, would write his parents the latest news on the home front, from the cat's point of view.¹⁴ Messages from "Mr. Chi Chi Bu, Gentleman Siamese Cat," would appear in Mona's columns and broadcasts, and he had his own series of publicity photographs. Eventually, he began to receive fan mail.

☙

The letter inviting Mona to audition was equivocal about the role of Monica Mugan's replacement. "It may or may not be a commentator's spot."¹⁵ This open-ended situation offered Mona the freedom to place her own stamp on the program. It also promised a lot of work. She had to carve out an on-air identity for herself that would sustain her through a punishing broadcast schedule. The show was only ten minutes long, but it was on air six days a week, throughout the year. This included Easter, Thanksgiving, Christmas

Eve, and New Year's Day. Being in the public eye brought her a great deal of freelance writing as well.

Radio shows on private broadcasters at the time were actually produced by advertising agencies, so that Dodi Robb, Mona's producer, was an employee of MacLaren Advertising. Aylesworth and Peppiatt, on staff at MacLaren, cut their comedy-writing teeth creating humorous promotional spots for *Listen Ladies*, and Mona herself had to generate reams of ad copy for various Christie's products. Another accepted convention of fifties programming was the regular announcer, who chatted back and forth with the host. Mona's partner was the actor Howard Milsom. In the banter which peppered every show, Milsom would play the role of the irrepressible naughty boy, with Mona keeping him wittily in line. They would rib each other mercilessly about their clothing, hairstyles, and anything else they could think of. Every so often, there would be an extremely tame *double entendre*. This is a typical introduction to a program.

MUSIC: THEME ...

MILSOM: Listen Ladies

MUSIC: THEME

GOULD: About – Dolls in Distress – Help Wanted.

MUSIC: THEME

GOULD: Hello, everyone. Hi there Howard. You interested in dolls, at all?

MILSOM: Well now, Mona ... That depends ... What sort of "dolls" ... blonde or brunette?

GOULD: I might have known. I mean REAL dolls ... the kind little girls are interested in.

MILSOM: Oh well ... those!

GOULD: Well, Howard, skip it. We popped into the Doll Hospital on Yonge Street last night, just see how the doll casualties were getting along, and had lots of fun chatting with the Harris Shafrons who mend broken heads, and put on missing arms and legs ... and refurnish faces and wigs.[16]

The show goes on to describe the activities of the doll hospital, interspersed with ads for Christie's biscuits.

Soon after Mona took over the job, she instituted a feature called "Woman of the Week," in which listeners would be invited to write in about a woman they admired. This was often a woman facing an obstacle or an illness, who still managed to lead an active life. Some husbands wrote letters of admiration about the courage, intelligence, and resourcefulness of their wives.[17] For those chosen as women of the week, it meant basking in attention, if only for a short while. And receiving – naturally – an enormous box of Christie biscuits. Annie Black of Hamilton wrote that she had "never had such a gift in my life." She concluded by saying, "Thank you for all the nice things you said, don't know whether I merit them or not. I'm just an ordinary person trying to 'make the best of a bad job.'"[18] Bob Kesten wrote, "Mona's new 'Woman of the Week' feature on *Listen Ladies* is going great guns."[19]

One Christmas Eve, Mona declared her mother "Woman of the Week." She proudly listed Ellen's accomplishments: weathering the loss of her own mother when she was still a child, moving as a young wife to Saskatchewan, where she spent long stretches alone with two small children and pregnant with a third. At one point, she was forced to shoot a timber wolf prowling about their property. According to the script, Ellen had taken over the family business after her husband's death in 1939.[20] All this might seem uncharacteristic, given Mona's stories of her troubled relationship with her mother, but she was capable of moments of great generosity and warmth, even to her worst rivals.

And Mona's stories of her conflict with her mother were, after all, only stories. All the evidence, from letters, to this script, to personal accounts, shows their relationship as loving. Ellen may have held back from praising Mona because of at the risk of giving her a "swelled head," but her pride in her daughter's accomplishments was obvious to anyone else who knew her. Douglas McTavish Junior told me he had resented Mona when he was a child, because the fun of his visits to his grandmother's house had been marred by Mona's radio shows. "Along one wall was a beautiful console radio that was a source of great frustration to me. It was silent except for a brief period in mid morning when all play came to halt and my sister and I were expected to sit motionless and silent on the living room floor. A woman's soft voice arose from the radio console. Aunt Mona had arrived! Grandma sat in her big chair at the end of the room enraptured, straining to hear every word and looking dreamily right through me as though I wasn't even there."[21]

When she moved into radio, Mona's readers became her listeners. The barrier of the page was removed and the relationship became one step closer. Mona's style, on air as in print, was to speak to the ordinary person. She assumed that the ordinary details of people's lives were remarkable and worthy of attention. And her own life was a constantly mined for material. She talked about amusing little things that happened to her day to day: the opening of the flower shop downstairs, the antics of people passing by on College Street, the plays she saw, the meals she prepared, the friends she had over. She created a couplet about the strange dichotomy of intimacy and distance she felt with her audience. "You speak to the mic with its bland, mute face/ straight into the ear of the human race."

She invited children to write in about their pets, for a regular Friday spot. She also broadcast from the Canadian National Exhibition, Simpsons' Homemaker's Show, and Honest Ed's discount department store.[22] She did a special broadcast about Owen Sound, which brought resounding praise from the local chamber of commerce as well as from numerous acquaintances in town.[23] Mona included a healthy measure of culture in her broadcasting. She read aloud her own poetry and that of various women poets. In the winter of 1949-1950 she adapted and serialized two of Katherine Mansfield's stories, "The Doll's House" and "Mrs. Brill," to be read on radio.[24]

She was flooded with fan mail. Often, the letters contained requests for copies of poems she had read on air. The phrase, "Would it be asking too much?" appeared frequently. Even after all this time her most popular poem remained "This Was My Brother." In sharing her feelings about her brother's death, Mona had established her identity as a person who understood loss. She began to write memorial tributes to public figures when they died, and this developed into a whole vein of occasional poetry – not only for deaths but also for births, weddings, anniversaries, and birthdays. Her poetry was seen as a voice for others who did not have the same facility with language. "Lament for the Death of our Good King George the Sixth" was printed in newspapers and church bulletins after the king's death in 1952.[25] In response, Isabel Woodrow wrote, "Your beautifully worded expression of our national bereavement has satisfied something inside me."[26]

Women wrote to Mona, confiding in her as if they had known her for years. One woman's letter told the story of how she was "got into trouble and had no place to turn." A well-to-do lady had paid for her child's keep until she could work again. Recently, she had met a man who loved her and was raising the child as his own. The laboured handwriting and choice of words show that this woman struggled with basic literacy. She closed, "Good luck to you xxxx."[27]

Mona's broadcasts inspired feelings of nationalism in many listeners. M.E. Carter of Toronto was downright militant in her sentiments. "I am so glad you radio people are fighting against this frustration that has been with us so long. When are we going to build up loyalty in our own. If they were wise the people that have talent will stay here now and fight it thro' for we are sick to death of Yankee Ballyhoo and only need leaders to take their proper place ... I'll be looking for you to point the way to others and prove that you can prosper here and not have to be like sheep and run across the Border."[28]

Christie Brown moved to *The Wayne and Shuster* show in 1952, which meant that *Listen Ladies* lost its sponsorship.[29] CKEY retained Mona in the lunch-time spot however, on a new, longer program called *Carousel*. The show was introduced with the words: "Strike the Symbol, ring the bell, it's time for Mona Gould's *Carousel*, that sprightly little fashion magazine of the air, so ..." Thus would begin a compendium of poetry, witty stories, tips on dressing and decorating, along with plenty of advertising. Sometimes Mona would take a break from the item at hand to read an ad, and sometimes drop a mention of a product in the body of the show.

Mona's scripts for *Carousel* are never in the form of full pages. After one or two items, the paper is sliced off and there is no way of knowing what belongs to what script. Mona must have found the shorter pages easier to work with. Sometimes, she typed a long row of dashes along the paper, and tore it along the dashes. At other times, she cut the paper with pinking shears, presumably with the idea that if fabric would not fray when cut by pinking shears, then paper would be less likely to fall apart as well. The opposite is true. I found hundreds of script fragments which fell to pieces as soon as I touched them.

The new program won the affection of even more fans. Kay Heal of Hampton Ontario wrote: "I must just take a minute to say how very much I always enjoy your programme. Your original way of describing everything is such a delight and your voice!! It is so very lovely, what is the magic in it that pulls so at the heartstrings, and so often has the tears in my eyes. It must be that it comes straight from the heart. Forgive this sloppiness, but you do get me."[30]

For *Carousel*, Mona had to sell her own ads. This meant getting in touch with all kinds of businesses, large and small, including Nestlé, Helena Rubenstein, Tintawn floor coverings and Westclox clock manufacturers – among many others. These advertisers complimented her on her ability to put people at ease, as well as on her unique way with words. Mona may have made it sound easy, but the skill involved was not lost on Gordon Sinclair. In his Radio column for *The Toronto Daily Star*, he wrote: "Mona Gould in her new thing at CKEY ... Carousel ... has hit on that profitable thing called 'believability.' The 25-minutes show is entirely written and spoken by Mona, including ... most important of all ... the commercials. As a result, the blurbs, so often an irritation, becomes [sic] part of the show. If Mona doesn't believe what she has to say then she won't say it. The pay-off works advantageously three ways ... listeners, sponsors and Mona are all happy."[31]

Mona's genius with sales sprang from her sincerity. She took – or masterfully feigned – a rapt interest in products and services which she must have had trouble, at times, keeping straight. After a beauty demonstration, a representative from Elizabeth Arden promised to send her along some lipstick in the new, pale colours.[32] I wonder which of Mona's friends ended up wearing that lipstick, since Mona would never be seen in anything but blood red! Her background as a teenaged adviser to homemakers served her well, since she had to uphold the illusion of being passionate about housekeeping. The Vice-President of a company called O'Cedar of Canada wrote: "In all the years we have sold and advertised polish, we have never thought of referring to a piece of furniture as being 'as bright as a new chestnut'. I can't think of a better way to more vividly express the appearance of a well-polished surface." He thanked her profusely and offered her free polish if ever she should need some.[33] Consumer products flooded their home, as they flooded the marketplace in the 1950s.

Being in the media also meant that Mona had a personal relationship with many of the city's shops, restaurants, and theatres. Life abounded with free meals, complimentary tickets, and treats of all kinds. She never lost the feeling that every business in the city was ready to fling open its doors to her and shower her with freebies. Mona placed large business concerns in the same category as she placed her father. She trusted and admired them. They were strong, protective providers who gave her plenty of opportunity to express herself. There was never any doubt in her mind that they had the best interests of the consumer at heart. Even Mona was dismayed in later life by how impersonal and profit-oriented corporations became, but the fifties was a more innocent age. Many people believed that more progress – and more stuff – was simply *better*. Advertisers saw themselves as educators, and the business itself was creative and stimulating: an ideal outlet for anyone with energy and talent. An interview Mona did with Margaret Thornton, Direc-

The "feminine miker" at home. Chi Chi Bu was
pressed into service in what appears to have been
an endorsement for Colgate soap.

tor of Women's Promotions for Ronald's Advertising for Canada, is suffused
with idealism about the profession. "In the Agency we always have wonderful creative sessions where everybody talks off the top of their heads and
the sparks start to fly and you suddenly get hold of the kernel of a good solid
idea and everybody moves very fast and everybody gets very excited … It's
terrifically useful. I'm sold on advertising. I believe it's a good wide wonder-

ful business to be in and very much tied up with our economy and our country. It's educational and informative, too, and helps raise our standard of living." Thornton goes on to say that "self improvement" is the purpose of advertising: "The improvement, I mean, of the race ... in general ... people ...That sounds awfully high flown but I think it's perhaps the ultimate aim. A little altruistic, but ..."[34]

Among the mounds and mounds of *Carousel* scripts, I found the beginnings of what I consider Mona's greatest art form: the unintentional poem. In her later years, I would read aloud fragments of her letters, just to enjoy their quirky rhythms. Even her rambling speech, with its seemingly out-of-control momentum, was full of surrealist images and obscure metaphors worthy of Gertrude Stein. I remember her telling the story of how the squirrels visiting her deck were sad not to have any peanuts. "A squirrel came right up on my deck and stared in my window, and two big grapes rolled out of his eyes and down his cheeks and rolled on to the floor of the deck and out into the garden, and the raccoons started playing with them, batting them around the garden, and it was a big dance of all the animals in the gardens of Farnham Avenue." After listening to her for hours, I would find myself dazed, as if I'd taken a mind-altering drug. At this point, the images she conjured would seem more and more real in my imagination, as if the story were actually unfolding in front of me. She sent postcards which resembled Bukowski collages. She would alter the original image by drawing over it, or overlaying it with pictures from magazines stuck on with masking tape.

The *Carousel* scripts were written in a rush, and more than likely through a haze of alcohol. At times, they became an uncensored outpouring of thought resembling the work of the Beat poets. The scripts' subject matter, of course, never touched on the Great Themes of sex, death, and alienation; instead, Mona would riff on the latest colours available in soft leather gloves or area rugs. But somehow, the results were not that different. These writings reached down into the rich, chaotic subsoil of language. Mona was a poet, first and last. She could not prevent the anarchic qualities of poetry from slipping through the constraints of commercial writing. This is what she wrote as part of her ad campaign for Bovril. I have done my best to duplicate the curious markings she made on the page in pen, on top of her own typescript.

you] "with your eye on a guy" – Gotta, dime?] Of course-you HAVE!] Just] ONE Subway ride], this, is going to cost you. O.K. then]. Put, the dime in an envelope.] Address it, to mona gould – CKEY – Toronto.]

Ask for] the <u>Bo</u>vril <u>coo</u>kbook; "For Go<u>o</u>dness S<u>a</u>ke" (. That's, its <u>name</u> – For Goodness Sake".) It's 'WAY a<u>head</u>] of any ole "witch's <u>BREW</u>-book] out of the <u>holl</u>owest <u>tree</u>] in <u>Chri</u>stendom.] (<u>Now</u>, then.) R<u>o</u>ll up your sl<u>ee</u>ves.] To wo<u>r</u>k, Gi<u>r</u>l! Pr<u>a</u>ctise] w<u>hi</u>pping <u>u</u>p,] t<u>e</u>mpting, satisfy-ing – beefy-rich] d<u>i</u>shes] with B<u>o</u>vril: B<u>o</u>vril] gives that "<u>X</u>" quality] fl<u>a</u>vour] that makes a man's heart] m<u>e</u>lt ri<u>ght</u> o<u>u</u>t of his s<u>h</u>irtfront!][35]

❧

Mona was among a number of radio personalities to leave CKEY and move to Foster Hewitt's station, CKFH, in 1957. (Though generally remembered for his hockey broadcasts, Hewitt was also a station owner. He had launched CKFH in 1951, with twenty-four-hour programming including music, news, and sports.) At CKFH, Mona took on a more ambitious daily program called *Be My Guest.* Anyone famous who came through Toronto would be invited to make an appearance on her show. She met Louis Armstrong, Eleanor Roosevelt, the Andrews Sisters, Irving Layton, Julie Harris, Gratien Gélinas, and Dr Lotta Hitschmanova (whose heavily-accented radio ads for the Unitarian Service Committee are remembered by those of us who grew up in the 1960s). There were many others whose names are less familiar today.

She is marvelous. Marvelous. Through aphasia, and all his complex feelings about Mona, my father had seized upon this one word to describe her. She had once been charismatic, larger-than-life, and never more so than in her days as the host of *Be My Guest.* I felt excited as I sorted through her transcripts of these programs, as if the papers themselves contained some kind of magic. In a sense they did, because they brought my grandmother back to life: a version of my grandmother I had never met. This was as close as I'd ever come to seeing Mona in her witty, expansive prime.

In addition to the transcripts, she assembled and carefully preserved a col-lection of eight-by-ten-inch photographs of herself, taken with her illustrious guests.[36] These were not new to me; I had seen them more than once before encountering them in the library. Her interviews with famous people – Arm-strong and Roosevelt in particular – formed the pinnacle of Mona's memories in the 1950s, just as the appearance of "This Was My Brother" crowned the previous decade. She listed the famous guests on her show almost every time I saw her. Even as an old woman she was still basking in their reflected celebrity.

Mona was proud of her broadcast career, yet her reminiscences of that era focused on the people she met, rather than her own remarkable achievement in being in a position to interview them in the first place. The reason, I think, was her refusal to ally herself with feminism. She could never really acknowledge that she was exceptional, because to do so meant acknowledging the position of women in society at large. But even though she never spoke in these terms, her sense of triumph in the fifties must have come – at least partially – from knowing she was thriving in a man's world, and that she was one of a very few who did. To make matters still more complex, she went through the decade representing herself as an ordinary woman, just as she had for her whole career.

Maintaining this position required a subtle dance on Mona's part, and looking at the scripts of *Be My Guest* allowed me to trace her steps. She may not have overtly questioned the position of women in society but she always assumed women were smart, and needed culture and stimulating discussion in their lives. An ad for the show encouraged a plucky attitude in Mona's listeners, if not an outright rebellion against their housewifely roles. Time listening to Mona was time for themselves. The ad showed a hand of cards fanned out as if for a bridge game, the front one bearing Mona's face. "It's Mona's Deal," the slogan read. The ad went on to say, "Here's bright, new radio entertainment for modern homemakers from Mona Gould. It's just good listening – absolutely *no* household hints! So throw down your mop, forget the dishes and visit with Mona's famous guests. You'll hear poetry, theatre news, occasional book reviews, plus other exciting goings-on about town. Yes, for 25 minutes every morning at 11:05 'cept Saturdays, radio is *yours* – when Mona tells about the fascinating world beyond your kitchen sink. If you like to live, you'll *love* Mona, now on CKFH's Radio for Grownups."[37]

Mona interviewed numerous women who had accomplished impressive things or led interesting lives. She always asked them how they balanced work with maintaining a home. Overall, the message was yes, it was possible – as well as fun and fulfilling – to have both. The editor and writer Lotta Dempsey told Mona in an interview that she did not do her own housework, that in fact, she had a male housekeeper. Dempsey did not complain about any unfairness in her business, though she commented that there should be a special school for children of professional women – and she defined these as women who worked because they needed the money. These schools would have shorter holidays so that the mothers would not have to worry about what to do with their children all summer. Many of Mona's guests were men, but she would still slant the interviews toward topics that touched on women's lives. While she did not challenge anyone directly, Mona got her point across with a quiet subversiveness that a guest might not even notice. In an interview with Irving Layton, she asked which poets he admired. He launched into a list of literary titans: Dylan Thomas, Robertson Jeffers, Wallace Stevens, T.S. Eliot, W.H. Auden. Mona let him finish, then asked, "Do you find women poets trivial, Irving?"

LAYTON: Well, that's too large a statement! I think some women poets are very good. I wouldn't certainly call Emily Dickinson a trivial poet. Or Edna St Vincent Millay. Or Emily Brontë. It's not "trivial." I think that they don't (some of them) go deeply enough into experience. They are afraid of the raw encounter with experience. They're not brutal enough, perhaps. But then I suppose one shouldn't expect women to be brutal and raw and masculine. For myself, I'd like to see one woman poet come up, to-day, like Sappho, and speak very frankly about sex, about love, from a woman's point of view. We haven't the poet like that yet!

MONA: Not yet. Tell me this, now, is it your wish to be loved as a poet that speaks of the masses? The kind of poet that your book is carried around in pockets 'til it's all dog-eared ... and read ... all the time?

LAYTON: Most certainly! I would far rather have my books dog-eared by some young man courting a girl under a beech tree and reading a poem of mine than to be commented upon by a whole battery of professors and critics. That's precisely what I want. I want somebody to carry my book in his pocket and read it to the girl that he loves!

MONA: "Read me ... do not let me die" ... hmmmm?

LAYTON: Yes!

I wonder if Layton ever realised he had used a line by Edna St Vincent Millay to sum up his poetic *raison-d'etre*![38]

There was no doubt that Mona could hold her own in a demanding business – and even the macho journalistic profession had to acknowledge this. In one column, Gordon Sinclair wrote admiringly, "Mona Gould scored a beat Tuesday with the first on-the-air story about Mrs. Eleanor Roosevelt's arrival in town. Mona had to get it the hard way, driving out to Malton, grabbing Mrs. R. on the fly, and being raced back to town while she wrote her copy."[39]

In another column, Sinclair recounted Mona's success in managing an adversarial interview. The comedian Danny Kaye was in town doing a benefit for the Variety Club. Mona was the only one to get any results from a press conference which proved too much for many of her male colleagues. Kaye arrived late for the conference.

> Among those ready to work and be nice to him were some pretty good names in these parts, Phil Stone, Wally Crouter, Mike Wood, Mona Gould, Keith Sandy, Monty Hall, Don Insley and others.
>
> Danny decided to try his district attorney act. When Monty asked who was his favourite entertainer Kaye snapped ... "By entertainer, do you mean singer, dancer, actor, radio stooge, comedian, commentator or what?"
>
> He was serious.
>
> Mona Gould had even less fun. She started by asking. "How do you like Toronto, Danny?"
>
> The answer was partly a yawn and partly a snort so Mona asked it again.
>
> Another yawn and another snort.
>
> Mona tried a third time.
>
> "Who is this Danny Toronto?" asked Kaye ... "Do I know him?"
>
> ... Maybe in type this reads as though it was amusing or even funny but had you heard the bite on the Kaye voice you'd have understood why some of the home town names took a quick powder and didn't bother to try the interview for which their gear had been set up.
>
> In fact you can hear part of it. Miss Gould got a few quotes for her 12:15 spot ...[40]

In her professional life, Mona was expected to play the role of sex object, and somehow find a way to be "one of the boys" at the same time. As part of the observance of Canada Book Week in 1950, she interviewed Morley Callahan. Bob McStay, one of the celebration's organizers, wrote to tell her that this represented a coup: Callaghan never did anything for free. McStay's description of Mona may have helped get past Callaghan's defenses. "He wanted to know if you were blonde and beautiful; I told him you were brunet

[sic] and beautiful; better bring along your pearl-handed revolver! This, of course, is kidding."[41]

By the latter years of the decade, Mona was a polished radio commentator, and a local celebrity. According to John Aylesworth, there were billboards with Mona's face on them all over the city.[42] A story by Nancy Phillips in *The Toronto Telegram* features a cartoon of Mona, and an interview. It gives a portrait of Mona at her most formidable. "She sits down at a table on which a microphone is placed, waits imperturbably for her split-second cue, and then leaning forward slightly says (as she has had said daily for the last two years over CKFH): 'and this is Mona Gould, asking you once again to ... *Be My Guest*.' Across the table from her sits the person she is about to interview, or the 'victim' as Mrs. Gould sometimes refers to her guest of the day." Phillips goes on to say that Mona puts people at ease with her "delightfully relaxed technique." The secret of Mona's success is that she enjoys doing this work; it is both her hobby and her job. Phillips tries to summarize Mona's impressive biography, but fails. She concludes, "Watching my frantic attempts to record her non-stop biography, Mrs. Gould let out a jubilant shout of laughter. 'You'll never sort this out. I've lived too long and done too many things.'"[43]

❦

Mona was over fifty by the time this article appeared, and consciously or not, she had decided that bravado was the best way to face the encroachment of middle age. The cult of youth is by no means new. Mona's age, and that of her colleagues, was more than once a matter of public discussion in Gordon Sinclair's columns, though he did add a respectful note at the end of this one. "Not to be unkind about it, the average age of this able foursome (Claire Wallace, Jane Weston, Katie Aitken and Mona) is about 50 and it's puzzling to this scribbler of like age that no youngster can make the break into Toronto radio in the chatter field. Leigh Stubbs, June Dennis and Su Fletcher are younger but none could be labeled sub-debs and so far as I know there are no really fresh young things in the chatter field at all. What the young ones lack is poise and self-assurance."[44]

In certain ways, the 1950s was a more forgiving era, before plastic surgery and hormone replacement gave women the option – or the pressure – of looking much younger than their years. A middle-aged woman might be the subject of contempt, but she could at least settle into her unhappy condition in peace. Overall, though, it was a horribly prescriptive time for women. On the backs and borders of Mona's newspaper and magazine clippings I found numerous ads warning women of the dangers of smelling bad, *without knowing it*. The sheer number of these ads startled me. Women were encouraged to freshen their mouths with Lysterine, their vaginas with (of all substances) Lysol, and their underarms with Mum deodorant. There were painstakingly detailed articles on grooming and behaviour, all taking it as a given that a woman's sole aim was to find and keep the attention of a man. One headline on the back of one of Mona's articles reads: "Wives Mentally Lacking." It warns women of the damage they might be doing to their husbands' careers by confiding in their friends about being unhappy at home. No wonder women were terrified of metaphorically "leaking" an unpleasant effluence!

Mona wrote about fashion and cosmetics. She was part of the industry which perpetuated this reign of fear for women. Yet she herself never succumbed to it. At least on the surface of things, she sailed through her working life with her confidence intact. Mona's handiness in creating a fictional persona may have helped her. It was the same ability that made it possible to write passionately about the household details she knew – and cared – nothing about. She was able to dissociate herself from the realities of her appearance; indeed, of her body itself. This would come to haunt her in later years, when she became dangerously overweight and dressed in a way that was downright bizarre at times. In the 1950s, though, Mona's relaxed attitude to grooming only enhanced her image. She was above petty worries about her own appearance, yet was also a voice of authority in the field.

Mona herself never tried to sell anything with scare tactics. Her ads were all about the pleasures of using a product, not the bad things that could happen if you did not. Her message was that a woman could and should enjoy looking after herself and her home. In a context where a kind of paranoia was being fostered amongst women, Mona's attitude was – as always – subversive. It gave women the message that pleasure and confidence are a source of power, and she provided a model for this in her personal style. She wore her hair shoulder-length and styled it herself, simply pinning it back from her face. She did nothing to colour it, leaving in all the gray streaks that were beginning to show. A wide-brimmed hat, red fingernails, lipstick, and high heels were essential to Mona, but they were just decorations; she never fussed over meticulous application of foundation and rouge. Where most women suffer the tortures of the damned in high heels, Mona was one of those rare people who could wear them as comfortably as slippers. Nor did she try to stay slim. As the years passed and she spent increasing amounts of time in Malloney's and Old Angelo's, she accumulated a considerable girth. This too was worn as a badge of confidence. She enjoyed eating and drinking, and never carried herself as if ashamed of her size. Jean Aylesworth recalled the bold way that Mona was able to carry off her personal style.

Mona always looked marvelous with a white blouse and some kind of black jacket on, and a real knowledge of who she was, how she looked, and it wasn't that this was all that casual. It was calculated. She knew this looked good on her, with her bright red lipstick that became her trademark. It had to be the same kind. Something like "Cherries In The Snow" by Revlon. It was Revlon ... And it was just so exciting because she played the part ... She loved the ... Algonquin Round Table – that sort of thing was exactly how I thought of Mona. A Dorothy Parker. And I think she thought so too.

Did You Notice?

Did you notice that I made part of that chapter up? Well, I didn't make it up, exactly. I fudged some facts I wasn't sure about.

I don't know whether *Listen Ladies* and *Carousel* overlapped, or whether one show replaced the other. I don't know whether Mona sold ads for *Carousel*, or whether Dodi Robb continued to be her producer. I tried to get it right; I looked up radio and television annuals, called stations to get their archives, pored over schedules on microfiche. But I never really figured it out.

More importantly, do you care? Mona certainly didn't. She never talked about *Carousel*, period. Like so much other information, it simply dropped out of her history. She said she had taken on an extra program to help send John to Europe after art college, but she never mentioned what that show was. She never talked about losing her sponsor for *Listen Ladies* either. She never talked about switching to CKFH. It drove me crazy not to know exactly what had happened. I longed to talk to someone who had been there. It would have been so easy if I could just have asked someone, instead of picking through all these disparate files, checking, cross-checking, and possibly still misinterpreting what had happened. That's what it came down to; I had the nagging feeling that I was getting everything wrong.

I went to visit Dodi Robb in Collingwood, where she lived in a seniors' residence. Dodi first met Mona when she became her producer on *Listen Ladies*. As joyfully as Mona took to her job, Mona and Dodi took to each other. They stayed in touch for many years, and, by seeming co-incidence, always lived in close proximity to each other. As it turned out, the nursing home where Mona spent her last weeks was a stone's throw from where Dodi had settled.

The day I was to meet Dodi, I put on a jacket with padded shoulders and Mona's Mexican pin. I arrived early in the afternoon for our interview, and the staff directed me to a dining room where Dodi was just finishing lunch. There were a lot of people in the room, yet I recognized her at a glance. Her friends and colleagues had led me to expect an imposing figure, tall and stout as my grandmother had once been. They also warned me she had recently had a foot amputated, and that she had lost an eye many years earlier in an accident. None of these descriptions helped me identify Dodi. The woman I approached was tiny, delicate-boned, with a translucent quality to her skin. She gave no sense, in the way she moved or talked to her neighbours, that her vision was impaired. It was her *way* of looking that drew me to her. That intense gaze could only belong to a person of extraordinary intelligence and probing curiosity. A person like Mona.

"Dodi?" I asked. I glanced down, wincing when I saw the pant leg that had been tied off at the bottom. As soon as she began talking, I forgot all about it.

"You're Mona's granddaughter!"

"Do you recognize the pin?"

"The pin? Oh no. It's *you*, honey. You're the image of your grandmother. I knew you right away."

I pushed Dodi's wheelchair along the hall, seeking a quiet place for our interview. At last we settled in the corner of a lounge. It was chilly, but relatively free of background noise. Seeing Mona in each other, we began talking as if we had known each other forever. The interview never officially started because we were too busy chatting. Dodi spoke of her connection with my grandmother.

"My mind delighted her. She was very pleased with me. We had the same interests about a lot of things, including our attitudes to men, careers. We shared a lot, even before we knew each other."

"What was her attitude to men?"

"I think it was always very healthy. She was sexually very interested in men. I don't think she had many deep lifelong female friends ... I think that her life would have been bereft without the company of men, as I did. My career – if it has been successful – one reason was that I liked men and men liked me."

She sat in a thoughtful pose, elbows on the arms of her wheelchair, fingers meeting each other in a triangle in front of her chest. Her voice was that of a much younger woman, as Mona's had been in her old age. It was not just the strength of her voice that gave me this impression but the confidence, the ready flow of words. Talking had been her job, and she still did it well.

"Did Mona consider herself a feminist?" I asked.

"Yeah, but not really. I think she was always an artist first. She was a poet, of considerable stature. I think she didn't live up to the potential that she had. I still read through her books. I don't have them all. I wasn't as careful with some things as I should have been."

"Why do you say she didn't she live up to her potential?"

"That was a rather frivolous thing to say because who's to judge who's living up to whose potential. That's a pompous thing to say, but maybe you only live up to your potential when other people think you have done your best ... I don't know ... I would say that Mona was a minor poet, as opposed to a major. I say that again in a pompous way in my elevation of myself."

So Dodi struggled – as I always had – with the role of critic. She continued, taking a slightly different tack. "The poet is always lonely. If he's serious about his work or her work, he will work at it seriously. Life's pain and joy will teach you time and time again. It will teach you to evade the popular because it's popular. The poet I will take to my grave will be Millay." This love of Millay, of course, was another thing Mona and Dodi had in common. "May I recite?" she asked.

"Of course. Please. Please do."

Dodi removed her elbows from the arms of the wheelchair so that she could place her hands in her lap. She sat up straighter, and recited what amounted to an abridged version of Millay's poem.

Love is not all
It is not meat nor drink nor slumber nor a roof against the rain
Or yet a floating spar to men who sink and rise and sink again
It well may be that in some troubled hour, pinned down by pain and moaning for release
I may be driven to sell your love for power, or trade the memory of this night for food
It well may be
I do not think I would.[1]

In a sense, Dodi had created a whole new poem, yet it said what it needed to say. It evoked Mona's sensibility, the particular combination of passion and detachment we both knew. It also answered my question about Mona's potential. She could have been another Millay, but was not.

The reason for all this was easier to pin down. Dodi said, "She was anxious to get out of work. She wasn't that disciplined ... She aggravated me because she was a bit dissolute. She liked to carouse, drink a little too much. That wasn't her finest hour. It killed off a lot of the creativity ... You can't write anything very good if you're half-tanked. I never could anyway."

I asked about Graham. "Well, I found him not nearly the colourful and endearing person that Mona was, and I don't say that with any dislike of him ... Mona was the person I was interested in, as a friend and a colleague. I was interested in her mind, and I was interested in her as a communicator. I could see that she saw always an interesting side of things and she was always willing to look at another little step that would unearth quite a good story."

Grinning, I sat back in my chair. This was just the reverse of what so many women have to endure, living in the shadow of their more flamboyant mates. In her marriage, Mona was the colourful one. To hear a woman talk unapologetically this way brought a kind of physical release. Yet immediately, I came to the defense of my gentle grandfather.

"He was actually an unusual man for the time. This was the fifties. He very much supported her getting the attention."

"Yes."

"He didn't compete with her."

"I agree, and as far the relationship between Mona and Graham, there was never any rivalry. I thought 'That seems to be a good marriage,' complicated because she was complicated."

I had a whole list of questions still unasked, questions about station ownership and schedules. I kept telling myself I should launch into them, but a feeling of immense fatigue settled over me when I even considered it. I realised that I would have to give up on knowing these details. They were insignificant details, in the long run. If someone had asked me about radio schedules from even a year ago, let alone a half-century, I could not have begun to answer. These facts were simply not that important. Or that interesting.

Meantime, the chill in the lounge started to become intolerable. I found myself drawing my hands into my sleeves, pulling my jacket close around me, and I saw Dodi hunkering down deeper into her cardigan.

"Are you cold?" I asked.

"A bit, dear, now that you mention it." It was then I noticed that a window right next to us was open, and that a March breeze was blowing right into the room.

"Well, this might be why," I said, closing the window.

Dodi's body folded in on itself in silent peals of laughter. She thumped the arm of her wheelchair.

"That's great!" She said. "And we were both sitting here freezing and not saying a thing! Isn't that just the type of people we are?"[2]

A Talent to Amuse

Mona's third book of poetry was a collection of light verse reprinted from *Gossip* magazine. It was also titled *Gossip*. Since the 1930s, Mona had contributed poems to this indomitable little publication. Slimmer and less polished than *Chatelaine* or *Women's Home Journal*, *Gossip* was basically an advertising vehicle, enlivened by articles, poetry, fiction, line drawings, and photos of society ladies and their children. *Gossip* did not change much over the years like the larger magazines, but – unlike many of its contemporaries – it survived for decades. The magazine took a chatty tone and was aimed at a privileged class, or those who aspired to it. These were ladies with time on their hands and money to spend on facials, lingerie, and the latest couturier fashions. The publication looked like a newsletter, and its informal design reinforced the feeling that *Gossip*'s readers were members of a private club. There were some display ads, but most of the copy took the form of genteel announcements – not so much selling things as making a select group of people aware that they were available. Many Torontonians sold and rented their houses through *Gossip*. Of course, most of the magazine's contributors and staff were busy working women, writing as if they were members of a leisure class. *Gossip*'s editor, Mona Clark, was a respected member of the women's business community.

Appearing in time for Christmas, 1949, Mona's *Gossip* poetry book was the brainchild of Mona Gould and Mona Clark. (Much was made of the collaboration between "The Two Monas.") First mentioned in 1946, the idea was shelved for a period and then picked up again after the Goulds' trip to Mexico in 1948. Mona Gould was the one to initiate the process, though Mona Clark enthusiastically jumped at the idea.[1] Apart from their initial correspondence, I found little information about the publication. One letter from John Gray of Macmillan indicated that the women had approached him, probably with the idea of publishing the book at their own expense. Gray wrote to Mona Gould on 8 February 1949, saying he would consider the poems she had sent, but "Until we have done that I won't even do any guessing or hunching, but as soon as possible we shall let you know something."[2] Either Macmillan entered into a purely commercial arrangement for the book's printing and production or it was eventually produced by the two Monas on their own. Neither my grandmother's archive nor the Macmillan papers at McMaster University has any other record of the book's origins. The final result is hardbound, yet resembles a pamphlet because it has no copyright page, and no date, publisher, or printer is mentioned.

The poems in *Gossip* are reminiscent of the work of another one of Mona's idols, Dorothy Parker. Though Mona modeled herself on Edna St Vincent Millay, she had been familiar with Dorothy Parker's poetry since childhood. (Her brother Douglas gave her a copy of *Sunset Gun* in 1928 when she was ten years old.) As she approached middle age, Mona became increasingly attuned to Parker's witty, world-weary strains. Like her idol, she had lived hard in her youth as if expecting to die at fifty. Also like Parker, she discovered she had a strong constitution that did not seem to be letting her quit. Dorothy Parker's name was mentioned in connection with Mona's again and again. In her "Whimsy" column Sally Townsend wrote: "We are familiar ... with [Gould's] sense of whimsy and her Dorothy Parkerish satire. Then, as suddenly, she will grip your heart with her sensitive awareness of beauty and the closeness of beauty to pain." Townsend went on to say, "This is not great poetry; it may not even be poetry in the accepted sense, Mona Gould follows no set form nor recognized pattern in her work, but she catches your ear; she holds you for a moment as someone whistling down the street on a clear morning, or as the sound of a sobbing child. She achieves effects in contrasts."[3]

Mona was praised for being less acerbic than Parker. Another newspaper item commented that Mona's poetry was like "Dorothy Parker without the sting."[4] Dorothy Parker's "sting" was, of course, what made her work so satisfying to read, but these newspaper items were not the first to use the language of mediocrity in a positive sense when describing Mona. The same thing happened during the promotions for *I Run with the Fox*. When Mona's talk to the women of the Lyceum Club of Owen Sound was covered in the local newspaper, the journalist wrote, "As a minor poet, she herself sings her songs for people whose problems are known and for her own generation, not, as so many poets frankly write for posterity."[5]

Mona, it seemed, was to be praised for not trying to be too much of a "tall poppy," for not becoming inordinately accomplished. She was loved for staying at the level of the ordinary reader not only in her form and subject matter, but in the very quality of her work. Townsend's reference to whistling is ironic. B.K. Sandwell, in one of his letters, had likened Mona's satisfaction with her own poetry to a child's thrill at learning to whistle. He expected Mona to take her work further than the initial rush of inspiration. But the raw, unprocessed quality which Sandwell deplored was seen differently by other critics, who found Mona's childlike immediacy appealing.

This attitude may have appeared even more in personal relationships than in print. Mona might have been praised for writing poetry at an early age, and for getting her work published, but she was probably discouraged in many subtle ways from excelling at it, or from developing the personality it takes to excel. A sensitive nature and a love of beauty might have been considered attractive in a young girl, but not a need for hours of solitude or an anxious, haunted drive for perfection.

An undisguised hunger for attention was frowned upon most of all. Today, most would agree that a writer needs a strong ego, if only to survive the rejections and criticism which will inevitably come her way. Yet Mona came from a time where "egotism" was a serious transgression, Indeed, when I worked with a group of women of her generation who were writing their memoirs, I had a difficult time convincing them to use the pronoun "I." It was as if I had asked them to pepper their prose with obscenities, or to reveal their bodies in some immodest way. I believe that a similar sense of shame prevented my grandmother from discussing the diligent way she built her career. She cultivated a liberal image, admitting readily to sexual urges and indiscretions. She never acknowledged her desire for attention, though. Instead, she created a version of reality where the world came to *her*; not the other way around.

Her third book, which was miniature in size, sold for $1.50. The epithet "verse for the purse" was used to describe it. One ad depicts a stork delivering a baby. The copy describes *Gossip* as an "itsy bitsy book ... just the right size for a handbag."[6] The promotional material was accompanied by a photo of Mona with artfully painted lips, hair swept back from her face, wearing a large black-and-white hat. The expected readership was women, and the book was meant to amuse rather than to challenge. Its commercial aspirations were made clear in the poem, "Sufficient Reason."

> I prostitute my Art
> Because it's tactical
> For starving in a garret
> Isn't practical![7]

The publication of *Gossip* marked a change in the way Mona situated herself as a poet. She was moving away from "serious" poetry (serious both in the sense that it was geared to a literary audience, and serious in its tone and subject matter). Increasingly, she was known for light verse. Her themes did not move much beyond vague heartaches, musings on everyday middle-class life, and the pleasures and frustrations of Ontario's four seasons. Her verses were short, and followed a simple meter and rhyme scheme. Mona continued to write poems based on her darker emotions, but more and more, her published work consisted of amusing rhymes. There were scores of these to every serious poem. She concluded *Gossip* with this poem:

> This book is little
> Light and small
> Not for the critics.
> Just for all
> Those ones who like to read and run:
> I really wrote it ... just for fun![8]

I cannot help reading between the lines of this seemingly lighthearted poem. It acts as a kind of disclaimer, warning the reader not to expect too much. Mona was suffering a crisis of confidence in what mattered to her most. Over the next decade, she stopped trying to share a large part of what she had to offer.

Though she lived another fifty years and wrote more than two thousand poems in that time, she never published another book. The negotiations regarding *Gossip* were the closest she ever came to trying to publish with Macmillan again. Ellen Elliott had retired in 1947,[9] which meant that Mona's primary contact at the press was gone. She had left graciously but – as Ruth

Panofsky put it – her departure was probably "less than voluntary." It is likely she was pushed out of her position and replaced by John Gray.[10] Mona kept no correspondence with Elliott about her leaving Macmillan, though she did hear in intimate detail about the health problems that had forced her editor to take a leave in 1946. Mona may well have intuited (or feared) that the new regime at Macmillan would not be friendly to her work. Interestingly, she did not sidestep Macmillan entirely. Rather, she approached Gray with a commercial proposition, for a book of light verse.

Still, she had made excellent sales with her two serious books, and critical response had been good; there was no reason why she should not try for a third – if not at Macmillan, then elsewhere. E.J. Pratt, a great supporter in the forties, would doubtless have helped her. By the fifties, however, Mona's correspondence was primarily with Viola Pratt. Nor did she correspond with anyone at Ryerson Press, which published the work of Dorothy Livesay and Miriam Waddington. Both had begun, alongside Mona, in *Canadian Poetry*, but went on to establish more visible and long-running careers. Of course, neither of these two poets limited herself to light verse.

As well, there were more and more periodicals publishing poetry by the 1950s. *First Statement* and *Contact* were thriving in Montreal, and this led to the formation of Contact Press. P.K. Page was published in *First Statement*, while Louis Dudek and Raymond Souster became involved with Contact Press. All three of these poets had also appeared with Mona in *Canadian Poetry*. But Mona did not follow their path. In periodicals, she did not look much further than *Chatelaine, Gossip, The Montrealer,* and *Women's Home Journal*. Nor, as the years went on, did she approach the *Tamarack Review, Contemporary Verse,* or any of the other literary magazines that began to spring up all over the country.

The reason for this retreat may have been the schism which developed between literary and commercial markets in the post-war era. Mona made a choice between them, allying herself with the commercial camp. This made absolute sense. She was committed to being a mainstream, popular poet. Yet it was not a good career move. During the war, her feelings had found an echo in the emotions of the whole nation, but the great uniting force of war was gone, and poetry itself was dropping out of the mainstream. The "tactical" markets were proving less and less fruitful, and this trend was to grow stronger over the coming decades. The Massey Report, released in 1951, and the formation of the Canada Council six years later, ushered in a new era of public funding for the arts. Under this system, literary magazines flourished.

The commercial magazines, on the other hand, received a critical drubbing. As Dean Irvine points out in his book on women editors, the post-war literary climate was blatantly hostile to Mona's aesthetic. He quotes from 1945 review by John Sutherland of Anne Marriott's collection, *Sandstone*. Sutherland's torrent of criticism derides Marriott's allegiance to the "lady writers" affiliated with the CAA. "Magazine verse" is also dismissed with contempt,[11] because some of the poetry in Marriott's collection had appeared in magazines such as *Saturday Night*, which regularly printed poetry among its articles. These magazines were, of course, Mona's primary markets. Certainly, Sutherland would have put *Chatelaine* in the same category, not to mention the local newspapers where Mona frequently published. If Mona had her ear to the ground in those days, she would have known that for a "lady writer" such as herself, making forays into the new literary markets could prove to be critical suicide.

At this crucial time in her career, Mona continued to identify with poets from other countries without taking part in the new literary activity emerging around her. Mona's contemporaries Dorothy Livesay, Anne Marriott, and P.K. Page faced their own challenges after the war. They did not simply seek outlets for their work, however; they created them. They were active in starting and editing little magazines.[12] But Mona did not do this. It may be that lines were already so firmly drawn that Mona felt she could not gather enough sympathetic colleagues. Whatever the reason, she stood in danger of stagnating.

The disclaimer in *Gossip*, and her failure to pursue other opportunities, may have come not so much from the sense of a hostile publishing climate as from an inner feeling of being stalled. What was she to write about? And how? Mona's life had become complicated over the last decade. She had experienced grave losses, many of which offered her no outlet for her true feelings. She might have felt free to express her grief at her brother's death, but the death of her baby had been dismissed as "just not to be." No doubt the miscarriage that followed had been treated the same way. As neither wife nor fiancée, she had had to keep her pain at losing Jim to herself. Her own husband had come home from the war, an occasion for celebration. What place was there for her grief when she found him a changed man? In the face of all this complexity of feeling, Mona would have had to reach deeper into the uniqueness of her experience, or broaden herself intellectually, or make some breakthroughs in form – or all of these things – in order to develop as a writer. She did none of them.

Rather than pushing the limits of her ability, Mona stuck with what worked. Her background in print and radio journalism may have contributed to this choice. She had always been driven by deadlines. Over the years, she had become attached to her habitual ways of doing things, ways that produced the expected results in the prescribed amount of time. From the boxes and boxes of drafts that Mona saved, it is clear that she did not rewrite her poems, apart from the odd word change. She prized the initial rush of inspiration, and refused to tamper with it. This could not fail to limit her. Dodi Robb had called Mona undisciplined. She liked to party, she liked to get drunk, and all this went along with valuing immediate gratification, easy success. When it came to slower, more painstaking tasks, she backed down.

Maybe fear of failure was masquerading as lack of discipline, or as high-handedness. Maybe it was fear of success. Or maybe John Aylesworth was right; what you saw was what you got, with Mona. Maybe she just didn't *want* to write serious poems. Her couplets were written with a lot of skill, and delighted many people. In the face of her personal sadness and that of the world around her, she may have decided that – in the words of one of her favourite Noel Coward songs – "a talent to amuse" was her most valuable asset.

◆

Financial pressures in the Gould household continued to mount. In middle age, Mona and Graham were now enjoying a more comfortable lifestyle. Their summer retreats to Muskoka had been succeeded by more expensive annual junkets to New England. They ate out often, and went to as many plays and films as their schedule allowed. Mona loved her taxis, her beautiful shoes and lipstick and flowers; she also loved to make grand gestures, give generous gifts. Most pressing of all, though, was their commitment to financing their son's education. John lived modestly and worked in the summers at hard and sometimes dangerous physical labour, but there were still many expenses to be met. It was generally accepted in the 1950s that every young artist must spend time in Europe, viewing the works of the great masters first-hand. Since John's chosen medium was drawing, he dreamed of having an opportunity to attend the Académie Julian in Paris. So when he completed his studies at OCA, his parents sent him to Europe for a year of travel and study.

Meantime, Graham's energy and motivation were sinking lower and lower. When he left his position in Owen Sound, he had expected to find an equally satisfying one in Toronto. This had not happened. He got a job selling cars at Yorktown Motors, but it was a step down from what he was used to, and he did not enjoy it. Mona did her best to make him feel part of the opportunities that were coming her way. In the spring of 1951, the couple did a series of four radio broadcasts together. Dubbing themselves "The Kaiser Travellers," they reminisced about their trips to Muskoka, New England, Mexico, and Quebec. Sponsorship came from Century Motor Sales. The unifying element in the series was that all four trips had been taken by car.[13] Gordon Sinclair was disdainful when he wrote about the shows: "Mona Gould and Howard Milsom have been re-engaged for *Listen Ladies* to begin September. Meantime, starting Saturday at her usual time on CKEY Mona will do a husband and wife thing with her own hubby. Seems to me Graham is an amateur at the mike or at least a freshman."[14]

Gone were the days when Mona and Graham could cheerfully pool their talents in a local theatre production. They were no longer equals. Public speaking came so naturally to Mona that she may not have noticed how many skills she had developed since they last worked together. In the intervening twenty years, she had become a seasoned professional. Perhaps in response to Sinclair's dig, Mona and Graham worked to remedy the unevenness of their program. Mona wrote in a letter to John: "They've had good publicity for the travel show. Put the mike closer to G this time and we rehearsed for HOURS ... so he's coming 'up and thru' much better and with more punch. I think we've got the beginnings of something GOOD and TRUE and FINE there, as our pal Hemingway or Pappa would say! ... Just heard our show and it sounded Okay to me."[15]

My father recalled epic, drunken fights between his parents during those years. He also spoke of the pleasure they took in one another's company, and the way they consistently supported each other's efforts. Despite a stormy relationship, they were still in love. Graham was unstintingly encouraging of Mona's career. When he went on selling trips, he wrote letters home describing his experiences in detail. In one letter from Quebec, he included as much support for Mona as he did his own news. She had learned that one of her poems (probably "Lament for our Good King, George the Sixth") would be broadcast on the radio. Graham wrote – perhaps assuaging her disappointment about some other venture – that this was "almost better than having it published because when people hear something they <u>have</u> to do something about it, whereas if they read it, you never know except when someone, months later, says 'Oh I liked that poem you wrote on the King.'" He concluded, "Wish I could hear Carousel this week and hope and trust that both you and John are feeling okay. p.s. Just hung up the phone after talking to you and I miss you <u>very</u> much. Much love, the Groint [Graham's nickname]."[16]

Some time in the fifties, Graham also started writing prose. Mona kept a story called "The Sunny Room," a memoir of a visit he made to a military hospital while he was a paymaster in the army. More cleanly typed than Mona's own manuscripts, it also has pencil marks that show Graham was thinking of adapting it for stage or film. The title refers to a nursery within the military hospital where "the instinct to live ... to survive ... to procreate goes on ... war or no war." A child is born to a young nurse and a soldier, who is gravely wounded and dies. The young woman finds herself in a terrible predicament because her father is an elder of the church, and she knows she cannot tell her family about the baby. A middle-aged, single nurse offers to take the child home and raise it as her own. At the end of the story, it is not clear whether the plan succeeds.[17] The story is touching, and written in a straightforward, unpretentious style. Some minor work with an editor would have helped Graham liven up his prose and clarify the ending, but Graham never published the story or adapted it for theatre; nor did he ever seek out a community of colleagues who might have helped him develop as a writer.

Mona never spoke of Graham's dwindling energy or its effect on her. The pressures on her in the 1950s may indeed have "punctured" her imagination – as Nancy Durham once put it – but her reputation as a poet was still strong. "This Was My Brother" continued to be reprinted on a regular basis. Publishers contacted Mona about using the poem in schoolbooks and anthologies. Some poetry by Mona was featured on a late-night CBC program in Montreal on 30 March 1950. Charles Miller of CBC Montreal wrote graciously to Mona thanking her very much for letting him see her books and suggesting she listen in to the reading, which he dubbed "Mona Gould Corner."[18] In 1951, the composer Michael Head set to music Mona's poem, "Small Christmas Tree," which he performed at the Museum Theatre on 7 April 1951.[19]

In addition to her radio shows, Mona published a column called *Listen* for a group of southern Ontario weeklies, in which she chatted about goings-on in Toronto. This clever piece of freelance strategy allowed Mona keep her contacts alive in smaller communities and draw, without much effort, on the work she was doing on a daily basis for her radio shows. Her contributions were substantial, often running across two columns, the full length of a news-paper page.[20] Columns collected from *The Paris Star* in 1951 and 1952 cover such diverse subjects as the death of Edna St Vincent Millay and the open-ing of Toronto's Royal Winter Fair, along with other art shows, concerts, and the celebrities that Mona met, such as the Group of Seven painter Fred Varley. The final word always went to Mister Chi Chi Bu, with couplets such as this one: "Mister Chi Chi Bu our gentleman Siamese cat says: 'Sometimes when I lick myself clean, I get hairs in my liver and spleen: Then I wheeze and I cough and I know that straight off I'll be given some … UG … Vaseline!'"[21]

Mona stopped writing *Listen* in 1952 but maintained her relationship with the smaller papers, producing a poem a week. These *Poet's Corner* spots were always accompanied by a photograph of Mona in her hat and lipstick. Here is a sample.

Spring Hits the Front Page

Spring is taking quite a chance
Judging from just one hasty glance
At headlines … screaming hate and fear
Across the turning of the year.
Murder and treachery … wrath and riot;
It seems like rather a scurrilous diet
To feed the starving minds of men
With promises of war … again.

And yet … each crocus lifts her cup
And goes on, bravely … coming up![22]

This project could not have been particularly lucrative but for Mona, every penny counted, and she operated on the principle that she should get as much exposure as possible, all the time. She also continued to contribute to the *Montrealer*. Alvah Beattie was buying poems in batches of five, and paying her twenty-five dollars for the lot. Her rate of payment had not increased in

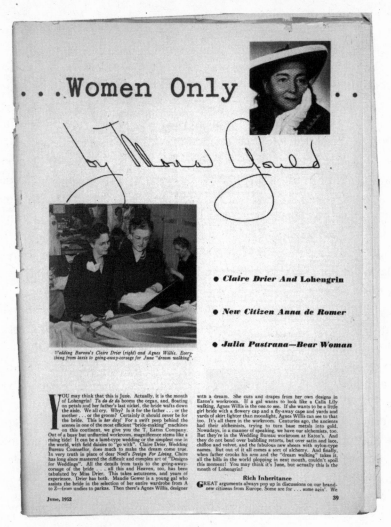

This issue of *New Liberty* was one of the few
magazines that Mona kept in its entirety.

thirty years, but she accepted this without complaint.[23] She also published in
Cats magazine, in exchange for a free subscription.[24] The section to which
she contributed was called "Few lines 'bout Felines."

᪥

Mona had withdrawn from writing *Listen* because she was offered a position
as editor of the women's pages of *New Liberty* magazine. In his correspondence with Mona, editor Keith Knowlton cautioned her that she must always

use the full name, *New Liberty*, when referring to the magazine. This was so that people would be sure to distinguish it from New York's recently defunct *Liberty* magazine.[25] Mona wrote all the copy for the pages herself, so her role was essentially that of a columnist.[26] The section was to be called "Women Only." Knowlton negotiated with Mona about the design, which was to include her signature, and possibly a different picture every month (this idea was later dropped). Mona's signature was extravagant and unique. She always wrote at an angle, using a book to line up the letters so that they were strangely flattened at the bottom. She would add the tails of the letters – the parts that would appear below the line – afterwards. This made her handwriting almost illegible in her tipsier moments, because the enormous tails would not always connect to the letters they belonged to, and would cut through three or four lines of handwriting beneath. For *New Liberty*, the signature made a striking graphic (though it was printed horizontally, rather than at its usual angle). About the content of the column, Knowlton wrote that Mona was welcome to write about men, reassuring her that Kate Aitken had always done so; besides, "I've seen no statistics that show that women are only interested in women. Dull world and short-lived if they were."[27] (Kate Aitken, seventeen years Mona's senior, was a CBC radio host. Keith Knowlton was not the only one who looked to her to set standards. During the height of her fame in the 1940s and 50s, thirty-two percent of Canadians who listened to the radio tuned into her nationally broadcast women's program.)[28]

Mona's column was the written equivalent of *Carousel*, full of amusing tidbits culled from the news, and chatty musings about anything she might think of. The tone was what Mona would have called "saucy" and the subjects changed rapidly, sometimes after a paragraph, and sometimes after only one sentence. The overall effect was like listening to a monologue by someone with an extremely short attention span. In a November 1954 column, Mona interviewed both Jack Fabian of Scotland Yard about female murderers (they tend to poison rather than stab or strangle their victims), and Mary Lou Chapman, who designed fabrics for cars. Frances Highland, a Regina actress premiering at Stratford, also received mention, along with the pantomime artist Jan Chamberlain and hair stylist Henri Gabor. Gabor – described as a "suave bachelor" – remarked that Canadian women's hair was easier to style than that of Swedes and Danes.[29]

Like her radio show, the column was an excellent vehicle for Mona, and an efficient form of self-promotion. Her columns often included mention of her projects in other media: for example, a poem adapted for piano by composer Ada Twohy Kent in a book called *Tiptoe Tunes for Tiny Tots*. Mona promoted the book both on air and in her column.[30]

In *The Monthly Epic*, his historical study of Canadian magazines, Fraser Sutherland does not have much good to say about *New Liberty*. It was sensationalistic, escapist, and it saved on fiction rights by running stories by long-dead authors like Edward Allen Poe.[31] He quotes Hugh Garner's withering description. "[*New Liberty*'s] circulation was a miracle, for hardly anyone ever admitted buying it, but claimed they'd just happened to pick up a copy in their barbershop or dentist's waiting room ... It was a strident, vulgar, thumb-to-nose little periodical, just the right size and heft to be read in a bus or train."[32]

The magazine was on the cutting edge in one area: it ran liquor ads, an illegal practice in 1950s Ontario. It was only through merging *New Liberty* with a Quebec publication that the magazine's publisher, Jack Kent Cooke, was able to get away with this.[33] The ban on liquor advertising only served to reinforce the commitment to drinking in Mona's profession. Drinkers were prone to claiming they were defending their freedom as individuals, and in some cases, as artists. Garner, for instance, linked drinking with the writing life. There was, he wrote, "no other career which would have interfered less with my drinking."[34] Mona's ability to down massive amounts of alcohol was a career bonus, if not a necessity. Doris Anderson, in her autobiography, *Rebel Daughter*, writes of lunching with her boss, John Clair, who "insisted I match him drink for drink." She would routinely go to the ladies' room and make herself throw up afterwards so that she could get some work done in the afternoon.[35]

The fifties, Sutherland writes, was a very lucrative time for freelancers. He quotes Max Braithwaite as saying that these were the halcyon days of magazine writing: "Plenty of work for everyone, reasonable prices, loads of opportunity, so that even a freelancer could make a good living, raise a family, and have a lot of fun."[36] All the same, no freelancer could afford to be a snob when it came to choosing markets; magazines were starting up and closing down at an alarming rate.[37] Mona's relationship with *New Liberty* did not last. In 1955, she disputed with the magazine's new editor, Frank Rasky, over the content of a column about cooking expert Madame Benoit. Rasky wanted Mona to provide more details, and she refused. She kept a draft of a letter to Rasky in her files. In high dudgeon, Mona defended her choice of material for several paragraphs, and concluded that this would no doubt end up being a letter of resignation. "It's a matter of journalistic integrity to me. I've worked with some pretty fine editors. I've learned over a long period of time, a craft for which I have tremendous respect. Almost a reverence. I refer, of course, to writing. I feel that the variety of kinds of writing I have done: the variety of personalities I have met, qualifies me to BE a columnist: and as such to choose whom I shall interview and what I shall pick and choose to have published about them."[38]

Ironically enough, this letter seems to have been written with more care than Mona's columns. She claimed to have done an informal survey of eleven people, asking them to comment on the disputed material. This is more thorough and detailed research than she did for most of her periodical writing. She may have been bluffing when she mentioned resignation, but if so, Rasky called her on it. The column continued to appear through April 1955 and then stopped. There is no way of knowing the nature of their relationship, but one thing is certain: Rasky held the power and his boss, Jack Kent Cooke, was owner not only of *New Liberty* magazine but of CKEY as well.[39] Later Cooke went on to buy Consolidated Press, publishers of *Saturday Night, Canadian Home Journal, Farmer's Magazine*, and eight trade journals.[40] Mona lost her sponsor with CKEY shortly before this, but the two events may not have been related.

Hugh Garner recounted how the new editor took over. Cooke seated Frank Rasky at a desk next to Keith Knowlton. It was not clear who was really in charge. Without saying anything outright, he made it impossible for Knowlton to continue doing his job. Garner commented in Sutherland's book that he (Garner) would have stayed in the job and forced Cooke into taking responsibility for his actions, but Knowlton ultimately resigned.[41] This meant that Mona had reason to dislike the new editor from the start. There may have been other factors. The presentation of Mona's column became less attractive in 1954. By August of that year, Mona's signature graphic and photograph had been removed. Soon after that, the name of the column was changed to "Only Human," and there was much less of Mona's text. From what I know of Mona, she would not have been able to hold out any better than Knowlton if Cooke had been trying to squeeze her out of her position. She would undoubtedly have taken the bait and found an excuse to resign.

Prior to the break with *New Liberty*, Mona was turned down for an opportunity to be a Paris correspondent for Consolidated Press. Cooke's reply to her application was curt. He wrote that they had already appointed their correspondent. "He is Earle Birney of the University of British Columbia, a choice which I am sure you will applaud."[42] Cooke may not have meant to be unkind in his last line, but it is not hard to imagine Mona feeling stung by the implication of Birney's clear superiority.

Mona appealed to Alvah Beattie to let her do a similar column in *The Montrealer*. "Couldn't YOU use a nice, bright, ebullient column from moi-meme? I'd snag you a pix or two of top flight personalities each issue: Keep it crisp, contemporary chatter ... I'd adore doing it for you. I think the Montrealer is the nearest thing we have to the New Yorker. I'd be plumb proud to represent you! How about it? Give in ... PLEASE DO!" Mona's cajoling won her a respectful answer, but not a positive one. On the back of her letter, Beattie replied that he could not offer her a column at present, but did not close the door on the possibility. "In the meantime, flood us with poetry – you write very well indeed but some of your poems are par excellence."[43] A *Toronto Telegram* column by Stan Helleur mentions that Mona was to move her column to *Mayfair* magazine in May 1955, but it never actually appeared there.[44]

Nevertheless Mona, the indomitable freelancer, continued to cultivate opportunities. A new magazine called *The Royal York* appeared on the scene in early 1957, with Jeann Beattie as editor. The magazine was to appear in guest rooms at the Royal York as well as CP trains, CPR hotel suites, and Empress ships traveling between Montreal and England. Beattie contacted Mona at once. "Obviously you were someone I wanted to alert about the book," she wrote. Mona has made a note on this letter in red pencil: "Soon!"[45] She took Beattie up on her offer. A version of Mona's *Be My Guest* interview with Lotta Dempsey was published in November, 1959.[46] Throughout 1959 she published interviews with several visiting celebrities, including Emelyn Williams and Julie Harris.[47]

In 1955, Mona applied for a scholarship to travel as a visiting poet to the Netherlands with the Royal Society. She did not receive the scholarship, which was a shame, since an opportunity to concentrate on her poetry at this juncture might have put her back on track. Letters of support from Clare Bice and Eric Rechnitzer show how highly respected Mona had become. Rechnitzer wrote that Mona "has a rare creative ability and has developed a high degree of literary excellence, particularly in the field of poetry and verse."[48] In addition to praising Mona's intelligence and many personal achievements, Bice wrote of her son John's accomplishments and promise as an artist. He noted that she must have sacrificed many opportunities in order to raise him, "Yet she herself is still young and very lively and personable and open to fresh ideas, and I would think she would be an excellent person to receive one of these government fellowships.[49] In this letter, Bice showed a lot of sensitivity. He took into account the efforts Mona had made on John's behalf without defining her in terms of the achievements of the nearest available male in her life.

Mona, on the other hand, made a point of mentioning John in any contacts she had with the press or people of influence. No one who knew Mona in this era was permitted to ignore the fact that she had a budding artist for a son. This was certainly intended to help John's career, but it did no harm to her own, either. Whenever Lotta Dempsey, Gordon Sinclair, or any columnist mentioned Mona, they also mentioned John. He was featured in the publicity for her *New Liberty* columns as well. The 'H' is dropped from his name in these press appearances, and at one point, he is credited with an additional two inches of height.[50]

Mona and Graham were open-handed with their financial support, assuring John in letters that they wanted him to do more than just subsist; they wanted him to enjoy life as a young artist. He expressed his appreciation in every letter home.[51] He did whatever he could to contribute to the family's well being, as well as to his own expenses. One summer he went to live with his grandmother in London, selling music lessons door-to-door to save money for the coming year, helping her around the house, and keeping her company. In years to come, Ellen was to remember this period as one of the happiest of her life.[52] To his parents, he wrote long, detailed accounts of his summer jobs, of his life at school, of his travels in Europe and, in later years, to Mexico. He made it clear to Mona and Graham that they were in his thoughts all the time, and through letters, he took them along on his travels.

The correspondence between John and Mona in the 1950s glows with loving attentiveness. While traveling in B.C., John wrote to his mother in response to some doubt she must have expressed about her poetry. In a respectful way, he nudged her toward devoting herself more consistently to her art. "You owe it to a complex, frustrating world to keep on writing these beautiful, simple things. They are not 'fully orchestrated' but then neither are the line drawings of Picasso or Matisse. And yet – the information is all there – as well as the beauty of form."[53]

A few years later, John was living in Montreal, finding whatever opportunities he could to get his work seen by dealers and critics, and peddling his services to art directing firms. Mona wrote to him with heartfelt encouragement, "Don't be discouraged, Dear, if it takes a LOT of tromping round! ... Be, like the little green snake at Muskoka, that I clobbered over the head with the canoe paddle, remember? Just keep coming up AGAIN and AGAIN each time, a little closer to the guy who is whacking you. Finally, his astonishment will be such that he will just sit down and give up. That's when you come ONCE more, right at his foot, and stick your tongue out! Then he'll put you on his payroll, to get rid of you!"[54]

Mona adored her son, and her feelings intensified as he matured as an artist. She was determined not to cling to him, though, and this came at a cost. She missed him terribly when he was away. After one of his long spates of traveling, she wrote:

The Gift

"He's coming HOME" she said
And all her face went BRIGHT with pleasure:
This was the measure of her heart's delight
So slight a thing could make her sing!
And yet ... not slight ...
For when a mother's "flock" is one
(And that, a son)
Knowing, that he will sleep in his OWN room
In his OWN bed ... to-night ...
This, is DELIGHT!
Swept IN from the stream of time,
Beached on his OWN land:
You could have offered her the WORLD (instead)
Frosted with diamonds
And SHE withhold her hand![55]

And that a son. That single phrase speaks volumes about Mona. She believed, quite simply, that men were *worth* more than women. For this reason, her hero-worship of her son may have contained a seed of envy. As a man, John could become the great creative genius she did not believe she herself could ever be.

Mona had reached a crucial point in her development. She saw both what she had become, and how far she was likely to go. Though she did all kinds of writing, she still identified herself primarily as a poet. On some level, she had always hoped that her enthusiasm and talent would be enough to ensure not only that she would be widely recognized, but that she could make a living from what she did best. This quixotic dream had carried her a long way; still, after thirty years it had not come true, nor was it likely to. Mona was working long hours, spreading herself thinner and thinner, with no possibility of a secure income, pension, or benefits. Then, a sudden crisis in 1956 made it clear that when it came to Mona's relentless work schedule, there would be no end in sight.

This Bleak Design

For years, Graham had not been well. His blood pressure was unstable and he suffered from a general lassitude which made life as a salesman more and more difficult. He was prescribed Rauwolfia, an anti-hypertensive drug which did nothing to help his blood pressure but acted as a sedative, sapping his energy even more. In 1956, when he was only forty-eight years old, Graham's working life was abruptly derailed. His blood pressure rose uncontrollably one night, and he had chest pains. It was several days before the doctor could see him, but Graham was hospitalized soon afterwards. In those days, people were responsible for their own medical fees. This came during a time when Mona was saddled with an enormous tax bill, her income from freelancing having been very high the previous year. She was angry that Graham, as a veteran, was not receiving more support. In a letter to John, who was living in Montreal at the time, she reported: "Dr. P. says the war probably gave G this whole deal." The doctor felt all the men should have been tested for heart problems at war's end, "at the expense of the same fair Gov't that 'ucked me out of the income tax dough and tied our hands tight, for the nonce."[1] In response, John offered to come home and help with the family finances and with caring for his father, saying "It would not be duty with me; it would be an honour and a pleasure, and might just put some 'direction' into my life too."[2] Mona wrote that it would only alarm Graham if John came home.

Mona could have used help from some quarter, however. Her mother's health was also failing. After spending some years in Michigan, Ellen had returned to the family home in London. She wanted Mona to spend more time with her, but Mona had many obligations in Toronto and not much support. Ellen's letters are difficult to read; the handwriting is large, and crowded into a small space. She wrote in pencil most of the time, and her notes are full of non-sequiturs, making it impossible to tell what she was saying from the context. The tone of the letters is affectionate and encouraging, but a guilt-inducing undertow is always present. One letter thanks Mona for the "lovely flowers." She writes that she is praying for Graham, and sympathizes with his having to wait for medical news, since she herself has gone through the same thing. Ellen listens faithfully to Mona's shows, she writes, but "I surely would have been glad to have you mother's day. In fact life is so terribly dull for most of the year ... no family to enjoy it with.[3]

Mona did her best to appease her mother. She rearranged her schedule to go and visit her whenever she could. She wrote to John, "Poor old Sweet! Y'know, she's trying so hard to cope, but I'm afraid she won't be along with us very much longer."[4] Eventually, Ellen was hospitalized, and Mona went to London to look after her. After checking her mother into the hospital, she spent the night in the house where she had grown up. Later, she wrote about lying awake, filled with the sobering thoughts that come with caring for an elderly parent. In her father's last illness, she had comforted him when he was getting a needle, just as he had comforted her when she was a child. Now Mona had come to another milestone in her life. She realised that Ellen was no longer the "competent, cool and dignified" woman who had raised her. "It was when she was obediently undressing at the nurse's request to get into bed. She handed me her belongings one at a time, to fold and put away for her. For the first time in our lives our positions were reversed and I felt that She was MY daughter, not I HERS."[5] Ellen Howard McTavish died in 1957, at the age of eighty-four.

Mona wrote to John that she planned to move to the country and care for Graham full-time, but she continued to take on freelance work at a furious rate. Retiring from work would have been impossible; she was the main breadwinner and leaving Toronto even for two days to see her dying mother had been difficult. Mona wrote a poem during this time suggesting what she must have been going through.

She was adept at nursing, animals or trees;
But let disease creep like a terror on a human one
She was undone!

If flesh sat sweetly on the proud clean bone
The tone of her voice, strong as a staunch sea buoy
Easy, she was, and quick with her word and warmth
This was her "climate" ... this her wind of joy!

Dumb ... in the presence of decay and pain
Walked she a hell, private, despised of all
Tiptoing fearfully past the cobwebbed ill
Feeling her way ... a-down an airless hall.

This, was a flaw, a deep and hurtful flaw
Bred in her heart when she was child in womb:
Anything ailing made her marrow freeze
Shutting her spirit in a dusty tomb:

Born out of hate ... and in a wintry month
She was conceived ... surely against her mother's will
Thorned like a curse within her mother's flesh
Bitterly nursed she felt this loveless chill.

Small ... she could burrow in a Collie's hide
Seeking ... blind as a beggar for some sign:
Tenderness ... somewhere this was surely hers
Somewhere she fitted into this bleak design.

Still, when the years went over and her mother aged
White as a Sybil in her wintry land
Still was she helpless to traverse this gap
Tho' she stood longing ... with an outstretched hand.[6]

Mona was being hard on herself in this poem and, looking for a place to lay blame, was correspondingly harsh about her mother. Yet in the midst of this "private hell," she maintained a façade of bravado at work and devoted service at home. And she did her best to numb her complex feelings by drinking.

Graham was greatly weakened by his first bout of illness. He was placed on three doses of Phenobarbital a day. He was unable to cope with even the slightest stress. A social visit from his boss sent his blood pressure soaring and it became clear he would have to leave his job at Yorktown Motors.

Photographs from the time bring to mind Mona's image of the "cobwebbed ill." Mona tried to stay cheerful. She wrote to John about their day-to-day life, "[Graham has] been looking good, lately and feeling tolerably decent, most of the time: He's being sensible about things: going out a bit more to the show with me: down to Angelo's to eat, the odd time: to the Library: it's not exactly HILARITY, but it's LIVING! And it's circulating! Which is GOOD for G!"[7]

This description was cushioned before and after by several paragraphs expressing concern for John and giving advice and encouragement for his career. "If it doesn't 'jell' take off on a new tack: Don't be downed! You can REALLY DRAW, kid ... I don't know much, for SURE, but that, I DO." It was as if Mona wanted to protect John as long as possible from the role reversal she had just experienced with her own mother. She finished: "Let me know if you get strapt for dough, Jon. PLEASE."[8]

Mona worked hard during those years, becoming more highly charged and extraverted all the time. Meantime, Graham moved toward quiet introspection. Anyone who remembers him from this time uses a single word to describe him: "sweet." His brush with mortality was the occasion for a lot of self-searching. The relentless enthusiasm demanded of a salesman had never run very deep, with Graham, and at times he must have felt like a failure. Now, his illness forced him to probe beneath the machismo that drove the men of his generation and come to terms with the vulnerability beneath. Through illness and a haze of medication, he did his best to note his revelations. "Mr. Hemingway wrote about courage. It is his big theme. It is a fine thing but to me – to go out as he did to observe it – is something like look[ing] ... a man in his long underwear taking a crap. I found another [unclear] Steinbeck ... another theme – love."[9]

Graham had to make changes in his lifestyle. First came a low sodium diet, which he described in a letter to John as "a real fiend idea ... The taste is merely removed from all food. It's uncanny what they can do – even bread – even butter. I eat fruit – vegetables – rice. Nature Boy that's me."[10] More importantly, he had to quit drinking. He joined Alcoholics Anonymous, and began to pursue – if not a formal course of psychotherapy – at least an exploration of himself and his history. He called AA "My last adventure and my greatest." His notes on AA were brief and sometimes written in the third person, but they captured the essence of Graham's process at that time. They mentioned feelings of anger, resentment, and failure for which "no money no love no power can compensate." "Big emotional denunciations or fights" were listed as symptoms of alcoholism, as well as a loss of direction or purpose. Graham noted that his Presbyterian upbringing was followed by "hedonistic revolt" in the 1920s and 1930s.[11] Now, Graham asked himself:

> Could I admit <u>possibility</u> of God?
> Could I live as if there were God?
> What is there to lose?[12]

Sober and salt-free, Graham tried to mobilize himself again. Mona wrote to John about a conference he was planning on attending with some former colleagues – probably from his days as a car salesman. She mentioned few details about the event itself, only that Graham was nervous as he got ready to go.[13] (This is not surprising, given that the event would probably be focused on drinking.) For a while he sold insurance from home, and it seems that at one point he even went on another grueling road trip. In April 1959, he wrote on a postcard to Mona that he had covered a hundred and fifty miles that morning.[14] All this activity was short-lived, however. As one doctor put it, the life of a salesman was "murder" to Graham. By the summer of 1959, his health was in sharp decline.

His faith in Mona was unflinching, however. I found a piece of paper, folded and refolded, perhaps wept-over so much that it had fallen to pieces. The scraps were pasted on a piece of construction paper and a second copy had been typed out on Mona's typewriter. She never spoke about the existence of this, Graham's last message to her.

> My Darling Mona
> You must always believe in yourself you know because a lot of other people do. You must always remember when other people don't – that – it is people like you who go ahead of the scientists. You must remember that poets are blessed – that God tells the poets before he lets others know.
> There are different styles of thinking – and if you change with every style – you are a <u>mirror</u> – but if you are a <u>poet</u> – people – being people – will discover you again – and again – and you will be in style and out of style. But there is only one truth.

You are a poet. So you must always listen to the voice in you. <u>It is right</u>.

Graham died 29 September 1959. He had just turned fifty-one.[15]

Social Pages

One day, I lifted the last of the seven boxes onto my cart and saw the raw wood of the palette it had been lying on. I gazed triumphantly at the empty spot, at the blankness of those boards, stripped of their messy obligations.

The feeling did not last. There were thirty-one boxes still to go. They were housed in a far corner of the library's basement. I booked a time to meet with Edna and retrieve them. Each pushing a cart, we walked through a labyrinth of shelves to find a storage area, cordoned off from the rest of the basement by wire mesh. Edna unlocked a gate in the mesh with a key and hung a red tag on the outside. This was, she said, so that anyone passing would know there was someone in there.

I enjoyed this little ritual, which seemed a tacit acknowledgment of the hazards of archival work. Did people get lost in the storage room? Did they pass out from lack of oxygen? I had no doubt that this was possible. I followed Edna through the cardboard landscape, winding our way among piles of boxes. Edna turned on lights to illuminate each area, then turned the lights off, obscuring the path behind us as we moved on. At last, we stopped in front of a huge stack of boxes: Mona's remaining papers. Edna nodded at me, gestured to the pile. I felt like Sisyphus at that moment, as though my task would never end.

❧

But it did. Over time, the pile of boxes in the basement dwindled. Over four years' time. What happened during those years? More of the same. My mother's bouts of illness became longer and more severe. Finally she was sick all the time. I remember sitting in emergency wards and doctors' waiting rooms, waking up breathless with anxiety or staring, exhausted, at a computer screen, willing my mind to function. Daily, Margaret Atwood's words echoed in my mind: "This above all, to refuse to be a victim." The possibility seemed very real that I *could* become a victim. Of what? Of my elders and their needs. Quite simply, of the past, of its ability to infiltrate the present. I fought against this, snatched moments of fun and love and friendship greedily. The ongoing state of emergency heightened my senses and made every moment seem significant. For every particle of my attention that the past took, I felt I must create an equally compelling activity in the present. I signed up for every course I could, took every possible free-lance contract, initiated projects to fill every spare moment.

One day, I tipped the dust and cat hair out of the bottom of a box, broke it down and carried it to the recycling bin. The last box. Somehow, I had got through it. Somehow, every piece of paper had found its way into a file, and I had come up with a rudimentary listing of what was there. I could not allow myself to feel relieved, even for a moment, though. I wasn't finished. Not enough order had been made. Each category – prose, poetry, journals, letters – still needed to be placed in chronological order, and I needed to produce something called a Finding Aid: a list of all the files and what was in them.

But I could not do it anymore. My thesis was overdue. My mother was sicker. I had started dating a man who, I could tell, was an ideal partner for me, yet I spent what little time we had together enumerating my worries and doubts. I knew I was probably ruining a good thing, but falling in love was the last thing I wanted. I had little enough control over my life as it was. In my journal I wrote: "It seems like anyone can take anything from me, any time." In the winter of 2001–2002, I stopped going to the library, though the archive was as present as ever in my mind. The boxes were still there; the disorder was still there. When I passed the corner of St George and Harbord streets, I imagined that I caught a whiff of Mona's smell, reminding me there was still a lot to do.

❧

I am not sure how it dawned on me that I could ask for help, but one day, I realised I had brought the project to a point where I did not have to do it on my own any more. In exchange for editing services, two of my clients, Suzanne Andrew and June Barnett, took on part of the sorting. They agreed to list the contents of some of the rough sections which I'd created. This seemed like the greatest gift anyone could give me. June became a dedicated admirer of my grandmother's work. She spent weeks in the library, putting the thousands of copies of Mona's poetry in sequence. Far from being happy that I'd found someone to share my burden, I felt angry at Mona. June's reaction seemed one more sign of her ability to take everything a person had to give, and more.

Mona had one personality on the page, another in the world. She was sweet and compassionate and sensitive in her poetry, and this was the persona June had come to love. But the real Mona spoke in a high-handed, contemptuous way of anyone who tried to help her, to *give* her anything. I hesitate to write down the things she said, because they might seem silly – or downright delusional – but she really believed them. When invited to do a reading in a school, she would declare that the children had all sat at her feet, trying to touch the hem of her clothing. The boys had pushed their way to the front to catch a glimpse of her beautiful legs (this, when she was over eighty years old). She said that once a friend had stood outside her door for a half hour in the rain with a meal for her to eat while Mona pretended she was not home. A man who helped her with something practical would be called a "little" man, a woman, a "poor little thing." Even the plant that thrived on her windowsill was a weed she was trying to kill. Yet people still gave her time and money and things she needed. They forgave her for the way she treated them, over and over again. Even after death, Mona continued to exert this power over people, and June seemed to have fallen, unquestioningly, for her game. I could imagine Mona's voice speaking with contempt about June.

"Stop!" I told her, "I can't let you spend so much of your time on this."

"It's okay," she insisted, her voice choked with emotion. "This poetry has changed my life. I feel like I've made a new friend. Even though Mona is dead, it doesn't matter. I feel like I know her, like she's still alive, and she understands everything I'm feeling, everything I've gone through in my life. I laugh and cry every day when I sit there reading through her poems. It's as if she's speaking *for* me, saying what I would say if I could."

June produced a cross-referenced binder listing about two thousand of Mona's poems.

⌘

I didn't have much of a thesis committee: just my own advisor and one other professor, David Olson, who came on board in the last month. I met Dr Olson just before I was to hand my thesis in. While he finished a meeting with another student, I sat in his waiting room reading an article about apes; about how, when they are trying to convey a new idea, they can point to two seemingly unrelated images on a communication board, linking them in a way that resembles metaphor. I wished I had included this in my thesis, which was called "The Problem of Metaphor in the Philosophy of Mind." It was too late now.

My advisor had said I should, out of courtesy, cite something Dr Olson had written. I devoured his book, *The World on Paper*, particularly the section where he mentions studies which test children's ability to distinguish a speaker's intention from a hearer's interpretation. A five-year-old child, for instance, will tend to assume that what she means is exactly what the listener hears. A few years later, children are able to distinguish "what the speaker said from what the speaker 'should have said,' 'meant,' or 'wanted.'" The way to find out the level of a child's understanding is to use indirect speech, irony and metaphor.[1]

He called me into his office and we had a short conversation. As I put on my coat and stood up to leave, he began grilling me with questions about my paper. Unprepared, I answered as best I could. I felt sweat dripping inside my clothes, a combination of performance anxiety and what I could no longer deny was a hot flash. My concentration fragmented long enough for me to think, "I'm too old for this," and then I went back to answering his questions.

"Okay," he said.

"That's it?"

"Sure." And I realized that my thesis defense had come and gone.

Peggy Lee died a few weeks after that. Her rendition of "Is That All There Is?" was played often on the radio. Fitting, I thought. Yes, that *was* all there is, but it was enough. I realized that the short citation from Olson had answered a question that had been nagging me for years, and that this question had probably been my reason for pursuing my degree in the first place. It had something to do with being able to make a distinction between intention and interpretation, word and meaning. Something about identifying this as a developmental phase. I had my answer, though I still could not articulate the question.

ʚ̃

It was December, 2003, the first anniversary of my mother's death. My life had changed in the past year. I was married. I had a home. Gradually I had built up a list of publishing credits, and now an arts grant was going to enable me to work full-time on Mona's biography. I would like to point to some moment of decision: a watershed that allowed me to fix all my problems. That is not how my story went, though. Exhausted, I had lost my sense of the larger picture. Instead, I just plodded along day to day. Eventually I found myself in a new place. I dreamed I was a refugee, living in safety but longing for my native country, knowing I would be killed if I ever tried to go back there.

The morning of the anniversary, I could not get out of bed. I had a cold, a bad one. I fell asleep. I woke up. I coughed. I made my way, hugging the wall, to the bathroom. I slept again. I woke up. I coughed. My husband joked that he should put some posters on the ceiling of our bedroom because that's what I saw most of, these days. He put a laptop computer on the end of the bed and showed me children's movies on DVD. I watched them for a while, then sheepishly admitted I found them too sad.

I dreamed I was trying to find Mona in a kitchen cupboard. Suddenly tiny, I climbed into it, picking my way up treacherous, miniature flights of stairs. I felt desperate to find her. I woke up and wrote on a slip of paper, "I dreamed that Nanna died before she died before she died," then fell back on the pillow again. I remembered another time in my life when I had been this sick, felt this helpless. It was when I had measles, at the age of five. "Rubella" was the name I heard whispered around my bed, and I knew it made me dangerous. My mother and sister had to move somewhere else, to get away from me. I spent my time in a darkened room and was told to avoid moving my head. One day I felt a stabbing pain in both ears, heard a sound like waves crashing. I stumbled out into the hall in the forbidden light. The walls seemed bent at odd angles and the ceiling felt like it was sloping just above my head. I picked up the telephone. 924-1738. Nanna. Comfort. I couldn't hear her voice but soon, everything got better. There was penicillin for my burst eardrums, and I was no longer left alone in my room. Nanna fixed it for me. I turned to her when my mother was not there. Now, my mother was gone for good.

What did I mean, "Nanna died before she died before she died?" It had something to do with her stories. There was something petrified about them. Dead. And also, dead*ly*. They were about the past, and sought, in some way, to fix the world, to stop it from moving. And to fix me, the listener. To define me, possess me. Some part of me realised this, and pulled away from her at an early age. I don't know how old I was, but I know I was young; too young to make the kind of distinction David Olson talked about, between intention and interpretation, word and meaning. Yet I *had* made some sort of distinction, had been forced to, because of the gap between what Mona said, and what my senses told me. What had happened, then? I came to mistrust stories – everyone's stories – but most of all my own.

From then on, I spent most of my life humouring my grandmother, going through the motions of being close. She felt it, and it hurt her, but she could not – or would not – understand why. And I could never tell her. How old was I when this happened? I could not put a date to it. It was early enough that in the meantime, I had forgotten what it was like to trust my grandmother, to believe her. Until now.

❧

One morning, I woke feeling I could bound over to the library. My lungs, for the first time in what felt like forever, were clear. Cold had descended on the city. The sky was a brilliant blue. It was time to go back, to complete the finding aid and make some order in the series of chapters I had cobbled together. I walked the hour and a half to the university. Although I could feel the skin on my face freezing, I was not bothered by the cold. Edna Hajnal had retired, and Jennifer Toews had taken over as curator of manuscripts. I told Jennifer I wanted to work in the basement, and right in the stacks. I craved the darkness, the obscurity, even the lack of oxygen in the place. Maybe here, in this strange vacuum, I could begin to see the shape of Mona's story emerge.

I elbowed a space for myself among the boxes and files which crowded the table. Jennifer walked by, ostensibly on her way to drop off a cartful of manuscripts, though maybe she was checking to see if I was alright. We began to chat, and lingered – we both admitted – longer than we should. I asked her how she could stand working among all these unsorted papers.

"Oh, this." She gestured to the rows and rows of shelves that stretched out behind us, and presumably, to the fenced-in area beyond. "It'll never be completely organized. You can't let it bother you."

"Sometimes I wonder what's the point of keeping all this stuff."

"Oh ... you'd be surprised. Sixty years from now, someone's going to come looking, trying to find out what it was like being a freelance writer in the 20th century. And they'll find exactly what they need."

I found this hard to imagine, but – I realised – my own opinion of the archive didn't matter anymore. It belonged to the library, and to scholars of the future, who would use it long after I was gone.

Mona's papers took up two bays of a metal bookshelf, with a few boxes spilling into the territory of neighbouring collections. One box, which contained newspaper clippings, was so large it had to be housed in a completely different area of the stacks. I decided to start with this one. The newspapers were all in tidy files, but I could not remember having put them there. I came upon things I had sorted several years before as if I were seeing them for the first time. Sometimes I admired the logic I had used in grouping clippings together; sometimes I shook my head in disbelief that I could do anything so strange. *What was I thinking?* I wasn't. I was just getting through it all.

At some point, I had put the social pages of the Toronto *Globe* and *Telegram* from the summer of 1958 at the bottom of the box. These were about my parents' wedding. They contained the requisite information. My mother was "the former Miss Hetty Ventura, daughter of Mrs. Ventura of London, England and of the late Mr. Harry Ventura." The couple was married in St Andrew's United Chapel by the Reverend Bruce Hunter, who had married Mona and Graham thirty years before. In the absence of the bride's father, she was "given in marriage" by her father-in-law, Graham.[2]

Wedding stories are stories of completion. And even if "happily ever after" gets derailed, you can still appreciate – for a few moments at least – the story leading up to the wedding itself. There are overtones of destiny at work, the destiny that makes ordinary lives extraordinary. My mother told me many times how she met my father. They were both working for CBC in the 1950s. Those were the early days of television, when programs were broadcast live and work was a constant party. My mother was a script assistant for the Variety department. My father worked in the paint-shop. She met him at an art opening and knew, across a crowded room, that she would marry him.

This part I remembered clearly. But the stories of my parents' wedding had become strangely fossilized inside me. I wondered if I remembered them correctly at all. My mother said she had suffered such a terrible attack of cold feet that she tried to jump out of a moving car, crossing the Bloor viaduct on the way to the church. Graham had pulled her back into the car and held her there while he drove the rest of the way. Everyone was so drunk that she almost married John Aylesworth, the best man. She also spoke of how she loved Graham, and he loved her, of how – in her words – they "understood each other," and of how, at the wedding reception, which was hosted and paid for by Mona and Graham, Mona presented her with a jar of pickled snakes. This, Mona said, was a delicacy, given to my mother in honour of her artistry in the kitchen. But its venomous symbolism was not lost on anyone.

From Mona I heard how on the steps of the church after the ceremony my mother announced – for the first time – that she was Jewish. Mona's story was peppered with significant pauses, and the word "Jewish" pronounced as if it were a combination of "leper" and "axe murderer." "I wouldn't have minded," Mona used to say, "If only she had told me before. It was the lying that got to me."

I had never seen any photographs of the wedding. Even when my parents were still together, there was no album in the bookshelf, no framed picture on the wall. That morning, in the library's sub-basement, I discovered my mother's wedding photographs. I had to roll my chair away from the table to avoid staining the newspaper with my tears. In my mother's eyes was an expression I had never seen during her lifetime. She looked happy.

⚜

My parents' marriage in 1958 was the first in a relentless series of losses for Mona. As far as she was concerned, my mother was taking her son away from her. I was born a year after my parents' marriage, in June of 1959. There are pictures taken that summer outside Mona's and Graham's apartment. My father holds me next to his face. I was told that Graham held me, too, whenever he had the strength, though there are no pictures of that. And there are no pictures of my mother with her newborn at all. In my sorting, I came across some notes Mona had made years later, about those months in which she felt her husband's life ebbing away, at the same time as her son had turned his attention toward his own home and family. She wrote, "I held Maria over my heart like a human poultice."[3]

—Jean Gainfort Merrill.

Both with radio station CBLT, Mr. and Mrs.
John Howard Gould were married in St. Andrew's
United Church, are now honeymooning in Mexico.
The bride is the former Miss Hetty Ventura, daugh-
ter of Mrs. Ventura of London, England, and the
late Mr. Harry Ventura. The groom's parents are
Mr. and Mrs. John Howard Gould, the latter the
well-known author and radio personality, Mona Gould.

The *Globe and Mail* 7 July 1959

Diminished but Not Licked

The newly widowed Mona did nothing to slacken her pace of work. A photograph taken within weeks of Graham's death shows her interviewing the Andrews Sisters in a booth set up at Honest Ed's discount department store. She is smiling in the photograph but her face is mask-like, her eyes glassy. There was a roller derby going on, on the floor above, while she was trying to conduct her interview.

Mona continued functioning, but she was in the throes of grief. She kept up appearances during the day, but her nights were filled with flashbacks of Graham's last hours. There had been a jolting trip in an ambulance with sirens blaring and frantic attempts to save him. The pain of separation closed in on her unbearably when she was alone at night, and she was haunted by memories of the last, tragic months in which Graham let go of life. At times, she felt strangely numb. At other times she was seized by fear – without knowing what she was afraid of.[1]

Mona would have done well at this point with a steady, predictable routine, surrounded by people she knew, but instead, as a freelancer constantly on the lookout for work, she had to put on a daily performance, much of it improvised, and often in unfamiliar environments. And even in her most intimate circle, Mona felt she was forbidden to express the raw edge of her grief. She wrote that showing her grief – especially to John – made her feel like she was becoming her mother. Her notes from this period are almost all in the third person. "She had hated her mother's tears. Now, she found herself, weeping wetly – copiously – disastrously! And all the while, without being ABLE to stop – she felt she knew her son was hating her tears – and despising her for stooping so low – as to ALLOW their shedding!"[2]

John was the closest, most trusted person in her life, and she now turned the full force of her needs upon him. For years, Graham had grounded her in reality, pulling her back from her extravagant fantasies even if it meant a fight. His constant expressions of affection had kept her insecurity at bay and satisfied her ravenous appetite for attention. Just as Mona began depend on him, though, John became less available to her. Whether because of the galvanizing effects of marriage and parenthood, or the death of his father, or the support now offered to young artists, he felt a new sense of urgency in pursuing his career. He stopped taking on other work and devoted himself exclusively to drawing. As if to affirm the wisdom of his choice, the Elizabeth Greenshields Foundation awarded him a scholarship. The expatriate life beckoned, as it did for many Canadian artists at that time.[3] John decided to take his wife and one-year-old daughter to Spain for as long as the grant held out.

At about the same time as the Greenshields scholarship was announced, a media buzz appeared around Mona's imminent departure for England. Elizabeth Dingman featured Mona in her column called "Getting Around." "John and I got our break together," Mona told Dingman, "and he was more thrilled at my chance than his."[4]

Although Mona described her trip to England as a "break," she orchestrated the whole venture herself. She proposed to CKFH that she would continue her daily broadcasts of *Be My Guest* from England. Though Mona's shows were popular, CKFH was hardly in a position to send her abroad as a foreign correspondent. The studio agreed to pay her a modest retainer, but she would have to pay her own travel expenses. The logistics of recording the shows and mailing the tapes were formidable; however, nothing deterred Mona. She wrote of her adventures in a piece called "The Iron Maiden and Me," which she pitched to various magazines but never published. She had to purchase a tape recorder herself for five hundred dollars. While in England, she was to produce a tape a day, to be shipped to Canada wrapped in tin foil, at her own expense. She would also pay for the batteries that her tape recorder was to – in her words – "devour like peanuts ... every time I did an interview."[5]

The strategy of picking up stakes in response to a loss had worked for Mona and Graham when they went to Mexico. Now, lonely though she was,

Mona was also free. While her husband and son had both had a chance to see Europe, Mona had stayed at home, entrenched in work and family obligations. Now the timing seemed ideal to take her show on the road. Mona would not be the first female broadcaster to take such a trip. In 1950, Kate Aitken had gone to Paris to comment on fashions for her CBC program. Why not Mona, too?

These were the surface reasons for the trip but there were probably other, less positive ones. While playing role of adventurous traveler, Mona was making a move that would bring her within a few hours' travel of her son. And no one looking at the Elizabeth Dingman interview could escape thinking that a desire for attention played a part in her planning. She wanted to compete *for* John's attention with all the new demands on him, as well as to compete for the public's attention *against* him. John had begun to appear in the newspapers not just as Mona's son but as an artist in his own right. Where she had always thought of him as a child and therefore in need of her protection, he had now broken an unwritten law by declaring his attachment to another woman.

Family relationships grew strained as the departure dates approached. My parents and I spent the summer of 1960 at Manitou-Wabing, a fine arts camp near Parry Sound, Ontario, where John was working as a teacher. This meant that we were out of town during Mona's final preparations for her trip. John wrote often to his mother, and they talked on the phone as well. His letters were full of affection and encouragement, but Mona seems to have been unsatisfied by the quality of their communications; he was constantly apologizing for not being attentive enough, and making up for this with expressions of love that many would consider out of place between a mother and son. I am not sure whether my father was aware of this dynamic, or whether he was so deeply enmeshed in their relationship that he thought it normal. He may have been trying to counteract any romantic tone in his letters when he cast himself in the parental role.

I have all the feelings for you that Bogie [Mona's father's nickname] would have had, and perhaps, to an extent, Nanna. Mixed feelings, feelings of real true joy that you are going to see some beautiful things at this time, feelings of sadness that we will be separated even for a while, feelings of strangeness at what can happen so quickly to people's lives – feeling of great hope for your future. You see, we have been so close for so many years that our lives have dovetailed, our thoughts interwoven, our existence interdependent. The lives of you and dad and I were like a beautiful drawing – complete and vital. Now, of course, the string has broken and we remain.[6]

The decision to take the trip made Mona feel better, at least at first. There were a lot of details to look after and the challenge energized her, taking the focus away from her grief. She closed down the apartment on College Street in a lightning, two-week period,[7] departed on schedule, and rallied support everywhere she went. She was traveling by economy class, but her situation attracted the attention of the shipping line's management and she was given access to the first class lounge to produce her shows. She made seven tapes on board ship. On her arrival, she spent a week or two with relatives in Much Hadham in the south of England. During this time, she used every possible contact to generate material. Her biggest coup was an interview with the sculptor, Henry Moore. Much as she enjoyed the English countryside, London was Mona's goal. She arranged to live as a "paying guest" with the Leeds family in Chelsea. In their beautiful Edwardian house, she immediately created a home for herself. The Leeds became life-long friends, and she won the hearts of the couple's two children.

Mona's agreement with CKFH did not allow her any time to establish herself in London before starting her broadcasts. This was not easy. "In Old London, I was on entirely my own. Only my face for a FRONT. No chain of influence, to lean on. Just the Iron Maiden and Me, and a great LONGING to succeed in my London Venture. Scared (I was) and damp, most of the time, for when I was in England it rained more than it had in 200 years, and that is a lot of rain!" The London Venture did succeed, though. Looking back, Mona wrote,

I interviewed: sculptors and writers, explorers and designers, architects and flower sellers, historians and curators of Museums and Art Galleries, Painters and Poets and Hindu Seers, a marriage bureau gal, sculptors and antiquarians, scientists and directors and producers, river barge-men and thatchers of the Hansel and Gretel country roofs, hop pickers and hatters, ceramists and educators, models and fashion magazine editors, booksellers and actors, artists and cat breeders, whodunit writers and illustrators, coffee bar proprietors and picture restorers to the queen ... I manufactured my own "chain of influence" and the whole thing "snowballed" satisfyingly.[8]

The "Iron Maiden" deterred Mona from doing many on-the-spot interviews. Aside from its weight, it was complicated to operate, and she had not
much affinity for electrical equipment at the best of times. Mona turned this
obstacle into a strength. With fewer interviews to draw on, her shows became
more narrative, more literary, as she strove to create a verbal picture of the
world around her. She wrote to John about how sad and lost she felt on a
visit to Paris, but her broadcasts showed a different side. For listeners at
home, she transformed the moments of loneliness and alienation into occasions for excitement. She wrote about her last taxi ride through the city. Her
driver's name was Henri.

> Still with us, HM? You're in Paris, France ... To have one last look
> down onto this exquisite city, now flowered into a million white sun-
> bursts of light! To drive once more into the heart of the twelve Avenues:
> where they converge. Slipping, "eel-like" (thanks to Henri) into and
> out amongst a million cars. The statues now, eagling OUT beyond the
> Arc de Triomphe, looking bone-white in the illuminations: a sort of pu-
> rity comes down. The gendarmes in their own special ballet de nuit,
> with each Gendarme the prima ballerina of his own Theatre D'auto-
> mobiles; with what an elegant flourish he keeps these mechanical mon-
> sters from entanglement: his performance is flawless.[9]

In London, Mona observed the shifts that were happening in social and
cultural life years in advance of their hitting Canada. She did a broadcast on
the Picasso exhibition at the Tate gallery, turning an observing eye on the
onlookers, as well as on the paintings.

> "Seated man with Glass" is a huge oblong canvas, dizzy with many
> colours: light and attractive, but it has every aspect of a patchwork
> quilt put together under glass. "Crazy man" says a blue-jeaner, with a
> toss of his duck-tail hairdo: incidentally, men in London wear their hair
> in as many individualistic fashions as Picasso himself has invented. They
> wear it long and involved, finger-waved and tossed and teased and spit-
> curled and with bangs and cut short to the skull and tinted and dyed
> and if you have HEARD of any other ways: they're here on masculine
> skulls, too.[10]

She wrote about the new system of public health which was coming into effect in England. This was soon to come to Canada, too, and having just seen her husband through an expensive series of hospitalizations, it was of great interest to Mona. She quoted an aristocratic young lady as hating it; an elderly relative had died without any painkillers because a doctor refused to come out after hours. But a flower-seller on the street had his daughter's life saved by a series of miracle operations done by the Harley Street physicians who normally operated on the "aristocracy." Sexual mores in London were, Mona noticed, far in advance of staid Toronto. "There are plenty of places in London where young men go about VERY openly with their current 'boy friends' and where young ladies date their current Girl Friends. This does not raise a single eyebrow, here."[11]

Mona was constantly short of cash. The allowance from CKFH in no way met her needs. Decent lodgings in London were in great demand, and housing prices were high. Her rent ate up a large percentage of her income. There were also numerous expenses associated with making the shows. Transportation was a challenge. Her budget did not extend to taxis, and she was forced to lug the heavy tape recorder up and down the stairs of "The Tube" and the London buses if she wanted to tape an interview. Some interview subjects required payment. Still, she experienced a sense of accomplishment. She wrote notes about her feelings, referring to herself in the second person.

It was possible to carry on, but just. At night fright lay down beside [you], and in the morning, rose when you did. In the streets, sometimes, it seemed that you would never get back to your lodgings. Soaked to the skin, shivering with cold and exhaustion and carrying the everlasting Tape Recorder, to and from Interviews. It would seem too much. A bellyfull. But always when morning came, the effort was made. The day began and ended, and you were still there, and diminished but not licked. Not by a dam sight![12]

Mona was living alone for the first time in her life, testing herself in the greater world, and she was making a go of it. Distance was taking the pressure off family relationships. In the fall, the younger Goulds took up residence in the village of Rincon de la Victoria, in the south of Spain. Miles away from Mona's day-to-day demands, it was possible for both John and Hetty to pour out all their warmth to her in letters. John encouraged her to be patient, and Hetty comforted her with memories of her own experiences as an immigrant adjusting to Canada. *Hang on*, was the message from both of them. *Things will get better.*

They regaled her with stories of day-to-day life in the small fishing village, of the lean times waiting for installments of the grant, of the moments of triumph when the sale of a drawing in Canada would bring a windfall. They wrote of making friends with other expatriates, and getting to know the local fishermen and farmers. John wrote about his work, his way of revealing his soul to his mother and cementing their bond. Hetty wrote thanking Mona for her advice on child-rearing. I was teething, often sick to my stomach, and anxious in new environments; she never knew whether she was doing the right thing. Although she appreciated the beauty of their surroundings, my mother was showing every sign of depression. Her own mother had recently died, and she had given up a fulfilling job and a circle of friends to spend all her time looking after a toddler while protecting her husband's creative time and space. In many letters, she mentioned her own attempts at writing: the journal she was keeping, the ideas she had for children's stories; however, she wrote, "My brain has gone to sleep." She was in chronic pain from arthritis. Her letters were full of brutal self-criticism. She accused herself of laziness, and felt guilty for not doing anything to "earn her keep." At the end of a long, doleful letter about toilet training, Hetty's tone perked up when she inquired about the intrigues in their social circle back home. She went on for a paragraph about various love-triangles and betrayals then concluded, "We hear no news from Toronto. You are our sole correspondent – although I have written to most of our friends."[13]

Mona showed a great deal of delicacy, reading between the lines of Hetty's letters and volunteering the advice that there was nothing wrong with wanting a break from full-time motherhood. She should find a babysitter for a few hours a day. The plan worked brilliantly. My mother began to learn Spanish and venture into the town on her own, and I got over my fear of strangers. Hetty wrote: "Boy, do I need you. Actually, Maria loves you so much, and constantly mentions you, and I think in her own babyish way misses you ... Believe me, Mona, any advice you have time to give in your letters I will soak up."[14] A plan had taken shape for Mona to join us for Christmas.[15] It was a bright spot on the horizon for everyone to look forward to, and it got Mona through the short, damp days of autumn in Britain. She

Mona in a Spanish café. This is a rare appearance without lipstick and nail polish.

worked furiously and banked nineteen tapes to be broadcast during her time off. She promised to send more tapes from Spain, as well. The fall had been wet in Spain, as it had been in England, but as soon as Mona arrived on Spanish soil the sun came out, and she slipped into the leisurely rhythm of life on the shores of the Mediterranean. The Goulds drank wine with friends on the patio of the villa, ate fresh fish daily, and explored nearby towns and cities whose very names sounded like poetry: Torremolinos, Marbella, Sevilla, Mijas. On Chistmas night, we were all invited to have dinner at the home of Lola, whose family looked after our house. Mona, as the *abuela*, was given the place of honour at the table.

Mona remembered the Christmas of 1960 as a golden time, but the return to London brought nothing but difficulties. Mona wrote about a dispute which came up with the management of CKFH. According to Mona's version, the station cancelled her show just prior to the trip to Spain because she wrote a letter asking to be reimbursed for her expenses there. She described how she made the decision to return to Canada, after spending Christmas in Spain. "Back in London, I felt such a surge of love for the city and my life there, that I fought against a feeling that I MUST STAY. I dared not. Fear had me by now in his hands. I could not take a chance. My will had flickered down too low. I fled home by jet."[16] Fear of what, she did not make clear, but in another set of notes she implied that the loss of her job had undermined her confidence, making it hard to seek out freelance work in London. "My courage was oozing," she wrote.[17]

But Mona did not lose her job. Throughout her stay in England, she received cordial letters from Barry Nesbitt at the radio station. He constantly assured Mona of how well her shows were being received. In a letter dated 24 November 1960, he politely turned down a request for holiday pay, saying she had taken all her holidays for that year, but advancing her a week's salary according to her request. This was the only sign of a dispute. On the contrary, it was Mona who decided to cut short her stay in England. She announced in the fall of 1960 (even before leaving for Spain) that she would return to Canada in the new year. Nesbitt expressed surprise at her decision, but said nothing about canceling the program. He remained enthusiastic about her work, and later mentioned that listener response on the shows from Spain had been excellent.[18]

In later years, another version of the story came to the fore. Mona used to say that she returned to Canada in order to be near the family. (In reality, she came back a full six months before we did.) In Mona's stories, her return was not framed as her own need but as John's, and sometimes even as mine. "I discovered that I'm more a mother than I am a writer," was the way she put it. The common thread of these two versions is that she never took responsibility for her choice to return. Mona's show did not continue when she got back to Canada, but the real reason was probably the advent of television, and not any dispute, personal or professional.

Ironically enough, she had a perfectly good reason to leave London. She was running out of money. There was no way she could support herself on her retainer from CKFH, and finding other work in London would have taken more time, energy, and connections than she had at her disposal. As the months went on, her freelancer's instinct was probably warning her that it would be disastrous to absent herself for much longer from her contacts in Toronto. She felt lonely, cold, and damp most of the time and, at the age of fifty-three, was living in a rented room without cooking facilities. Why would she simply not admit that she wanted a more comfortable life? Mona would never have done such a thing. She expected herself to rise above all material considerations, and felt ashamed of taking them into account.

It may have been out of a sense of failure that she shifted the responsibility for her return to Canada on to others. Her dream of going to England had been a young person's dream: grandiose, vague, and in the long run, impossible to realise. She was simply going to live the life of a writer, in what she believed to be the hub of all writing. She would be Hemingway, the foreign correspondent, Katherine Mansfield, the footloose Bohemian, and the sensitive, passionate Edna St Vincent Millay, all rolled into one. In formulating her plan, Mona turned her back on all she knew about the business of writing: that building a career takes time and constant application, and that a strong community is essential. Mona saw this trip as her big chance. Grief-stricken though she was, she may secretly have believed that marriage and motherhood had held her back from becoming better known as a writer, or simply from living the life of the "real" writers she admired. That life had not materialized simply by transporting herself to England. Mona had made the situation work for her as well as possible, but in the end, she could not sustain it. She had to return to the life she knew.

Once back in Toronto, Mona immediately regretted her decision. A year and a half after Graham's death, her grieving hit its most intense phase. She was mourning the loss not only of her husband, but of her own dreams. She stayed at the home of her friend Kay Middleborough, where she had no bedroom of her own. She wrote that she felt "like an extra foot." Her inner turmoil continued. "A civil war goes on in my mind and body," she wrote, and harshly exhorted herself to mobilize her energies. "I have always been so strong and healthy and fully of vitality – I love to pour it out and just now it's 'clogged up' – so it runs back in and is a sort of slow poison – but human beings could stand Belsen and return."[19]

Mona's reputation was such that she immediately re-entered the journalistic community without missing a beat. As soon as she came back, she was the guest on at least four radio and television shows, talking about her experiences.[20] She had written to Eric Rechnitzer of MacLaren late in 1960 about her impending return. He reassured her that he would certainly find work for her, and he did.[21] The newly formed Canadian Conference of the Arts required a publicist, and she worked with Alan Jarvis to promote the organization's first meeting in Ottawa. As well, she did promotional work for the Anglican Church of Canada. As a seasoned and well-respected publicist, she had no trouble winning these two prestigious accounts. In other words, Mona fell on her feet.

However, a pattern now set in of moving quickly from one job to another, always ending in some kind of bad feeling. The position with MacLaren was temporary. When it finished she was interviewed for a number of jobs and found another, but there were disputes with her new employer and the position did not last long. She wrote that she was not used to being "cooped up" in an office all day.[22] Mona was making hasty decisions and alienating people unnecessarily. She seemed, inexplicably, to be undermining her own chances. In typical form, she never spoke about what was really troubling her. Under the ministrations of "Doc S.," Mona had begun taking barbiturates. These were routinely prescribed as tranquilizers at the time and as a recent widow of menopausal age, Mona was a prime candidate. After a number of months, Mona decided that she needed to stop taking them. Two disconcerting incidents may have prompted her. Once she fell off a chair for no apparent reason, and on another occasion, fell and sprained an ankle while walking. She weaned herself off the drugs without mentioning her plan to anyone, though she kept notes in a journal. The ups and downs of withdrawal undermined her ability to work, and whenever she was not under the influence of the medication, her grief struck with redoubled force. On one occasion, she managed to get through the night without taking any pills, but experienced such a bad panic attack in the morning that she almost threw up. She had to take a double dose of the drug in order to be able to start her day.

Later, having come through the worst of the withdrawal, she encouraged herself in her journal: "Want to make a success of this back to health venture so very much. It will affect all the rest of my life. I know. Felt pretty average tonight on 1 beer – at home – 2 very teeny scotches (widely spaced) at dinner … one – count 'em – sodium amytol all day. Feeling of being of use the key."[23] Mona was a full-blown alcoholic by this time, and remained one for many more years, but she successfully overcame her dependency on barbiturates by sheer willpower. Apart from the odd over-the-counter remedy, she remained drug-free for the rest of her life.

Mona wanted more than anything else to be on air again. She sent some scripts to Gloria Harron, head of women's programming at CBC. Though she had no openings at the time, Harron wrote that she was anxious to put Mona to work as an interviewer, encouraging her to keep an eye out for good subjects. Unfortunately, this promising opportunity did not come to fruition.[24]

Although she was earning an income from all these various jobs, Mona did not find herself an apartment. Something made it impossible for her to settle. She also may have been waiting for the family's return, hoping that if she had not found a home she would be invited to live with us. She was. In the spring of 1961, John wrote from Spain, suggesting that we all live in a duplex together. We moved into a house at 121 Davenport Road which had an apartment upstairs for Mona, and one downstairs for us. It was here that I began spending a lot of time with Mona. My earliest memories of her come from this time. My mother went back to work at CBC, and my father spent days at his studio. I was in nursery school for half days, but whenever I was at home, Mona was my anchor, always wanting to see me, always there when I needed her. Mona wrote a poem during this period called "It Is Autumn in the Garden."

It is autumn in the garden
And it is autumn in my life.
My grand daughter and I are easy
In the garden.
We pick up the yellow leaves
And the sere brown
We exchange opinions
On the red ones
And exclaim over the striped ones.

Our Siamese cat
Leaps like a gazelle
He achieves the fence top
And clambers onto a poplar tree.

My grand daughter tells me
It is a "skunk tree"
"WHY do you call it a skunk tree?"
I ask my grand daughter ...
"Because it is full of skunk holes"
Says Maria, solemnly,
And she, should know!

The wind blows over the garden like an avenger
The tall trees ... toss and bend ... and leaves rustle down
    in battalions;

My grand-daughter and I quarrel over this pencil and paper;
She pokes with an aggressive forefinger
I have to stop writing
Lest I lose an eye!

And the leaves blow over –
And the wind sings –
And Maria and I quit the garden.
We hurry down the street
Leaf-light ... and hurrying ...
We sing a song to the wind ...
"Together" we sing ... "Toge-ther" ...

It is autumn in the garden
And it is Autumn in my life –
Most fortunate of women,
I hold love ... by the hand![25]

However, life at 121 Davenport was not as peaceful and loving as the poem suggests. Mona was trying to come between my parents, and to turn me against my mother. She encouraged two relationships: the one between me and my father, and the one between herself and me. This, effectively, excluded my mother. Hetty was there, as the person who had physically borne me, and she was around to take care of me, but she was not in the chosen circle. It was as if I were the child of Mona and my father, and my mother was a surrogate or a wet nurse. In the many hours I spent in her apartment, Mona would tell me that my mother was "not a lady." I understood that this phrase took in my mother's quick temper and raucous laugh, her wild, curly hair and olive complexion, and the aura of anxiety that seemed to hang on her at all times. Mona was a lady and so was I, but my mother was not. I remember another word my grandmother used: "Jew." Seldom spoken, it had the status of an obscenity. My mother's being Jewish, of course, made me Jewish too, but Mona did not acknowledge this.

My mother, for her part, felt that Mona was a bad influence on me, and on our household as a whole. I remember spending a weekend at a cottage, and waking up in the morning to find the screen door locked and Mona asleep on a reclining chair outside. Years later, my mother told me that she had locked Mona out of the house because she was so drunk. At Davenport Road, I often woke up early in the mornings and went upstairs to Mona's apartment. She could always be depended upon to be awake, even when my parents were still asleep. Once in a while, I would be distressed to find the door to her apartment locked. My mother told me later that when Mona came home from a bar, she would sometimes have a man with her. Of course this would be considered perfectly normal today; my grandmother was in her mid fifties, and had been widowed for several years. But my mother was scandalized, or perhaps just threatened. She may have made herself out to be worldly, in her letters to Mona from Spain, but being the wife of an artist in 1960s Toronto was more than she had bargained for.

Iris Nowell recalls Toronto's art scene in those days with relish. One party is described in loving detail in her 2010 book, *Painters Eleven*. Its host, Tom Hodgson, was one of the army veterans who attended OCA. (He graduated two years before my father entered the college.) "Festivities began when the women, one by one, peeled off their blouses, and Tom made sketches of their breasts." Then, Hodgson painted with watercolour on the breasts themselves, then a model named Linda, "one of Tom's especially endowed studio models," had slides projected on her breasts, and "[a]fter the show Tom and Linda headed into the adjoining small studio, and in a few minutes Tom appeared, announcing that lunch was served. On a coffee table lay Linda, her naked body covered with slices of ham, salami and cheese. Fanned around her head were stalks of celery, whose frond ends provided curly tips to her long blond hair, and piled between her splayed legs was a mound of oranges and grapes. Maraschino cherries bejeweled her breasts. One wag could not resist commenting, 'What a spread!'"[26]

Was my father at that party? Probably not. Marjorie Harris, who worked for Dorothy Cameron (my father's art dealer in the early 1960s) told me he did not socialize with many of his colleagues.[27] He was, however, certainly part of Cameron's stable of artists. His work was included in the Eros exhibition at the Here & Now Gallery in 1965, in which drawings by Robert Markle and Graham Coughtry were deemed obscene and seized by the police.[28] This was a time of sexual experimentation, of pushing boundaries. Whatever my father's degree of involvement, it was not a hospitable environment for a new marriage to thrive. Mona, for her part, was eager to meddle in my parents' ups and downs, and widen the cracks in an already unstable relationship. In 1964, we left 121 Davenport, and moved into the first of a series of short-term apartments in the Annex. My mother was pregnant with my sister Ellen. This provided the excuse that we would now need more room. The real reason was that it had become impossible for us to live under the same roof any more.

Liberty Hall

Mona was trying to come between my parents, and to turn me against my mother.

How do I know that? The simple answer is, my parents told me: both of them, together, some time after we moved into our own apartment. I was young – maybe six years old – and I suspect I asked why we did not live with Nanna any more.

After that, my memories arranged themselves around what my parents had said. Their explanation introduced me to a new way of looking at my grandmother. I was not to take what she said at face value. What my parents said about her was both a condemnation and an excuse: this is the way your grandmother is. We know it. We tolerate it. Now, you're in on it, too. They were doing me a favour, giving me a way to make sense of what I might already be feeling.

What did my grandmother say? I can't remember. I only have memories of her unhappiness. And her certainty that my mother was to blame.

Dueling narrators, I eventually came to call it. My family expressed its conflicts by telling conflicting stories of the past. Though it helped to hear my parents' view of things – it *did* make sense of feelings I was already having – I also came away with the impression that the adults in my life had different versions of reality, and that they were vying for my loyalty. My way of showing loyalty was to believe a person's stories.

At least for the time being – and at least when it came to Mona – my parents were still on the same side.

⫣

Mona had another version of her story, a daytime version, which did not include being rejected from her son's home. It went like this. Mona placed an announcement in *Gossip* magazine: "Poet and Gentleman Siamese Cat seek apartment with ship's deck overlooking garden. Elm tree a must." In another version, she announced that she wanted to live *in* an elm tree, preferably a three-pronged elm, though she would accept an apartment. Doctors Oriana and Harold Kalant answered the ad. They had just the place, the first floor of number thirty-nine Farnham Avenue.

Farnham is located a little north of the wide, curving streets of Rosedale. Lined with solid, brick houses, it runs between the thoroughfares of Avenue Road and Yonge Street, at the top of a hill which once formed the shoreline of Lake Ontario. Impeccably maintained apartment buildings lined these two main streets. It was in the most pleasant and respectable of neighbourhoods, and had its own local library, banks, and shops. Yet it was still in walking distance of Yorkville, Holt Renfrew, as well as an elegant little cluster of boutiques called the Lothian Mews. Mona got her deck, her elm tree with the requisite number of prongs, and as a bonus, two doctors living upstairs. (The Kalants were research scientists, but as far as Mona was concerned, it was the next best thing to having a staff of medical doctors in the building.)

The Kalants became the first of many friends on the street. They often stopped by for a glass of wine on Mona's porch on their way upstairs. Mona soon found neighbours who shared not only her literary interests but her love of whiskey. Her apartment was the scene of many impromptu parties. Ogden Hershaw, or "the Colonel" as she called him, would appear at her door on weekend afternoons dressed in his kilt, his uniform for serious drinking. At exactly 12:01 a.m. on January first, he would fling himself over her threshold, brandishing a lump of coal. "*Lang may yer lum reap!*" he cried, and accepted her offer of a "wee dram."

Another friendship came through me. One afternoon on Mona's high back porch, I witnessed the first communion party of Elizabeth Barry, who lived next door with her large family. All the children were decked out in formal wear and Elizabeth herself was dressed in what I concluded was a wedding gown. They arranged themselves in orderly rows in the back steps to have their photographs taken. I was spellbound, and felt honoured, a week or so later, when the miniature bride seemed willing to become my friend. I wanted Elizabeth with me every time I visited Mona. She made me feel less tired, less stuck in one place. For a change I wanted to go outside and play. My grandmother seemed more energetic too. Around Elizabeth, she became the kind of grandmother anyone would envy. With her cries of "Liberty Hall!" she encouraged us to run up and down the steps from the garden, bang the door as often as we wanted, never worrying about breaking things or making too much noise. Cookies, snip-doodle, and Mona's ice cream and ginger ale "floats" were available on demand.

Many years later, Elizabeth and I discussed those days. Just as I had been fascinated by the aura of tradition and stability that surrounded her family, she was drawn to the exoticism of Mona's home: the unfamiliar food, the stacks of books and magazines, not to mention the aura of frank sexuality that was evident as soon as you walked in the door and saw the enormous nude hanging over Mona's couch. Fortunately, Elizabeth's parents never got past the front porch, or they might have forbidden her to visit. It is even more fortunate that they never used the bathroom in Mona's apartment. Over the tub, she had taped a poster for a popular Yorkville hangout, the Unicorn Shop, featuring a woman clad in a floor-length gown with what seemed to be an orgy going on around her feet: five or six youthful, naked bodies all entwined in various combinations. Elizabeth told me: "I ... remember Kahlua bottles. She'd put candles in them. We never had candles at home ... Those great candlesticks with all that wax on that black table. It was an out-of-control kind of thing ... There was an element of being wild. We had candles on our birthdays and my father God love him probably had the fire extinguisher nearby ... To watch a candle melt down and play with the wax! All these things that I never saw. Naked bodies and a cat on the dining room table, and your grandmother would talk to the cat and it seemed to understand."[1]

Elizabeth was one of many children that Mona took under her wing. She called Elizabeth "Lillibet," reminding her at every opportunity that this had been the nickname of the queen when she was a child. She praised her "titian" hair and "creamy" skin, her easy manner with people. "In a family of a lot of kids she made me feel like an individual. And I was always so impressed that she was impressed, that she latched on to me and I latched on to her. She was very different from the Nanna that I had ... Your grandmother did not seem like an old lady at all. She used to talk about being old, feeling old, but she didn't seem old to me. She was so full of life! Her big brooches and her hair ... I was attracted to how different she was from the women in my life."[2] For Elizabeth, Mona was a role model, a woman with a fulfilling career, a career, furthermore in writing and public relations, which was to become Elizabeth's chosen field. She kept in touch with Mona all her life.

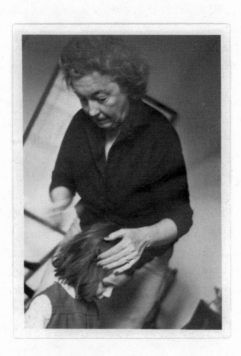

I spent many nights at Mona's apartment. In summer we sat up until late at night on the porch, eating potato chips and leaving a bowl of them out for the racoons. We watched their peculiar table manners across the expanse of floor, silently, while they watched ours. We slept outside, too, on a small cot. In winter we slept in Mona's bed next to the open window. Mona spent much of the night talking. She also kept the radio on. The station would occasionally be obscured by static in the middle of the night and Mona would declare that the radio was hungry. She would get a soda cracker from the kitchen to "feed" to the radio, and this always seemed to make the station come back clearly again. In the mornings she held up her opal ring to catch the early rays of the sun. One of the stones was tinged with pink at the edges. She said it was absorbing the colour of the sunrise to use later in the day.

Morning had a heavy quality when I had spent the night at Mona's. My eyes kept closing; I was not sure if I was asleep or awake. On weekdays, Mona styled my hair in a fantastical arrangement using pipe cleaners and stockings, and sent me off to school in a taxi, my lunch in a Crown Royal bag. I carried my head high, my neck stiff, to support Mona's hairdos. They seemed to have a life of their own which I had to carry upright and not disturb. Mona taught me how to fill out forms in the liquor store with special pencils which were attached to the counter with a chain. On each visit, she got me a few of these forms to take home and practise with. She also taught me how to eat in a restaurant. On Saturdays, she took me to lunch at the Lichee Garden, which I loved because of its richly upholstered walls and throne-like chairs. Mine seemed especially regal since it was built up with red, silky cushions. She ordered whiskey and milk for herself, and a Shirley Temple for me. Closing my eyes to bite the maraschino cherry off the swizzle stick, I imbibed the essence of my rich future. I knew that I was going to be a writer. A poet. "You will have," Mona told me, "a beautiful life."

At the age of about eight, I woke early one morning to see a robin on the windowsill outside my bedroom, the reddish light from the sunrise illuminating its feathers. A sensation in the middle of my forehead seemed to draw me up into a sitting position. The sensation spread through my whole body. I felt as if I were levitating from the bed, all of me greeting all of this moment. The moment, *my* moment had arrived. I had a poem. Later that day, I wrote a poem called "Sunrise." The poem was given to me; I knew exactly what to say. As soon as I could, I presented what I had written to Mona. She declared that I had surpassed her.

꒰ꂫ

Mona's house was one of the few constants in my life in those days. We moved often. Our homes were the dark, ground floors of Victorian houses in the Annex. I would barely learn my route to school when it would be time to pack and leave again. We had a housekeeper, Mrs Connolly, who stayed with us all day, and sometimes at night when my mother worked late. I loved Mrs Connolly – it was impossible not to – but I thought of her as belonging to my sister Ellen, just as Nanna did to me.

My parents always seemed to be either fighting or kissing, and I wasn't sure which bothered me more. They seemed so tightly focused on one another that there was little room for Ellen and me. There was a frantic edge to their laughter and high-jinks, as if they were trying to stave off the next wave of ill will that would inevitably come. When things felt bad in the house, my father approached and stood beside me, "Feel like a walk?" he would say, and I would wordlessly stop what I was doing and go with him, usually along Bloor Street to Christie Pits, where we would admire the dome of a Ukrainian church that was visible from the park. This is what I did: made my father feel better. There was never any question of saying no. My father had a power like the sun to warm and brighten my existence when he was with me, or leave it cold and dangerous when he was not.

And like the sun, my father came and went. Sometimes he went on long trips: to Mexico, Peru, Japan, and once to Pikangikum, an Indian reservation which he could only reach by airplane. Even when he was in the city, my father would stay out very late some nights, or simply not come home. My father had his absences and returns, my mother, her cycles of illness, anger, and tears. For a while she was in hospital, and then spent several weeks in their bedroom. Doctors came and went. Eventually, she got up and started to go to work again. I remember watching her get ready to go out, one evening. She straightened her red velvet dress on her shoulders and told me, "I'm not the same any more. I'll never be the same." My mother's unhappiness seemed part of her being ill, part of the same continuum. She was surrounded by an aura of something bad, and I didn't want to be near her.

But I loved being with my father. He had a studio in an old house on Markham Street, and I would sometimes spend the day there with him, breathing in the smells of turpentine and oil paint which permeated the building, watching quietly while he made drawing after drawing, his tongue creeping down over his lower lip as he worked. Some drawings he laid carefully on a cot that he had in the room; others, he crumpled and threw to the floor. He gave me paper and charcoal to draw with, if I wanted. I was also allowed to read, just as long as I was quiet. If I got restless, I crept over to the window to look at the totem pole which stood in one of the yards opposite, and at the customers going into Gaston's restaurant, or Honest Ed's department store on the corner. I had to stand beside the window though; never directly in front of it. If I forgot, my father's words, "Get out of my light!" would seem to shake the walls, and he would stare even more fiercely at his drawing until I moved my shadow out of his way.

I didn't mind. As I watched my father's crayon pass over the paper, I learned to see the creation of a drawing as a kind of story and loved to watch each one as it grew. I started to cry when my father seemed about to crumple up a drawing I liked. Once, I managed to get his attention and intervene. He looked at me intently. "You like this?"

"Yes!"

"Why?"

I scrambled for a reason. "I like her skirt."

"Okay. Maybe you're right." The drawing went on the bed.

Most of all, I knew the workday would eventually finish. The hours of sitting still and quiet were made worthwhile by the times when I had my father's attention. He listened to every detail of my long, fantastic stories, and every question merited a considered explanation, often supported with hand-drawn illustrations. He made me a series of books based on nursery rhymes, but using my own face and name. My father's sketches of me in childhood show what he dubbed "the look of ultimate concern." I was melancholic, anxious, and clung silently to my worries and grudges for weeks on end. My father understood that there was no teasing or cajoling me out of this. I needed a reflection, not an antidote, for my feelings. There were many nights when children's stories terrified me. Even the most benign fantasy presented a world too chaotic for me to tolerate at bedtime. Fairy tales were a sure-fire trigger for nightmares. My father would read me – with patient explanation of all the words – the melancholy Jacques' soliloquy: "The Seven Ages of Man," from *As You Like It*. "Sans teeth, sans eyes, sans taste, sans everything," I echoed, finally able to drop off to sleep.

At one point I got an eyelash in my eye and concluded that it would work its way into my brain and kill me. I am not sure how long I cultivated this terrible scenario in my mind. It felt like days. I remember lying on my bed, composing the words I would use to announce my condition to my parents. When I finally told them, I had worked myself into such a state that my knees gave way under me. My father quelled my mother's (probably relieved) laughter with a wave of his hand, and pronounced that I would need an operation. He washed his hands, and insisted my mother, sister, and I do the same. I solemnly brought sheets and a pillow and arranged myself on the couch where my father removed the eyelash with the corner of a handkerchief that had been moistened with my own spit.

We rented a cottage every summer in a place called Duck Bay, about a hundred miles north of Toronto. I remember getting out of the smoky bus, gulping my first breath of cool air. Before I was school age, my father and I spent our weeks alone there while my mother went to her job at CBC. She took the bus up north on Friday nights, when she wasn't working weekends.

I remember the nervous twitch that developed in her eyes after a just few hours at the cottage. She hated what she called "the country," her English accent returning to enunciate the contemptuous words. The country, she said, reminded her of being evacuated from London during the war. She hated bugs, barbecues, and boats, hated to appear in a bathing suit, could barely swim anyway. She missed movies and plays and parties, and her cappuccinos at the Coffee Mill restaurant. She missed her taxis. She missed her friends.

My father worked at his easel every day, and to start and finish the routine we took a long walk together. Forbidden ever to complain of boredom or fatigue, I learned to keep pace with him, and to keep going through any kind of weather. "You've got to learn to be a good walker," my father insisted. This included sessions of clambering barefoot over stones on the beach, "toughening up our feet." One day we took an especially long walk to a town called Waubaushene. Here we found a house with a "For Sale" sign outside. I remember venturing into the dark, ill-smelling interior, barely able to see in the gloom. I had an impression of green, peeling linoleum, furniture heaped against the walls. I felt my father's excitement grow. This was it! Our house. My father's enthusiasm spread and covered both of us like a blanket. We had found something. A house that we could own. My parents bought the house, though I doubt my mother was enthusiastic about the idea. As for my father, as soon as I mentioned Waubaushene to Marjorie Harris she said, "That house was his real love."

꿏

Along with many Toronto artists in the sixties, my father was becoming a local celebrity. His name appeared in the newspapers with increasing frequency. First, as part of a longer list of participants in group exhibitions, then with reviews of his solo exhibits, and features accompanied with photos and reproductions. In 1966, he hosted the CBC-TV program, *Home Movies*, as well as a series of "Wednesday Nights at the Workshop," in which he held public conversations with artists and filmmakers. These took place at the Artists' Workshop, which by then had moved to Markham Street from its first location on Bloor. Unlike many of his contemporaries, my father did figurative work, fine draftsmanship influenced by the classical masters. This went against the prevailing trend. Marjorie Harris told me that during her years at the Here & Now Gallery, John's openings drew a more conservative, older crowd, though the work sold well. "The other artists represented by

Dorothy would probably have thought of John's work as sentimental or derivative.[3] But this certainly didn't discourage Dorothy from doing a bang-up job representing him. He was a bit of loner, not one of the large spawn of artists who hung out at the Pilot Tavern close by. John always struck me as being a haunted soul. I have no idea why. We didn't talk particularly deeply about anything except work which, in this case, was his art."[4]

I asked her if she thought that being outside the mainstream had been difficult for him.

"Definitely," she replied.

Whatever John's own feelings, Toronto critics supported his decision to stay the figurative course. In a review of a group exhibition at the Art Gallery of Toronto in 1961, Pearl McCarthy praised the abstract pieces in the show but commented, "only men with very strong clear ideals hold out through the unpopularity of realist or figurative art." She wrote, "John Gould's drawings command respect."[5] Through the late sixties and early seventies, Kay Kritzwiser carried on the tradition of consistently favourable reviews.

When she first met my father, Marjorie had been surprised to hear how well-known Mona had once been. A relative newcomer to Toronto, she had never heard of Mona. By the early sixties, Mona's media presence had all but disappeared, whereas John's star was on the rise. "Of Hetty and John: they lived what I thought then of as the ultimate artist's life: husband is the artist, wife works to supplement their income. Their place was full of wonderful things they'd brought back from Spain where they could live on practically nothing."[6] Marjorie remembered that John talked about Mona a lot. She was "a formidable presence. Certainly in John's life and of course Hetty's." She was a "difficult" mother and mother-in-law. He was trying to separate himself from her.

It chilled me to hear that these conflicts were obvious even to John's work colleagues, and that they were remembered so vividly, almost fifty years after the fact.

The Heart Alone

Mona's career might have been less visible by the sixties, but she was still working hard. In 1962, she had taken a contract as a public relations consultant with Mothercraft, a day-care centre which at the time housed a training school for "well-baby" nurses. She stayed there through most of the decade. Mona made a great production of hating Mothercraft. *Moth-er-craft*: she told the whole story of her feelings in the way she enunciated the word. The first two syllables would be dragged out like a teenager's rebellious "Mo-*ther*!" The "craft" would be tucked in archly at the end, implying that all things motherly (and by extension, female), were crafty and conniving, and that the name of the organization was an apt – though unconscious – reflection of this. Mothercraft was the necessary drudgery that paid her bills. Mona always said she was doing them a favour, working there.

Given her disdain for the job, I was surprised at how many files Mona had kept of Mothercraft archives. There were newsletters, annual reports, press releases, and an advertising brochure, along with the many feature stories on Mothercraft that she wrote and placed in various publications. Mona kept her scripts of speeches to Mothercraft's board of directors, along with a great deal of correspondence. I did not recognize the Mona I remember from the sixties, in this material. My grandmother had seemed static to me, mired in her stories of the past, whereas the Mona I encountered in the Mothercraft files was active, articulate, positive, and confident. Nor did I recognize the stodgy, narrow-minded institution that Mona invoked in her descriptions. I learned that Mothercraft was nothing short of a radical organization.

From its foundation in the 1930s until early in the 1960s, women made use of the Mothercraft hospital after they gave birth. This facility enabled a woman to recover from childbirth and establish a breastfeeding routine. Not all the women who used these services were particularly well off: among them were the wives of labourers and students, who sometimes paid reduced fees.[1] At the hospital facility, the new mother could learn necessary skills in caring for a baby, and a woman with older children could rebuild her strength before taking up the responsibilities of housekeeping again. Before Medicare was introduced in the 1960s, "advice rooms" were universally available. These clinics provided basic well-baby checkups and information to mothers.[2]

I discovered that Mona had been involved in a movement to create a training program for midwives at Mothercraft, the idea being that Mothercraft could eventually offer a continuum of care through pregnancy, birth, and post-partum, up to when a child would go to school. In 1962, Mona made a trip to New York to research midwifery practices and reported to Mothercraft's board of directors on her findings. In New York, Mona came around to the view that though pain was inevitable when giving birth, it was nonetheless possible for a woman to be awake and relaxed throughout the process. "Birth should be ecstatic, not traumatic," she wrote, and returned to Toronto believing that midwifery should be adopted in Canada. Mona's report was impassioned, and probably went far beyond what was asked of her. This was a period when childbirth was medicalized, and both midwifery and breastfeeding were met with hostility. This may have been why – despite her best efforts – the midwifery training program at Mothercraft never came to fruition. She talked often of how much I had missed her when she went to New York, but never about the reason for her trip. This is surprising since it was arguably more exciting than anything that had happened to her in England or Spain.

"Feeling of being of use the key," Mona wrote, after her return from England. At last, she had found a context where the whole range of skills she possessed could be of use. When Mona worked there, Mothercraft's annual reports often contained original poetry, and one advertising brochure featured a verse by her on the front.[3] She acted as a mentor and counselor to the students. As part of their orientation, they attended a presentation by Mona encouraging them to do their best and reminding them that they were now representatives of an august institution.[4] They were also invited to approach her individually.

This kind of work suited my grandmother. All her life, young people had gravitated to her, and now she found herself in a setting where she could be paid for helping them develop. In one of her boxes, I found the draft of a letter Mona wrote to a girl who had withdrawn from Mothercraft training because of some personal difficulty. She shared some of her own sad experiences and reassured her that it was possible to survive disappointments and losses in life. Finally she gave the girl a biography of the author Joyce Cary, noting that Cary had faced many obstacles in his life and expressing her hope that "this book might sometimes be an inspiration to you – to go forward ... at any ... cost!"[5]

Having a well-known writer on staff was in keeping with the visionary policies of Mothercraft. To think that Mona would be uniquely suited to counseling the young was a radical idea, and providing a poet with a paying job, not only writing but communicating in person, was more astounding still. Vera Mackintosh Bell, one of the organizations' founders, considered Mona a treasure. Mothercraft was lucky to have Mona's talents, and Vera, lucky to have Mona's friendship. Sometimes she would write that an anecdote Mona had written in a letter was wasted on her humble self, and would send the letter back, urging Mona to use it for publication. Vera began her letters with endearments such as: "My dear girl," "My dear, clever girl," or "Ever-faithful one." She would then apologize for her own tardiness in replying with a phrase like, "You have probably given up on me," or "You will think me a complete flop."[6]

In addition to being a great admirer of Mona's work, Vera had an extra attraction. She was none other than the sister of Katherine Mansfield. Often, Vera would draw parallels between Mona and "K.M." in her letters, and once wrote that Mona had phrased something in a "KM-ian" way.[7] Nothing would have been more gratifying to Mona than to hear this. When Mona visited Vera in Ottawa, Vera gave her a book cover embroidered by the young Katherine Mansfield, as well as a copy of a letter which Mansfield had written to Vera's son, Andrew. Later, Mona donated the book cover to the New Zealand's Alexander Turnbull Library, where it was displayed in an exhibition of the author's memorabilia.[8]

After Vera died, Mona continued to correspond with Jeanne Renshaw, Mansfield's last surviving sister. I found notes from her scattered throughout Mona's papers, and in the end they filled a thick file. Jeanne and Vera both used the same sort of small, refined notepaper of the thickest quality. Jeanne used a fountain pen, and her flamboyant handwriting was difficult to interpret. It was clear, though, that she thought about "K.M." frequently. She also had spiritualist leanings. "There is no death," she wrote more than once, "only transition." She believed that Katherine Mansfield had been a deeply spiritual person, and that she was as present in death as she had been in life.[9]

Such beliefs had been popular in Toronto's artistic community since the earlier decades of the century and Mona would have come into frequent contact with them, even if she did not participate. Both E.J. Pratt and Ellen Elliot, Mona's editor at Macmillan, had at various times conducted séances in their homes.[10] Graham and Mona had come to believe in reincarnation on the basis of Graham's war experiences. He had been stationed in an area of England where his distant ancestors had lived. He arrived in a particular town after dark, but found the next morning that he knew exactly where everything was, as if he had lived there all his life. Mona often told me that as an "old soul," I had lived many times before. She listened attentively if I told her I had dreamed about being in an unfamiliar place. "You must have seen it in a former life," she would say, with a knowing nod.

As far as I know, though, Mona never did more than talk about her beliefs. She never tried to "contact" Graham, her parents, Jim, or her brother after their deaths. Instead, she focused on the way our experiences with people during their lifetimes keep them with us even after they are gone. "I'm right on the top of your head," she used to say, when I got older and saw her less often. She meant that she was with me all the time, even when not physically present. Implied was that she always would be with me, even after she died. Mona may not have believed that the ghost of "K.M." visited her directly, but the correspondence with Vera and Jeanne enfolded Mona in Katherine Mansfield's mystique. In her solitude, she must have felt that the spirit of the writer she idolized was, on some level, keeping her company.

&

I remember Mona expressing nothing but contempt for Mothercraft, yet it is clear she flung herself into her job with enthusiasm, energy, and love. The disconnect does surprise me. Mothercraft was a women's organization, and Mona felt obliged to deride all things female, at least in public. I imagine that Mona was not unlike the children being dropped off at Mothercraft every morning for nursery school. She protested loudly as long as someone was watching, but once left alone, she eagerly embraced the creativity and learning that the place offered.

Mona may have expressed contempt for Mothercraft specifically *because* her work there brought her close to the issues that had shaped her, Mona never complained about the conditions under which she gave birth to John: the cold steel table, the loneliness and isolation, the patronizing nurse, the doctor who showed up at the last moment, the sudden, overpowering introduction of drugs. The journal entry written when John was in his fifties was my first inkling that his birth had been less than a fairy tale. The story Mona told most often was that that her father, Alfred, arrived after John's birth and asked, "Were you a good girl?" "Yes!" Mona had declared proudly, meaning that she had not made much noise.

In the early 1960s life was next to impossible for unwed mothers, but Mothercraft offered them at least a slim chance of keeping their children. Mona herself had become pregnant out of wedlock. What would life have been like for her, had it been an option to raise her child on her own? What if marriage and conventional family life had been a choice for Mona, rather than something that society had forced on her? Of course, these speculations never entered her conversation. Nor did she ever admit to speculating on whether her second child's death might have been prevented. It is a human trait to rehearse over and over what could have been done differently, after a loss. Mona must have wondered whether, with better pre- and post-natal care, the baby that was "just too tiny" might have grown into adulthood.

꒰ꔸ

The genteel halls of Mothercraft would never be enough to contain the full range of Mona's talents, not to mention meet her expenses. She proceeded to find herself some private clients. One was the Walrus and Carpenter restaurant on Cumberland Street, on behalf of which she wrote ads in verse form for *Gossip* magazine and a similar publication called *Town Talk about Toronto*. Mona's status as the Walrus and the Carpenter's official scribe meant that there was at least one place in town where she could grandly sweep in and treat friends to a meal. For a verse a month, Mona could still be, in a small way, a celebrity.

She also wrote promotional material for Hiram Walker and Sons. In 1964 she wrote a feature on Lorne Duguid, Hiram Walker's president, for *Gossip*.[11] Soon after this she proposed to write a series of ads for Hiram Walker in verse form, and was enthusiastically accepted. This scheme provided her with a bit of extra money, and – more questionably – with cases and cases of free booze. As a family, we dreaded the week a new case would arrive. The whiskey would be opened first and quickly polished off. Then Mona would gradually work her way through the wines and sherries to the liqueurs. A sweet brandy called Cherry Heering was her least favourite, and she invented a dessert consisting of vanilla ice cream and canned cherries, topped by a splash of this liqueur, in order to use it up on visiting children. (It tasted like cough syrup, but helped dull the boredom of listening to adult conversation after dinner.) At some point she sidestepped her contact at Hiram Walker and corresponded directly with Peter Heering Jr. She tried to convince him that she loved Cherry Heering. In reality, she was angling for a free trip to Denmark. The company sent her even more Cherry Heering, but never sent her on the trip.[12]

The format of the *Gossip* ads was brilliant. Mona would write a new poem in each issue, always under the heading of "The Genteelwomanly Use of Spirits." This scheme got around what Duguid called Ontario's "outdated liquor laws."[13] (Liquor ads were beginning to appear in magazines by this time, but no one could be shown drinking. Instead, the ads would depict the drink's label, and sometimes a handsomely groomed male hand, holding a glass.) Mona's columns were the ultimate in "lifestyle advertising." Sometimes the columns celebrated the seasons, Mona's tireless standby when it came to subjects for verse. They praised the beauties of Canada, suggesting that everything was best enjoyed with a drink in hand. At other times, she would present a character sketch of an attractive, enviable woman, mentioning the vital part that Hiram Walker products played in her life. Here is one of them:

She's an actress.
A contemporary one
Yet, somehow
Elizabethan.
She has a great gusto
For life and living,
Her children adore her!
...
She is committed to her art
And yet to her family too.
...
She is easygoing about

Almost everything.
But a real tyrant
When it comes to
Cocktails.
...
Long ago, she made a choice:
"Crystal Gin," she said, is it!
And no one disputes
This great lady of talent.

She infinitely understands
The genteelwomanly use
Of spirits![14]

This "tyrant" hardly fit the mold of the idealized housewife of the 1960s, but – like all Mona's "Genteelwomen" – she was celebrated for her quirks and eccentricities. Bringing darker elements into advertising is a risky approach, but Mona carried it off. She never apologized for her poetic sensibility, her ability to see all aspects of life. It was part of what she sold when she sold herself as a writer.

In 1965, Mona joined the editorial board of *Town Talk about Toronto*. Smaller in size than *Gossip*, *Town Talk* was primarily an advertising publication which included the newsletter of the Association for Better Basic Education. Many of the ads and stories had an educational focus, and there was a yearly guide to summer camps. There were also ads for local restaurants, theatres, shops, and services (including Mothercraft). If an advertiser paid for the use of colour, it would be carried through the entire magazine. This meant that the print itself would sometimes appear in blue, red, or, on one unfortunate occasion, bright green with yellow accents.[15]

During the mid sixties, Mona's involvement with *Gossip* expanded. Filling in for Zena Cherry's "Much Ado" column, she would periodically contribute a compendium of short snippets under the heading "Out of a Reticule." She regularly contributed book reviews as well. Later, Mona wrote a series of interview-based articles for *Gossip*. As portraits of local luminaries they fit well within *Gossip*'s mandate, but they continued in Mona's tradition of subversiveness by broaching contentious topics. Many were about women in non-traditional roles. Among the fashion tips and ads for dress shops was Mona's interview with Dr Bette Stephenson, the first female chair of the

Ontario Medical Association, which appeared under the headline: "Position and Power in a Man's World." Stephenson is quoted as saying, "I guess I might be called a pushy kind of bitch. Certainly more aggressive than passive. I am definitely not going to take anything lying down, and I don't have any hesitation in saying what I think. But I'm also a sensitive person when it comes to principles." One of these principles was a woman's right to reproductive choice. Stephenson told Mona that "a bunch of male legislators in Ottawa" should not have the right to decide the fate of "a pregnancy that hurts both the woman, her future child and the children she already has."[16]

There was an article on Helen Sawyer, an astronomer at the newly built McLaughlin Planetarium.[17] Dr Henrietta Banting was also the subject of features on two separate occasions. Banting was involved in a drive to provide free pap smears to all Canadian women, a program which was gradually being adopted by all the provinces. Mona wrote of the dangers of cervical cancer and the importance of regular tests. At one point, Banting was asked whether smoking led to cancer, and she answered that the link was not proven.[18]

⚓

Meanwhile, Mona's Dieppe poem had become a textbook staple. It brought fees of fifty to seventy-five dollars every time it was reprinted. Mona also contributed other poetry and prose to various Nelson schoolbooks. Mona's childhood friend Margaret Stevens (now Tanton) had returned to Toronto after many years in Calgary, and was on the editorial board of these publications. She was also involved with a monthly ecumenical publication called *Rapport* published by the Ryerson Press. Mona's bi-line began to appear in *Rapport* as well. Its content reflected the increasingly liberal attitudes of churches in the 1960s. There were articles on jazz and poetry, references to the musical, *Hair,* as well as to eastern religions and native cultures. Margaret wrote an article meditating on loneliness. It included a remark that homosexuality "has its own loneliness" but that new, more liberal laws might help to alleviate this "by improving the public attitude."[19]

A column called "We Are Here" appeared first under Margaret Tanton's bi-line, then Mona's. Mona's contributions were lively, but decidedly sloppy from a journalistic point of view. She did a number of interviews on such topics as end-of-life care and the conditions faced by refugees. Her interviews were not attributed, and anyone who knew her could tell that she was simply interviewing the same people over and over again … if, indeed, she actually got around to talking to the people at all. She sometimes "interviewed" herself. One column recycled a story which she had told on *Carousel* years before about giving directions to an immigrant woman looking for the address where she was to start a job. This time Mona presented the story as if it had been told to her by a taxi driver, in the context of a formal interview.[20]

A significant coup was a commission to write a brochure for the centenary of Eaton's department store in 1969. Mona wrote it from the point of view of someone who had witnessed many of the changes Eaton's had been through, making good use of her ability to create simple, memorable turns of phrase.

To try and capsulate the Eaton story
Down thru 100 years
All the way from
Bustles to Bikinis
Is rather like trying to turn
An oak
Back into an acorn.
…
In a time of change and turbulence
Men on the moon
Next – maybe –
People shake their heads and say:
"What can a man … BELIEVE …?"

And then the Santa Claus Parade
Comes around again –

The brochure was well received, and she tried to parlay its success into further work, both with Eaton's and with MacLaren Advertising. She received rejections in both cases.[21] Mining a similar vein, she got a commission to create a brochure for the World Day of Prayer for the Women's Inter Church Council of Canada. This, too, was warmly praised, but did not lead to any more commissions.[22]

In 1968, Mona was approached by George Marshall of Columbia Pictures about her poem, "God Bless All Clowns," which had been published years before in *New Liberty* magazine.[23] According to Mona's notes, it was the producer Carl Reiner who first discovered it, and wanted to use it in a film called *Billy Bright*.[24] This was just the type of stunning surprise that Mona loved. All the difficulties in her life as a freelancer were made worthwhile by these occasional, thrilling opportunities. Even in lean times, though, she was not afraid to push her luck. Columbia Pictures initially offered her fifty dollars for the use of the poem, "subject to the proviso that you are, in fact, the authoress."[25] Sometime in the next two weeks, Mona not only provided proof of authorship, but increased the fee to two hundred and fifty dollars. The next correspondence came from Mona's lawyer, and a contract was drawn up, but Mona continued to want adjustments to it.[26] She had her lawyer add a clause to the effect that if the poem were made into a song, she would receive royalties.[27] In February, she was still holding out on signing the agreement. Marshall wrote a testy letter noting that given how much trouble his company had undertaken to find Mona, it should be clear they were not planning to make unauthorized use of her work.[28] The contract was signed the next day, and Mona followed it soon afterwards with a letter saying she was "keen to find a market for more of my verse in your business."[29] The film eventually came out under the title of *The Comic*. Mona kept a copy of the two hundred and fifty dollar cheque, reproduced at ten times its original size.[30]

Mona enjoyed a constant flow of work throughout the 1960s; still, she was living hand to mouth. It would be easy to blame this on extravagance. She drank heavily and ate out, bought her lipstick from Holt Renfrew, and liked to send bouquets of flowers for every occasion. These expenditures were just frills, though. In more important ways, her lifestyle was modest. She lived in a one-bedroom apartment whose rent was never raised. She had no car or cottage, bought no new clothes, and attended few plays or concerts. If she traveled, it was for work. The freelancer's life was really responsible for her financial troubles. She was without a regular salary or sick leave, and for every stretch of solid work there were numerous unpaid breaks. She was not good at budgeting at the best of times, but the irregularity of her income made it especially difficult to stay in control.

Margaret Tanton and Vera Bell knew that Mona was counting every penny, and wanted her to share in some of the comforts that they themselves enjoyed. Vera would often add a few gracious words to the end of her letters, indicating that she was enclosing a cheque. An anxious little economy seems to have existed between the two women. Vera would send Mona money, and would find a bouquet of pink carnations on her doorstep a few days later. She may have been trying – tactfully – to reimburse Mona for the flowers when she sent the next cheque. Vera also sent Mona clothes. She would give elaborate reasons why she herself could not wear them, and urged Mona either to have them made over for herself or to sell them. Since Vera was tiny and Mona quite stout, by this time, the latter option was probably what she had in mind. When Mrs Bell died, she left Mona her Persian lamb coat in her will. Mona did not sell the coat but saved it for my sister Ellen to grow into.

Margaret wrote that she would like to share her prosperity with Mona. She enclosed cheques in her letters and encouraged Mona to buy "a treat" for herself. The cheques – more often than not – probably went towards Mona's basic expenses, and no doubt Marg was aware of this. Now that they were both widows, Mona's friendship with Margaret Stevens Tanton took on redoubled importance for both of them. Their correspondence was full of tenderness. It was clear, and somehow agreed-upon, that Mona would be the Mary in this relationship, Marg, the Martha, and they played their roles without question. Mona was special. Marg felt honoured to have her as a friend. She considered herself less talented than Mona, her prose less musical. At one point, she sent Mona a few jottings from a novel or short story that she had been writing called "This Thing Forlorn," about a friendship between two women named Margo and Judy. The two are childhood friends, who then marry and live far apart. At one point, Margo writes to Judy: "I am sure that if I lived by you or even near I should very easily be satisfied with basking in the reflected glory of having a clever friend, and should never try to do anything myself."[31]

Marg was by no means less of a writer than Mona. Her contributions to *Rapport* magazine reflect her years of experience as a journalist, as well as a lot of hard work and attention to detail. The craft is evident, and the prose is more musical than she knew. She did not possess Mona's bravado, though. Mona was special because she *believed* she was special. Marg admired this quality above all else. Like Vera, she treated Mona's letters as personally crafted works of art, dedicated to her.

Mona was aware that her friend felt this way. One letter made its way back into Mona's archives after being sent to Marg. I believe it was written on the occasion of the death of Marg's husband. It is a declaration of Mona's love for her friend.

Communication is so important to me. I wilt like a poor plant ... lacking it – I feel YOU do TOO – so let us keep close to one another in this

strange world – where so many are dying of the coldness of no communication at all!

You must stand very steady – now – as Mook used to counsel me!
VERY steady! But <u>know</u> that I am AWARE of the ground whereon you
stand – have experienced it – have, trembled – have, somehow-stumbled
thru' it-scarred-shaken-out-survived – Therefore – when you need me
– just call or write to me, but for gawd's sake Martie – be sure to com-
municate!

...Oh Martie-Martie – how <u>far</u> <u>away</u> is London and Port Stanley –
and skating in Victoria Park and Central Collegiate – <u>Was</u> it <u>you</u> – was
it <u>me</u> – was it ... US??????

When I see you – like yesterday ... I KNOW it was ALL ... <u>so</u>![32]

The letter may have been returned to Mona by Marg's relatives after her
death, or Mona may have asked for it back. (This is something she did frequently. On the death of Vera Bell, Mona sent a letter to a friend in England
as well as to Dodi Robb, eulogizing Vera and then asking for her letters to
be returned.[33] The idea was that she might use them some day.)

By this time, Mona was having it known that she was writing her autobiography. Her freelance contracts had dwindled to the point where she had
little to fill her time. Still, she always said that she was busy working on her
book. She eventually sold the idea, in 1977, to a company called Consolidated Amethyst, the publishers of *Rocks and Minerals in Canada*. With the
working title of *The Sage of Saturday Night*, the book was to take the form
of a collection of essays on prominent Canadians Mona had known over
the years.[34] B.K. Sandwell was the sage in question. Vera Bell was also to
be included, and so was Fred Varley. Mona's essay in *Gossip* magazine
entitled "Vintage Varley" told the story of a falling-out she had had with the
eminent artist in the 1950s, and the charming way that the two had reconciled.[35] The memoir on Varley was the most complete of her portraits. The
rest of the book never materialized except in the form of fragments less than
a page long.

Creatively, Mona felt frustrated and trapped. She was a performer, and
there remained a part of her that would only be satisfied by performing. In
a journal entry from the early 1960s, she wrote of how grateful she was for
the job at Mothercraft; still, "Sometimes I long for a show of my own again.
It had its 'moments' but it was rugged, too! I used to dream of being free of
broadcasting + now? I sometimes dream of having a show again. Perverse,

we humans be – Very perverse!"[36] Despite her longing to get started again, she did not directly pursue any radio or television opportunities. Nonetheless, she did not drop completely out of sight. She appeared on Elwood Glover's *Luncheon Date* program, as well as on *Flashback* in 1963.[37] My mother, still employed at CBC television, may well have played a part in the invitations. Betty Kennedy did a story about Mona on her radio program *Living with Flair* in 1964.[38] These bursts of activity made her feel alive again, but they also whetted her appetite for more. And there was nothing more after the mid-sixties. In September, 1969, CBC *Matinee* used an interview she had done with Fred Varley. Since the date coincided with Varley's death, it was probably a rebroadcast from Mona's days on *Be My Guest*.[39]

❧

In the meantime, Mona was writing massive amounts of poetry. This volume increased steadily until she died. I have never been willing to spend the time it would take to winnow out duplicates and place all the drafts in order, or try to determine which poems were published where. Mona only kept an accurate record of her publications in the mid thirties Otherwise she just kept clippings of her published work, and her habit of cropping these clippings very close to the poems meant she left behind a lot of flimsy, two-inch square slips of paper, some of them falling apart. Often, the typeface on these clippings gives an indication of the publication and the approximate date, but here too, there are many duplicates. Her correspondence is somewhat helpful, but there are many, many poems not accounted for in acceptance or rejection letters. Of course acceptance did not guarantee that a piece actually appeared when – or indeed if – an editor said it would. It is increasingly possible to track down publications through digital archives but not all editions of the newspaper have been digitized. Even if they had been, it would take years to follows all the trails.

Still, given the excellent listing produced by June Barnett, I can make a rough estimate of Mona Gould's literary output. She wrote in the region of five hundred poems between her debut in 1920 and the death of Graham in 1959, including broadcasts, columns, and "poems of the week." From the clippings she kept, it seems Mona published eighty percent of what she wrote or presented on the radio. About eighty percent of that could be referred to as light verse. From 1960 to 1974, I estimate that she wrote another five hundred poems, about ten percent of which was published. This included her Hiram Walker ads, as well as publications in *Gossip* and other commercial magazines. Over the next fifteen years, she added another thousand-odd poems to the tally. (This number includes everything from typed poetry to handwritten drafts, and parts of her journal whenever they lapsed into verse.) One of these poems was used as part of an art installation, though it was never published. Finally, in her old age, she wrote about a thousand more poems. All of these were read to an audience, but never published. In other words, the more Mona wrote, the less she published, or vice versa.

She did collect seventy-eight poems sometime in the early seventies, listing them as if getting a manuscript ready to send to publishers. From the attractive presentation (not to mention the accuracy of the typing), it seems likely someone else prepared it for her. There is no record of correspondence with any publisher about this manuscript, though.[40] It consisted of lyrical poems in a serious vein – not the rhyming poems about cats and seasons that were still finding a home in *Gossip* magazine from time to time. Though she was now giving more attention to her serious work, Mona did not seek new markets for it. In a journal from 1964 she mentioned, in veiled fashion, an attempt to have some essays published by McClelland and Stewart. This ended in disappointment.[41] Maybe it was in response to this rejection that she decided to stop trying to sell her writing. In a journal entry from about 1964, she wrote:

Heart's content
I know now what to do! There has been this constant deep nagging [?] me ever since G died! That's why when I come home from the office at night I drink whiskey. It numbs the niggling like a thistle in the heart.

Because there is never any place to put it (my writing, that is). I have almost quit trying. My mind would give off ideas but I would try to put them to sleep. Shrug them off. "what is the use?" … But now I have come to terms with my self! It does not matter that no one will buy. What matters is – that I have been a practising writer since I was ten. Highly geared and aware. Full of new ideas and dreams.

So now I accept the frustration part and I ignore it. Now I begin to sing sweet songs to please my self.[42]

After reconciling herself to a life of obscurity, she concluded: "The descent into burning remembrance and loneliness is hell!"[43]

Mona longed for attention, but displayed a kind of inertia when it came to sending her later poetry out for publication. It seemed that she had lost her nerve. It is also possible that – painful as it was for her to lose her readership – a part of her welcomed the end of her literary career. At this point she had been publishing most of what she wrote for over forty years. This had been satisfying, of course, yet it had also meant relentless exposure, and despite the image of openness she liked to project, Mona was a deeply private person. She had always drawn at least part of her income from poetry; thus, the past forty years had demanded relentless production, as well. Even though Mona did not get what she wanted in the 1960s, I suspect that on some level, she got what she needed: permission to confront serious themes, and push herself past the mediocrity that had been reinforced early in her career.

These were the years when she told me the story of "This Was My Brother" – and the way it gave rise to her first book – again and again. Somehow, it did not strike Mona as a contradiction that, between these stories of past triumph, she also spent a lot of time enumerating her losses. The constant was that she was always in an extreme position: on top of the world or at the bottom. She was never ordinary, never just "okay." She portrayed herself as emotionally and physically fragile, permanently damaged by grief. As time went on, she began to treat everyday tasks like shopping, cleaning, even going out of her house, as heroic undertakings. She rarely attended funerals or made hospital visits (though she would write poems and send flowers for many occasions). She would say that she wanted to go, but "dared not." This could be difficult to put up with; Mona was essentially strong, and others around her had suffered every bit as much as she had. In retrospect, though, I understand why she clung so tenaciously to her status as mourner. Mona had always felt she should face grief stoically. Over the years she had lost both parents, her brother, Jim, two babies, and finally, Graham. Now she was aware she had passed the halfway point in her life. She wrote – in the third person – about the feeling of having so much grief come to the surface after being long repressed, "She had been, not only killing, but 'murdering' – time – getting her days and nights 'over and done with' – toward nothing. Her heart cold, her hands, empty. On the surface – she coped – and adequately – but her soul pricked her like a goad – tormenting – demanding – insisting – til she, enfin, 'surfaced.'"[44]

Grieving became the subject of much of her writing. While some pieces are dripping with self-pity, others are full of insight. Mona's magazine work was often sloppy during the sixties and seventies, but in her poetry and personal writings, she knew moments of greater clarity and skill than ever before. She did not send these works out for publication, however. In one essay, she combined poetry with her personal reflections, as well as quoting from other authors. The introduction to this piece suggests that Mona considered it to be the beginning of a longer work, and she may have felt that she had to expand it before she could seek a publisher. But it is complete in and of itself, and would have been much more suitable for *Rapport* than some of the hastily-tossed-off articles she contributed.

"Contrary to the general assumption," she wrote, "the first days of grief are not the worst. The immediate reaction is usually shock and numbing disbelief. One has undergone an amputation. After shock comes acute early grief which is a kind of 'condensed presence' almost a form of possession. One still feels the lost limb to the nerve endings. It is as if the intensity of the grief, fused, the distance between you and the dead. Or perhaps, in reality, part of one, dies." The challenge, for someone in mourning, is to continue to grow in the face of the loss, rather than being sealed off by "scar tissue." The new self which grows after the loss is like a child in the womb. But to grow after a loss calls for an unflinching willingness to experience pain. Mona goes on to list the various distractions that the mourner creates to avoid this pain. Self-pity does not help, nor does remorse. "Remorse is another dead end, a kind of fake action ... Like the food one is offered in dreams, it will not nourish." Ultimately, it is necessarily to "discard shields and remain open and vulnerable ... To grow, to be reborn, one must remain vulnerable – open to love but also, hideously open to the possibilities of more suffering."

The story ends with the loss of Mona's second child, and a poem called "Second Sowing."

For whom
The milk ungiven in the breast
When the child is gone?

For whom
The love locked up in the heart
That is left alone?
That golden yield
Split sod once overflowed on August field,
Threshed out in pain upon September's floor,
Now hoarded high in barns, a sterile store.

Break down the bolted door;
Rip open, spread and pour
The grain upon the barren ground
Wherever crack is found.

There is no harvest for the heart alone.
The seed of love must be
Eternally
Resown.[45]

❧

Though she never found another partner after Graham, Mona remained
a passionate woman. Her journals from early widowhood show that she
developed several attractions to men who either did not know she existed, or
gave her mixed signals at best. She was well suited to a life of romantic agony.
Her attachment to her father and rivalry with her mother predisposed her to
enter relationships which could never be consummated. For this reason, her
early marriage to Graham probably prevented her from making a lot of mis-
takes. Still, it did not protect her completely, and perhaps she did not want
it to. Unfulfilled longing had provided her with inspiration back in the days
of *Full Circle*, and she drew on it again now, as a source of creative energy.

Mona may have set her sights on unattainable men, but many others still
found her attractive. She kept letters from men who courted her in the 1960s,
along with journal entries hinting at several romances. (She never mentioned
them to me other than to say she had had "offers.") One man fell in love with
her during a single dinner party in 1962 and continued to write to her for the
next twelve years. He was not free, and lived some distance away, but openly
declared his love for her and offered her friendship and the opportunity to
confide in him any time. His overtures were based not on how she might
fulfill his needs, but how he might fulfill hers. There was a constancy and
tenderness in all his letters that must have lifted her spirits, even though the
relationship remained platonic.

Despite her age and swelling girth, young men were still magnetically
drawn to Mona, as well. Though they did not become sexual partners, they
were more than happy to flirt, squire her around town and do errands for

her. My grandmother's relations with her family were laced with complex layers of manipulation, but to those outside the intimate circle, she presented herself as a winner, free of the dark complexities that tend to scare men away. She expressed a healthy sexual appetite, and said in so many words that she got exactly what she wanted out of life. This had always been attractive to men, and continued to be so as she aged.

Displaced

For all her pain during the early years of widowhood, Mona had a lot of good things going for her, and she would have muddled through the 1960s quite well had it not been for the self-destructive tendency that grew stronger with each passing year. As the decade wore on, Mona gained a tremendous amount of weight. Her face became puffy and florid and her eyes hooded, with a cloudy look to them. Her relationship with Mothercraft was going badly. She painted the situation as a noble fight for her identity in an environment where every attempt was being made to co-opt it. Her integrity as an artist was pitted against the forces of narrow-minded respectability. She described her life there as "hurling myself against a wall of pablum."[1] It is hard to say what really happened, but I suspect she was just not functioning well anymore, because of her drinking.

In 1968, her last year at Mothercraft, Mona began to have severe nosebleeds. Doctors tried cauterizing a blood vessel in her nose, but without success. Her blood pressure was dangerously high, yet she never modified her diet of sweets, whiskey, and strong black coffee. The nosebleeds were a terrifying experience for Mona, especially since she lived alone. Eventually, she had to be hospitalized for blood transfusions. After a number of transfusions, she felt stronger; the cauterization eventually worked, and she simply went on as before. Over time, her life became more and more chaotic. It was the opposite of a race with death. She had constructive work and was surrounded by people who loved her, yet she seemed determined to outrun these positive forces and reach the finish line before anything, or anyone, could catch up with her.

Mona left Mothercraft on unhappy terms, soon after the nosebleeds. There is no record as to what happened, but the result was that she no longer had any regular income aside from writing the odd piece of advertising. Vera Bell came forward with money to cover her rent, and this helped for a while. Mona approached her brother Doug for a loan and from that point on, he enclosed a cheque in almost every letter, without being asked.[2] He often apologized for their not being larger. John Aylesworth, now a successful producer in Hollywood, also began sending her money every month.

In 1970, Mona was hired as the editor of *Gossip*. The magazine was in the process of moving to an office on Cumberland Street at the time, but she preferred to work from home and at very strange hours. She was continually receiving deliveries for the magazine in taxis at odd times of the day or night. I recall sitting up for what seemed forever one night at about the age of ten, barely able to keep my eyes open while I "helped" Mona read the galleys of *Gossip*. Mona sat with a drink at her elbow and a welter of paper strips in front of her, cursing the incompetence of "those stupid dames" who had done the typesetting.

The association with *Gossip* began hopefully. The press release from May 1970 described Mona as "a Canadian of unique literary ability," and anticipated the "polish and creativity" she would bring to the magazine.[3] The first issue under Mona's direction was promising. Mr Chi Chi Bu took his place on the masthead, and Mona's distinct touch was everywhere evident. By her second issue, though, the magazine had become slight, inconsistent, and messy in its design. A scant three months later, her tenure at *Gossip* ended, rancorously. Mona kept a copy of her letter of resignation, addressed to *Gossip's* then publisher, Gerald Campbell. The prose was lovingly wrought, and she delivered insults gleefully, in a kind of orgy of bridge-burning. "I remind you of your jaunty statement at our last 'business' meeting. I quote 'If you're SMART, like I am – you GIVE the ulcers, you don't GET em.' This is my written permission to give my set to some other misbegotten Editor!"[4] Mona wrote that the office was dirty and that she was not paid on time. She was receiving the salary of a hundred dollars a week. This was not princely, but it was enough to support her. If she could not depend on her payments, though, she would also have been forced to look for outside work. At the age of sixty-three, she probably did not want to juggle several jobs any more.

After her break with *Gossip*, Mona kept tabs on the magazine by inheriting Margaret's copy after she had read it. One issue, with Margaret's subscriber label on the outside is full of Mona's critical markings. "Fill!" she scribbled in the margins, "Hand-out!" "No identification of sponsor!" Soon afterwards, she was hired as the editor of "Up-to-Date," an advertising/editorial section of *Canadian Collector* magazine. Vera Bell's son, Andrew, had written for this magazine, and the connection undoubtedly helped her. This job, too, was short-lived. Mona hardly included any contributions from other writers. She wrote virtually one entire issue on her own. Articles were signed with various versions of her own name or initials: M.G., M. McT., and so on.

Between jobs, she tutored a number of students from nearby Brown Public School, as well as from Havergal College, a local private school for girls. Her business was not brisk, but she enjoyed the work and made a lasting impression on several young people who studied with her. As part of an after-school program, a group of children spent two hours a week at her apartment, studying creative writing.[5] One of these children was Maija Beeton, whose father, Bill, traveled and worked with my father. Maija recalled these sessions. "We'd read things and write things and we'd look things up in the dictionary. Going to the dictionary was a big event ... She'd make up ... crazy ways to remember words. Oyster: 'Oy I've got to stir the pot!' ... She would take words apart and play with them. It was hilarious. She thought they were so self-evident. The kids were all looking at each other thinking: *This isn't the first image that comes to our mind.*"[6]

Maija was another of Mona's chosen children. She had spent time with my grandmother since she was born, and our two families visited often. As soon as she was able, she began to take every opportunity to see Mona, independently of her parents. For Elizabeth Barry, growing up among rigid routines, my grandmother's home offered a fascinating dose of anarchy. For Maija, it was just as appealing, but for opposite reasons. Her own household was Bohemian, and she went to Mona's to escape its chaos.

To go to Mona's house there was a calmness where things could be discussed. There were no babies screaming. She would ask questions and seem very interested. It would make me interested in my life. There were things that seemed mundane but she would recontextualize everything. Then suddenly it would seem more exciting or there would be adventure in it. She always had space for me, even if other people would be over. I had a wonderful feeling of being a sparrow or a robin or a bird, something that's delightful and that is of nature and that has dropped by. I would get this wonderful feeling of being wanted, seeing someone smile when they'd see me.[7]

Tutoring did not bring in anywhere near enough money to support Mona, and for a while during the late sixties, she had to collect welfare. This represented a severe blow to her dignity. When one cheque was lost, she had to appear in the office to sign for a new one. She recorded this event in an odd little essay which she never published. She began her account in a chatty way, as if writing for the social pages of a newspaper, but then waxed grotesquely eloquent as she picked up momentum. As usual, the female characters got the brunt of her ire in the story.

It was like some perverted congregation gathering to worship at the horse blinder doors – behind which Welfare workers were guzzling coffee and stuffing their faces with food. How they could swallow in such smelly filth was a subject of some sort of amazement. Up and down Cubicle Alley the fattest ugliest women Welfare workers sashayed. They seemed to get some sort of sadistic pleasure out of twitching their gigantic flabby buttocks in purple patterned pant suits stomachs, ahoy! And breasts that bore no resemblance to breasts but were like massive blown up bladders or cow udders, hanging and banging. They wore hideous strapped and fancy shoes. Their hair was greasy and some ran combs through it as they munched and masticated. It was such a revolting sight, even Horrenemous Bosch would have hesitated before committing it to canvas![8]

⚜

At around this time, we moved to Waubaushene. Life was tough there, especially in the winter. The cottage was uninsulated, and far from any doctor, supermarket, bank, or laundromat. We had no car, and my father was away for stretches of time. There was a good two-room school in the area, but the bus trip to get there involved something my classmates called "the bumps." No sooner did he reach the dirt road just outside of town than the driver would speed up, creating his own midway ride as he tore over hills and around corners. I arrived at school each day headachy and exhausted.

Tirelessly gregarious, my mother made one or two friends in town, but there were not many playmates for my sister and me. Waubaushene was a hundred miles away from Mona, though, and this distance was something both my parents craved. Mona was less and less inclined to go outside her neighbourhood, and traveling by bus would have been out of the question. This did not prevent her from visiting us, though. She arrived one day in a taxi, along with her cat, a snip doodle, a bottle of wine, and my friend Elizabeth Barry, who had been given permission to stay with us for a week, as long as she attended both confession and mass.

My father was the third generation of men in his family to move their wives away from big-city life. Both Alfred and Graham had eventually returned to the urban environment their wives loved, but not John. We moved back to Toronto for a while and my mother started working again, but this only lasted a little over a year. In the summer of 1971, my parents separated. My father moved to Waubaushene and my mother took my sister and me away for what I thought would be just the summer. The situation was at first confusing. My father told me he and my mother were having a "cooling-out period," but by the time we got back, Ingi had moved into the house with her eight-year-old daughter, Melissa. He told me that nothing had changed, because he still loved me. He said, "Love is not a pie. Just because there are more people sharing it, doesn't mean anyone gets less." I could not stop myself from feeling I had much, much less, though my father said I was hurting him terribly by not being happy for him. The suddenness, the speed of his change in families, made me doubt everything I had ever known.

Mona responded with shock and horror to the separation. She kept letters from her friends saying that young couples took their marriage vows too lightly, that children were the real victims of divorce. Mona herself wrote a great deal about this. My own hurt was the subject of many of her poems. Mona's sympathy was welcome, but her intense focus on me left me feeling drained rather than cared for. There was something wrong, some false note in what she was saying, but Mona seemed to fill the air so insistently with her words that I could never define what it was. Later it became clear to me. She spoke as if my parents' separation had been an act of God, *Force Majeur*, with no element of human responsibility involved. She might acknowledge that I was in pain, but would never criticize her son, or admit that he had had a hand in causing it. Once, she asked me, "Do you feel displaced?" She may have used the word, "Re-placed." It was on her porch, a fall day. I remember shaking my head so that my long hair fell in front of my face. "Yes," I said, from behind the curtain of hair. This was as close as we ever came to addressing what was really going on.

But I knew exactly what was going on. From my point of view, the world was now clearly divided into the hurt and the hurting, the losers and the leavers. You could not be on both sides. Mona and I were not together any more, and never could be. Like my mother, I was in the losing camp, and we were fine as long as we stuck with our own kind. My mother and I had never been compatible, but now we had to depend on each other. Over the course of that summer, we became lifelong friends.

Mona wanted it both ways. She wanted to be part of her son's new family, and still have the old relationship with me. This is when she began giving me jewelry. The Mexican pin came to me when I was thirteen, and a year or two later, her opal ring. The more she struggled to remain the centre of my universe, though, the more Mona succeeded in pushing me away. I tried to avoid visiting her, or even talking to her on the phone, but through some bargain that must have been made among the adults I began spending Sunday afternoons and evenings with her: an interminable four or five hours. These visits were as awkward as my visits with my father, except that Mona was one who seemed to feel abandoned, and I found myself in the role of the guilt-ridden, estranged parent. I may have spoken up about how much I dreaded these sessions because she eventually began coming over for Sunday dinner to the apartment my mother, sister, and I shared, a few blocks from where she lived.

I remember her asking me once if there were any boys I liked at school and whether my "monthlies" had started yet. I responded with a shrug. The idea of becoming a woman felt suffocating to me, and I tried to ignore any signs that it might be happening. I was frightened of the world of uncontrolled desire that I was sure awaited me as soon as I crossed the line into womanhood. My clothing felt like inadequate protection. I was haunted by stories my father had told me of his training in Paris, when destitute young women would arrive in the entranceway of the Academie Julian. "*Desrobez!*" the concierge would demand, and they would – in all weathers – drop their clothes to the floor. Did I hear stories of the studio parties when I was a child; of the time a meal was served from the body of a model? Possibly. They had the status of urban legends, even when I was growing up. Iris Nowell's accounts did not strike me as unfamiliar. One thing is sure, those stories were never – then or now – told from the models' point of view.

I did not look forward to life as a dinner plate, or as a wife who spent her days waiting for, then enduring, rejection. And rejection was inevitable. I knew I would never be able to keep a husband. Marriage seemed rigorous to me – something like living in Waubaushene – and you had to stay on the lookout all the time in case someone tried to take your place. I did not have that kind of strength.

Nor did I want to be like Mona. She considered herself exempt from the rules that govern most people, exempt from reality itself. She made things up and treated them as if they were true. Even the colour of my eyes was a detail she felt at liberty to change. She wrote stories and poems about me and had pictures of me all over her walls, yet I felt invisible because I was not really seen. All of this hurt me, but from what I could tell, it hurt Mona worse. All my life I had heard stories of how special she was, how much she impressed people. Yet all I saw was a lonely alcoholic who seemed to have nothing more important to do than meddle in her family's lives. She was also poor.

These problems, I felt, had something to do with her being a woman. Mona had told me about other literary women like Virginia Woolf, Elizabeth Smart, Sylvia Plath, and Edna St. Vincent Millay. They were drawn irresistibly into madness, hopeless love, addiction, and early death. She talked about this as if it were inevitable, as if it came with the territory. Mona herself might have lived to be an old lady but seemed to be stuck like a needle on a broken record, unable to move forward, telling the same old stories again and again.

Meantime, I had made friends with a girl from school whose mother was a feminist. Their living room was always full of women in army clothes, drinking beer and talking, talking, talking. When her dad came home – which was seldom – they didn't even look up from their conversation. Various books appeared in my friend's room: books like *Free to Be … You and Me* and *Our Bodies/Ourselves*, and one that said you were supposed to look in your crotch with a mirror! This was scary, not to mention disgusting; still, I liked feminism. The idea that there was something wrong with the way women were treated made me feel like I could breathe again. It meant that the craziness and drinking and suicide might be part of a larger problem. And that you could fight back; you *did* have a choice. When I announced my new allegiance to Mona, though, she replied in a tone at once wounded and cautionary: "You're not becoming a lib lady, are you,

Darling?" I didn't reply because I knew it wasn't really a question. I just covered my face with my hair.

A kind of compulsive questioning of Mona's stories now went on in my mind, as if to preserve some territory from the control she seemed to exert. Her storytelling seemed an aggressive act: a colonization of the world through words. I had to find a way to stop her from colonizing *me*. Mona often asked me to share my poetry with her. "Bring over some of your stuff," she would say, in a casual tone. I was writing poems in a grey hardbound journal I had found in a stationery store. It was so beautiful I used a pencil in it, not wanting to mark up the pages too much. The poems were sometimes about missing my father, and then later they were about a boy in school who was friendly to me, but nothing more. The journal felt like home to me, and with three of us living in a one-bedroom apartment, it was my only way of being alone. Asking to see my journal was the worst thing Mona could have done. I ignored her requests. One day, heart thumping, face burning, I heard myself say, "No!" I had the sensation that something had been torn, some part of my flesh or hers, or both. I can't remember her reaction.

From her correspondence, I could see that Mona blamed my mother for my decision to withdraw from her. The irony was that Hetty was striving to keep her children's relationship with Mona alive. We always lived within walking distance of Mona, and Sunday dinners became an inviolable routine. At times, they were the most dependable social contact my grandmother had. Hetty genuinely loved her mother-in-law, and remained devoted to her all her life. During the troubled years of her marriage she wrote letters to Mona, even when they were in the same city. She took this initiative as a way of keeping the air clear between them. My mother would apologize for her outbursts of anger and officially forgive Mona for whatever she had done to provoke them. Because of her own willingness to forgive, her relationship with Mona endured, even after her marriage had broken down.

ॐ

Despite their sudden separation, my parents' marriage ended slowly and messily, with legalities that dragged on for several years. Mona was caught up in the drama, interfering at every opportunity. Yet she did not speak of a very pressing problem of her own. Maybe she was creating a diversion – for others as well as for herself. For several years, she had been experiencing digestive trouble, but spoke to no one about her symptoms. Then, in June of

1974 she was admitted to hospital for tests. Cancer of the bowel was diagnosed, and she had surgery a few days later. My father came to the lobby of our apartment building to tell my sister and me the news. Ellen was nine, and I was just turning fifteen. There were two couches facing each other, with mirrors over them. I remember feeling the blood drain away from my face. When I glanced in the mirror my shocked eyes stared back at me. Mona might die! This seemed inconceivable to me, yet at the same time, inevitable. I had already entered the long corridor of loss and this was just one more step along the way.

My mother said that when she visited Mona in hospital just after the operation, Mona apologized for all her past manipulations. "Probably the drugs," Hetty said, "acting like a truth serum," yet this was enough for her. From then on, the conflicts between them eased. Perhaps Mona realised that two daughters-in-law were better than one. Ingi, by this time, was placing her numerous talents at Mona's service. She cooked meals for Mona, sewed clothes that would accommodate her ballooning figure, kept an arms-length but protective eye on her finances. She enjoyed a short grace period before becoming the butt of a lot of unkind remarks, both behind her back and to her face. Certainly my father's second marriage represented a greater loss for Mona than the first. Complain as she might about my parents' union, its very instability had allowed her to stay bonded to her son in a none-too-healthy way. John's marriage to Ingi was for keeps, and they displayed a solidarity that my parents had never been able to maintain.

Mona came through the operation well and did not need further treatment. Visiting her in hospital I was dumbstruck, not knowing what to say in this world of sickness. Mona, at least for the time being, appeared to be silenced as well. I sat uneasily for a while by her bed. At last, dinner arrived and a slightly dwindled Mona popped out from under the covers in what she called her "split-ass nightie." A thimble-sized glass of sherry was served on the dinner trays of the women in her room. Mona darted over to the next bed. "You don't want that, Dear," she declared, downing her neighbour's drink before the lady had the chance to protest.

❧

Shaken by the thought of losing my grandmother, I vowed to do whatever I could to make her feel better. As soon as school let out for the summer, I spent as much time as possible in Mona's apartment. Sometimes I would do errands for her, but mostly I just kept her company, listening to her talk. On days when she actually felt unwell she would tell me not to come. I felt rejected at these times, blindsided by this hidden aspect of Mona's nature, her deep-down desire for solitude.

During that summer, Chi Chi became increasingly weak and lost his appetite. Mona phoned me one morning and told me that she had made an appointment for him to be "put to sleep."

"And I want you to take him."

"Okay, Nanna," I said. Saying no did not feel like an option. A few hours later, I took the shivering and weakened cat into the vet to be euthanized.

I told a friend the story over lunch when we returned to school in the fall. "No!" she declared, laying down her sandwich.

"Well ... it had to be done, he was ..."

"NO," she repeated, thumping the table, "it's not right! That's the type of thing parents do!" This had not occurred to me.

Among Mona's papers I found a poem she had written on the death of Chi Chi Bu.[9] The account of the last look they shared is poignant, but it leaves out the fact that I – and not Mona – had been the last to look into his eyes. Reading Mona's poem about her cat's death, I had a small glimpse of what it must have felt like to be Mona's forgotten sister-in-law, Dorothy Hammond.

When the fall came, Mona could not accept that I had to go back to school. She called me on the first day as I was getting ready to go out the door, listing a few things she needed me to pick up on the way to her house. I tried to explain to her that school had started and I could not come to see her that day. My voice dwindled as I talked to her. She was not taking in my words at all. I should be there, as far as Mona was concerned, and was not. The reasons why didn't matter.

In the years that followed I spent less and less time at her house. I had responsibilities at home. My mother was complaining of what she called "dampness." After her long days at work as a publicist at the Art Gallery of Ontario, she would lie straight down on the couch without eating anything. I prepared dinner, and on nights when I went to my after-school job, my ten-year-old sister would do it. Eventually, her strange collection of symptoms was diagnosed as lupus, but the cortisone drugs of the time carried side effects worse than the disease itself. Hetty decided to go off all medication and tough out the attack. Late at night, she paced the floor, terrified and in some nameless kind of pain. I would try to comfort her, not believing the reassurances that came out of me. I did not talk about it to my friends, or teachers, or to my father. It seemed especially important to keep the information from Mona. My mother did not know how to protect herself. I had to do it for her.

I now imposed on myself a strict regimen of five hours of homework per night. When my assignments were finished, I wrote out charts conjugating verbs in German, French, and Latin. One evening, I looked up from the books and papers strewn on my desk. *I am not a poet*, I thought, as I stared at the wall in front of me. Poetry had been with me for a while after my parents separated. It stayed around for just about as long as they were working out their divorce, but now that things were final, it was gone, like a fixed sum of money that had been used up. It had been over a year since a poem had come to me, and I hadn't even noticed. Now, I felt bereft. A poet was something that I *had* been – should still be – but was not anymore. Being a poet meant being special, and only as a special person did I have the right to feel good about myself. It had something to do with feeling at one: with the world which inspired me, with what I was trying to say, with how to say it, and with anyone who might read what I wrote. I no longer seemed to have access to this feeling. It was one more aspect of being a loser.

Maria and Chi Chi Bu, taken with a Polaroid camera, about 1974.

Mona's cancer operation marked the end of her working life. She was now old enough to receive a full government pension, and illness gave her a reason to quit looking for work. She began to volunteer at the nearby Belmont House nursing home, doing readings of poetry by herself and other writers. She eagerly read literature from the Canadian Cancer Society and received peer support from others who had had colostomies. She was outraged at the silence surrounding cancer, especially colon cancer, and insisted on discussing her condition in an open, matter-of-fact way. She named her colostomy "Charlie Brown" or "CB," for short. Her status as cancer survivor, just like her status as widow, was assumed with pride. It became part of her image as special, in need of extra consideration, and the warnings of her imminent death now began to multiply year by year.

Mona was assigned a general practitioner by the name of Naji Cohen, who followed up with her after her operation. He was a compassionate doctor who spent time getting to know Mona and encouraging her to share her deepest concerns. She dubbed him her "guru," and named Chi Chi's successor "Naji" in honour of the important place her doctor occupied in her life. Dr Cohen was a recent immigrant from Iraq. He was Jewish, yet he somehow put Mona in mind of the Lebanese Christian writer, Khalil Gibran. This, in turn, led her to thoughts of mysticism and meditation. The connections between all these influences were tenuous at best, but they worked for Mona. She began to keep Gibran's work on hand at all times, along with a number of popular Buddhist texts. Silent meditation was hardly Mona's style, but she was inspired by the *idea* of what Buddhism could offer. To calm her mind and live in the present moment became a goal for her.

When she was strong enough, Mona took a trip to the United States. She went on a long car trip with her brother Douglas and his son James. As the youngest member of the party, James was sent out nightly for cocktail supplies.[10] Later, she stayed at Doug's home in Oregon, and made the acquaintance of a new generation of McTavishes. Being an elder delighted Mona. To be an *ancien*, as she termed it, was a matter of enormous pride to her, and she was not above adding an extra year or two to her age when it suited her. She also visited John Aylesworth in California. There, she was treated to a stylish haircut and a new wardrobe (including four pairs of Ferragamo shoes, which she announced were the only kind narrow enough to fit her aristocratic feet). John noticed that she began drinking early in the day. "She called it her elevenses. Her elevenses became twelvses and oneses too. They progressed."[11]

Here in Canada, we already knew to call Mona mid-morning – after her first drink but before her maudlin phase set in. It was better to invite her over for dinner than to go to her house, because there was some chance of keeping an eye on the level in the bottle, not to mention making sure that the meal would be on the table before ten p.m. Everyone was resigned to Mona's drinking and never believed it would change.

Other things did. My mother's illness went into remission and she got a job managing the Forest City Gallery in London, Ontario. In a smaller city, she could own a home of her own. I went away to Bishop's university in Quebec. Riding the bus from Montreal to Sherbrooke, I looked up from the book I was reading to see the mountains of the Eastern Townships, the leaves all turning colour. Everything about the landscape – the curving roads, the steep mountains on either side, the very quality of light – was new to me. A recognition flickered tentatively through me. It was so unfamiliar that I pushed it aside at first, but it kept coming back. I was having a new experience. An experience of my own. I was seeing something new, going someplace new, a place where no one in my family had ever been and where no one knew me. I also saw where I was in the arc of my life: the beginning. I was, in fact, young.

This feeling lasted for a total of three days. One of the courses I had elected to take was acting. At the first meeting, the professor asked us to say our names, where we were from, and what plays we had seen that had moved us. One of the women in the class, Carolyn Rowell, had straight, sandy-coloured hair to her waist. Unlike the rest of us, she somehow managed to look good in her body stocking (the regulation outfit for the class). I had never met a woman who seemed so comfortable in her own skin. She frankly returned the not-so-subtle stares of the various men in the class – and men they were. Two actually had beards! She spoke of her travels in California back when she was married, and of the plays she had seen in San Francisco. After class, I raced off to the dressing room, making plans to go home. I would never, never be a match for these worldly people. And I could certainly never make friends here. Carolyn followed me down the hall, almost at a run.

"I want to ask you something," she said, when she finally caught up with me, "Are you related to Mona Gould, the poet?"

"She's my grandmother."

"And is she still alive? Did you know her?"

"Yes. She lives in Toronto. I've known her all my life."

"Like a book with half the pages still uncut," Carolyn quoted. "Such a simple image, yet it says everything, doesn't it? And your *grandmother!* It must have been amazing to grow up with someone like that."

"Amazing," I said, and imagined I heard Mona chime in, *I'm right on the top of your head.*

19

Who Sink and Rise, and Sink Again

I was finished. I had created the entire finding aid, listing Mona's letters, manuscripts, photos and books, typed it up in every detail. The listing could have been a lot better organized had I wanted to spend more time on it, but it served its purpose: files were grouped together in categories, and more or less in chronological order. By clicking the "find" button on a word processing program, you could search for the important documents and milestones in Mona's life. That – I hoped – was good enough.

Mona's stuff was in order. I was relieved, and very, very proud of myself for sticking with it. During my nearly six years' work on the archive, each day had been a barrage: the shuffled papers overlaying each other, each one with the power to evoke memories and emotions, to call for decisions. I was swept from one era to another, from one *Mona* to another with nauseating speed. In a half-hour period I might keep company with the menopausal widow, the spirited child, the housewife craving erotic adventure, and this in turn evoked my memories of Mona's stories about those periods in her life ... and the way they diverged from the facts. This was not unlike my experience of Mona herself. The living rooms where I sat listening to her would feel crowded with characters and scenes from the past, overlaying whatever was happening in the here and now. From one visit to the next, I never knew if I'd hear stories of triumph or loss. Then a neighbour might knock on the door, and a different Mona would suddenly appear to answer it.

Now, I'd sorted her out.

The day I was to hand the finding aid over to Jennifer Toews, I took one last look in the basement. And I saw there was something I'd forgotten, something big. Five boxes of spiral notebooks glared out at me from the corner of the room. Journals.

Can I really say I had *forgotten* the journals? No, I can't. I have to say that I had ignored them. Whenever I found one over the years, I tossed it into a separate box. Gradually, the boxes became part of the furniture. I had ceased to notice them anymore, cut myself off from thinking of them as part of my task. I lifted one notebook and flipped through it. Another. Mona's handwriting overlapped itself, dashes and swirls cutting into the lines above and below. The notebooks were in no order in the boxes, and the entries within the journals were helter-skelter. Some entries were dated, some not. Some books mixed the tight, pencil-written entries from the mid-sixties with the loosening scrawl of the 1980s. Chaos, again.

My first instinct was to throw them away, unread. Not everything had to be kept. Surely, as the archivist, I had the right to say that something was insignificant? Surely I had the right to declare that this was something no one would ever read? This work had taken me long enough, taken enough *from* me.

I didn't want to read these journals, sort them, or least of all, transcribe anything from them. They felt too private. They would take me back into Mona's inner world, all the anger and sadness and fear she had shared too much with me, too early in my life. *Was* it her inner world, though? Or was it just another performance? A performance designed to make me feel responsible for her, at the expense of myself.

I was forty-five years old, with more security and happiness than I had ever dreamed possible, yet the life I had created seemed, all of a sudden, to have no influence on my well-being. The past could instantly take over.

I asked Jennifer for her advice. "Well," she said, "There may be interesting stuff in there. It's up to you, but if I were you I'd have a look through them. You'd be surprised."

It took me some time, but in the end I decided that the journals were part of the task I'd taken on. I was still the same person, the one who'd said "yes" to sorting the papers in the first place. It was not with the same old, thankless feeling though. I had done enough sorting to know there could be unexpected rewards amidst the difficulty. And from what I'd learned so far, the only way out of certain situations is by going further in.

❧

I am now "Counting" — Time
finding my aloneness and solitary daily-ness — hurtful to the core — and so wounding — I willed time away — "hurry up", I would feel — "I'd let out it, maybe — tomorrow — a new day — I will not (be) by myself — or will be invited to go out with someone — or (be) somewhere at night such as tour" ... and so I fluttered hours away! "Shredded" them!
Now? I treasure time preciously — I "eke" it — out — in little "spurts" — meticulously — appreciating each hour — from before daylight till round 10. p.m. when I head to sleep!
I met a round little woman in the lobby. Her name? Dorothy. Her hair cut off to about an inch sticking straight up all over her skull "brow white"? this is clean as a Whistle e She tells me, "mix-up-ed-ly" that she will be 90, next week (3) parties for her! How will she ever grapple with such ladies celebration? It will be some occasion to remember someone speaking, first "she begins to blabble. The elevator comes! I jump in ascend!
If I live to be 90, will I be a "Dorothy" I wonder?

The last phase: a page from one of Mona's numerous journals.

Jon came up last night at suppertime – We talked a bit + then the B's came. We did have time to co-oberate our previous certainty – that I am a part of what Jon is "giving up" if you like – for his career! No strings must be attached." – He is "outwardbound" + sold on the certainty that he must not be bound by any ties.

...

I feel sorry for Hetty – very sorry! I could not have borne a love that "kept its cool" – Beyond me!

[later entry]
The abrasive quality – new in Jon – has come of his bitter battle of the sexes – with Het – He is always enfin – in deep combat – there – (natch) – so he has this newly built-in aggressiveness that makes it impossible to get <u>close</u> to him, even in conversation – he is alert to pounce – to be "on top" – He is learning a great deal – but is his heart?

...

I have a loving heart + this, I cannot change – ever. And I am glad of my loving + committed heart for it has brought me the infinite bliss. Great loves + of course enormous, heartache – but I have stood up to it + therefore it has all been most worthwhile.

...

[later entry]
May I please beg your vast indulgence-
My rent is due – over due -
But if you could

...

It began to pour down – a lush summer warm rain – so I went out into it + squitched happily upstreet in my old shoes from Spain – they're done, anyway. It was as good as being barefoot + I loved it!

[later entry]
Jon + I had our "date" – post-trip" we went to see "Warrendale" – the very controversial film on disturbed Adolescents. John Brown's equally farout treatment – Very absorbing film (terrifying, in spots) then we

went down to Jon's studio + saw all his Peruvian work – It's beautiful!
Exquisite – some. We went to a funny little Swiss hole-in-the-wall +
drank some beer and talked + talked + talked til 3. The lovely close –
old – always – contact of minds was there – I see now we can only have
this "celebration" about once a year! It is my Xmas! I was purely happy
– in bliss – all the time. I'm sure my eyes were never off his face.
...

[later entry]

Denied
She is the avenger
She is the <u>punisher</u>
This ugly woman
With the heavy
Flawed feet!
Let no one laugh.
Let there be no celebration –
Lest the walls shake
And the roof
Fly off!

Somewhere
She read
About Belsen!

Learn to pity
This
<u>Ugly</u> woman![1]

I recognized these incidents, these people. My father took a trip to Peru in
1967. The "ugly woman" was my mother. Her feet were twisted by childhood illness, and by being frozen during the war. She was terribly self-
conscious about them. She was ashamed, too, of being Jewish, of being the
bearer of so much ancestral pain. Mona reduced her to that pain, and robbed
her of it, in four words. Mona could do that. Mona *would* do that. In the
journals, I saw – in action – the mechanism by which she justified it. She told
herself she was under attack from baser people, people who were not of her

kind. Always, these people were women. Mona wrote about her cruelties to other women as achievements. There was a war on, and women were the enemy: "Resentment becomes part of it – because the whole psyche is 'on edge' – 'alert to hurt' fighting to survive – but so blindly – like a cornered animal. I must look out for this. It's easy – the Bullies – 'smell' this fear + if they are women – they pounce and hold you in their claws – + shout into your quivery face + torture you … For it is the lovers + the builders of life – who are able, somehow, to survive – to 'sculp' their lives into beautiful 'beings' that give out to others and light candles in all 'darks.'" [2]

There were two kinds of people in these journals: the noble, blessed, beautiful ones, and the ugly. The light ones, and the dark. My mother was not one of the beautiful ones, and could never be. Her "ugliness" sprang from anger and hurt, but Mona did not see the connection between anything she did and the way my mother felt. Every few pages she noted that my mother's back had seized up, that she had pain in her elbows or shoulders, or that she had developed a rash all over her palms. Mona lamented how inconvenient it was that my mother could not function, hinted that she was inept as a mother and wife, observed that the rash could not be from doing the dishes, since she had a housekeeper to clean for her.

I recognized Mona's voice. It was the one I heard so many nights staying at her house. This was the uninhibited flow of words, the words that shaped me, yet were missing from memory. And I felt ashamed, again. Ashamed to be related to someone capable of such cruelty. Ashamed that I had been privy to it. I raked myself with questions. Did I participate in mistreating my mother? Did I enjoy seeing her hurt? Was I, deep-down, like Mona? And, after all these years, was I still trying to make up for my connection with her – by spending all this time and energy trying to sort her out?

∝

Mona's bedroom. I am standing on her bed, facing my father and mother who stand in front of me. My eyes are level with my parents' eyes. I look past them to the window. It's night. The overhead light makes a brilliant, frayed white spot on the glass, and around it, black. Darkness outside.

"Your grandmother has drunk three quarters of a bottle of scotch," my mother whispers. "We don't want to leave the baby here with her. It's dangerous. There might be a fire."

"And you," my father says, "You can decide to stay or go."

I pause and pretend to consider it; then I take a deep, responsible breath. "I'll stay," I say. It's a rule, made wordlessly and long ago that the words my mother has just said must never be spoken to Mona. It would be like closing a door, and we can't do that. Someone – however small – must keep the door open. This is my job.

My father clasps my arm. "Are you sure?" He asks.

"Yes, sure."

I can't remember the faces of my parents. Whether they were grateful or worried or grim, only that they turned from me, quickly, then disappeared into the darkness of the hall.

It's night. I'm against the wall. Nanna is on the outside of the bed, her white face silhouetted against the dark window, her hands folded in front of her. She's speaking to me, but looking up at the ceiling. "Never use people ... Darling," she says. There is a space in which she wants me to speak. I'm to ask: "What do you mean, Nanna?" I say something, and though I don't know what it is, I remember her answer: "Your mother is using me to take care of you, so that she can ..." What did she say after that? It must have been something like, "go out to a movie with your Daddy." But there is darkness all around the memory. Around all the memories, impinging on their edges.

I remember the meaning of what she said. I remember the French and Spanish words she used, *enfin, nada*. The horrible silences that would come between her words, and how they'd stretch out forever, those silences. They meant, *the world is bad, and I am hurt, and nothing can be done about it.* In the silences between words, there was the sum total of Mona's desperation. A belief that this moment, this terrifying moment, would last forever.

Browning Island, Muskoka. Nanna and I are here for a whole week by ourselves. We are in a boathouse, a house made especially for boats. It is dark, here. The door disappears behind me as soon as I step into the darkness. The only way out is by boat. I feel the scratchy floor on my bare feet and see the mysterious shapes of objects hanging on the walls on either side. The floor stops a few steps ahead of me. The boathouse has only a narrow walkway around the edge, and an expanse of water where the centre of the floor should be. I know it is water by its lapping sound, but all I see is a dark patch. There is brilliant light outside. The opposite wall of the boathouse is made of white light. It blinds me when I look straight at it.

"Okay now, Darling," Nanna says, "I'm going to get into the boat, and then you'll come in after me." She steps off the edge of the wood floor and descends, step by step, towards the water. There's a paddle in her hand. Her blotch of white face shows in the dark.

"Oh, don't give me this," she says. "Come on, boys," and then there's a splash. My grandmother has disappeared. The water has swallowed her. For a while her "just a minute, Dear" holds me there. She said to wait, so I'll wait. But I know that my grandmother has gone into the water. The water has covered her, and there's no way out of the boathouse, for me.

In the story I tell myself, this is what happens: I begin to wheeze through my teeth, my belly heaving as air pushes itself panicked in and out and screams begin to come. But that's not what happened, that's what *should* have happened. In fact, I don't remember anything at all. There was a pause. A break. In my memory? No. In me.

I was there, and then not there, and then there again.

In the end of the story I tell myself, there's another big splash, and then some gentle splashing. And Nanna's back. She comes up the ladder again and wraps herself in a towel and crouches down to my level. She says, "Don't worry, Dear. I'm a really strong swimmer. I can swim across that lake and back and never be tired."

But I don't remember. I don't remember what happened at the end. There's a phrase by Millay that I heard for the first time from Dodi Robb. "Men that sink and rise and sink and rise and sink again." I hadn't heard the line back then in the boathouse, but I understood it. I understood that that there are people who sink and rise and sink again, and I understood that Mona was one of them. She may have come to the surface this time, but it was only going to be a short while before the water drew her back under. I was not one of those people – the ones who sink and rise – but it didn't matter, because wherever Mona went, I went too.

20

The Walnut-Shell Game

The journals from the sixties and seventies were difficult for me to read, but at least there weren't very many of them. I was comforted to learn that they formed only a small percentage of what the boxes contained. Most were taken up with the spiral notebooks which Mona filled during the last two decades of her life. She was, for all intents and purposes, now an unknown. Yet she kept writing. In the notebooks, Mona kept journals, short prose pieces, reams of poetry, generating more paper in those twenty-odd years than she did during the most active part of her career.

Some of the entries were the most vindictive of her life. Some were difficult to make out, some not legible at all. When Mona began to lose her sight, she also began using smaller notebooks. Sometimes, she would write in magic marker over top of earlier entries, done in pen. In time, the marker had faded and spread through layers of paper. These journals had a weird kind of beauty as objects in themselves, but could never be deciphered. Despite all this, and despite the intimidating volume of stuff, I came to see the importance of Mona's notebooks from this time.

Reading them filled a gap in Mona's story, and my own. Looking back was never easy, but I decided I would rather have more information than less. Besides, I was alright now. I had my happy ending. And this meant that my history no longer felt like a series of sore points, but a reminder of how good things had become. I was thankful to Mona for preserving it for me.

During the 1980s, I was less in contact with my grandmother than at any time before or since. This was a natural part of growing up. I was caught up in my own life and had little time for her. But I was also consciously avoiding Mona. It seemed to me that she had exploited my childhood attachment to her and demanded to be the centre of my attention before I had a choice. Moreover she was showing no signs of stopping. I was angry at my grandmother, had been for a long time, and did not want to hide it any more. I did not want to hide, to dissemble, period. Yet my relationship with Mona had always been made up of complex layers of pretending. I did not know how to disentangle myself, so I just avoided her altogether.

Now that Mona was gone, her manipulative bids for attention fading into the past, I was – quite simply – interested in her, and I began to feel that others might be too. Increasingly, I agreed with Jennifer Toews that there might be value in Mona's later journals, though they documented a life sadly devoid of stimulation. As a freelancer myself, I found them uncomfortable to read because they invoked the empty days, the silent telephone, the dwindling bank account that I would rather not think about. It was important to think about these things, though, and not just for me. Mona recorded what happens to an artist in old age: financially, creatively, emotionally. Her journals show what happens when a writer who has always had a context is left alone; what happens to a healthy person when there is no longer enough challenge in her life, when an expansive personality is confined to a narrow existence. Mona suffered in this situation, but she found a way to cope: she wrote about it. Her journals show, in intimate detail, what it feels like to get old.

ىك

After finishing university, I lived in Montreal for two years. This was the early 1980s. Apartments were plentiful, but there was no work to be found. Unable to think of anywhere else to go, I moved back to Toronto. The economic situation here was the just the opposite of the one in Montreal: I was immediately hired as the administrator for a dance organization, but felt stuck in the job because rents were so high. I seemed to be stuck in every aspect of my life, seeing no way to start the writing career I had thought would magically materialize as soon as I finished school. Then I fell in love, at first sight, and the feeling was mutual. My new boyfriend was a musician, with a fierce dedication to twentieth-century repertoire (which I knew nothing about). He was a vegetarian and resolutely condemned the use of alcohol and drugs. He read books I didn't understand, and introduced me to people so smart and sophisticated I was afraid to say a word. I was intimidated by him, but felt destiny was at work. I entered my new state with grim resignation, tinged with self-importance. In a single, defining moment I resigned the youthful freedoms I had come, tentatively, to enjoy. Everything now took second place to my love affair. I felt my loss of independence like an amputation, yet accepted my condition without a fight. In my journal I wrote, "My giving years have begun."

After a few weeks, the time came for me to introduce my boyfriend to my family. I was proud of him. To be able to find myself a boyfriend like this – and at least for the time being, keep him – seemed proof of something that had been in doubt since my teenage years: my own worth. I looked forward to showing him off to my parents, but my tippling grandmother was another matter. This was a rite of passage, though. It had to be done. I knew it would involve dragging him out of bed at what – for a musician – was an unthinkable hour, but I decided to arrange a visit as early in the day as possible and hope that Mona had not started drinking when we arrived. I phoned Mona to set up a time and got no answer. I tried again and again, over the course of several days. It was out of character for her not to be at home. Finally, one Saturday morning, I decided we must simply show up. There was no answer when we knocked at the front door, or the back. Finally, we jimmied open the window which gave on to her back porch. Walking around the empty apartment we saw the signs of a hasty departure. I phoned my father, heart pounding, and learned that Mona had been taken to hospital several days before, hemorrhaging again, this time from the site of her colostomy. She was resting, having transfusions. She was not in any immediate danger, but the situation was not good, either.

By this time, Mona was obese. Her blood pressure was out of control, and this had probably led to the hemorrhage. In consultation with my father, the doctor decided to use this scare as motivation for Mona to make a big change in her life. From now on, said the doctor, you stop drinking, or you'll die. Mona chose to stop drinking. She had been thinking about this change for a long time. As early as the 1960s, her journals show that she made resolutions to cut back, and sometimes even to "go on the wagon," but none of these lasted for long. She must have been living with a pernicious sense of failure for twenty years.

Now, she was ready. With all the determination she could muster, Mona stopped drinking in the summer of 1982. When Graham quit drinking, back in the 1950s, he joined Alcoholics Anonymous. This meant admitting that he was helpless against his addiction, "submitting his will to a higher power," and acknowledging that this power, in turn, was the only force that could restore his mental health. Mona and Graham had turned away from the stodgy religious customs of their youth, but they were still Christians at heart, and the AA notion of a higher power was one they could accept. Nonetheless, when the time came for Mona to quit drinking, she did not join Alcoholics Anonymous as her husband had. I suspect that she associated Graham's "submission of will" with his death soon afterwards. Mona had no intention of dying. Nor was she prepared to admit she was helpless. She did not seek counseling or any medical attention. She simply toughed it out.

I felt I should help Mona, show her I was proud of her, go *through* this with her in the way I had her recovery from cancer surgery, but I had done it once already and did not have it in me to do again – at least not for her. I forced myself to call her once in a while, but never as often as I knew I should. I remember one particular call. I felt horribly guilty, having left Mona to get through what must surely have been the worst of the withdrawal, alone.

"Hi, Nanna," I said brightly. "Just wondering how you are."

Because I could not mention – ever – that I knew what she was going through. The support had to be in the form of a casual call about something else.

"Fine, Dear," she answered, as if from very far away. I knew from her voice that she was decidedly not fine, but had no idea what to do about it. After that short conversation, we hung up.

Mona denied, outright, that she had ever had a drinking problem. "I never drank very much. It was just a social thing," she would say. Her reason for stopping was an order from the doctor, and the discussion went no further than that. She kept whiskey in the house, and would encourage others to pour themselves a glass before dinner. "Just because I had to stop," she said, "that's no reason people should not enjoy a drink in my house." Instead, she stuck to strong black coffee, drunk from a straw which would become increasingly stained with lipstick. I was grateful for Mona's hearty attitude, but I underestimated the toll that her denial was taking on me. In my dream just before her death, she had used the words, "I can't help it," finally admitting, as her husband had in his AA meetings, that she was powerless. This saddened me, but it also brought a sense of acceptance I had never felt around Mona during her lifetime. Even in our best moments, my resentment was always brewing under the surface. However, it was not *drinking* Mona admitted to in the dream, but an obsession with her son.

❧

Free of alcohol, Mona became more alert, healthier, and less disoriented. Not much else changed, though. She still told fantastical stories, still claimed to be too fragile to take on any ongoing commitments, and still surrounded herself with drama. There were always ups and downs, hates and loves, involving the people in her daily life. Now her apartment became the focus of Mona's emotional turmoil. She had lived on Farnham Avenue for twenty-odd years, and thanks to the generosity of her landlords, the Kalants, she had never seen an increase in rent. But finally the bathroom and kitchen needed renovations so serious that she would have to move out for several months to make them possible. This was traumatic for Mona. The thought of moving out, and then back in again, not to mention financing such a venture, daunted her. She could certainly have managed with the help of friends and family, but the prospect of renovation brought home to her how much she depended on her apartment's low rent in order to survive on her pension, and how few others options she had. Mona's typical response when she felt beholden to anyone was to become increasingly high-handed. This is what she did with her landlords. The whole situation became emotionally fraught, as if relationships hung in the balance and personal loyalties were at play, instead of tiles and floorboards. Ultimately, she decided to leave the apartment for good.

With her reluctance to go out of the house, however, Mona could not mobilize herself to hunt for apartments. Ingi began to look for a place for her. Mona did not want to move out of her familiar area, though local rents had skyrocketed. Her daughter-in-law combed neighbouring streets and ones further afield, finally discovering an apartment on Macpherson Avenue between Avenue Road and Yonge Street. Mona had what she wanted, which was access to her regular shops and businesses. (In fact, she had cab drivers and neighbours do most of her errands for her, but the idea that she *could* reach everything on foot was vital to her.) However the place was a basement, and tiny. At the age of seventy-six, she was going to live in one room with little natural light, and complete strangers living beside her.

Despite Herculean efforts to find a decent place in the neighbourhood, Ingi was accused of relegating Mona to a basement and insisting that she live under squalid conditions. Mona depicted herself as being at the mercy of a daughter-in-law who did not understand her needs and wanted to confine her to some kind of emotional and physical dungeon. In reality, the new apartment was all Mona could afford. And even at that, it was more expensive than her apartment on Farnham. My grandmother's situation went from shabbily genteel to outright poor, and there was no end in sight. She would have to survive on her government pension, with the odd infusion of cash whenever a poem was reprinted or a friend sent her a cheque. Living within a strict budget was soul-destroying to Mona. She was committed to *feeling* that life could offer her a bit of grandeur, even if this was manifestly not true. Now even her weekly *New York Times* and the odd trip to the movies were beyond her means. She kept spending money on these things anyway, but it cost her a great deal of anxiety, and at times left her short of money for food. The people close to her back then joked that she lived on strawberry ice cream and coffee. Sadly, she could not afford much else. In her archive I found notes indicating that at one point, she ate nothing but potatoes and milk for a whole week while waiting for a pension cheque.

Mona was energetic, and miraculously free of any trace of arthritis, but she was not getting any younger. She was developing cataracts, and this contributed to what had become a case of true agoraphobia. The city was growing exponentially, and technology was moving faster and faster, making everything from banking to going to the doctor a daunting experience. She might be coping day to day but sooner or later, Mona was going to need someone to look after her. She would never admit this though, and the machinations surrounding the issue were enough to drive any potential caregiver away. Mona would present strange demands, obviously trumped up, and obviously a bid for attention, yet never speak of what was really going on. Rather than initiating a frank discussion, she orchestrated dramas on separate but somehow related themes. Her stories had to be deconstructed, subjected to complex and subtle interpretation, in order to get at the truth. The whole enterprise was exhausting and frustrating.

When Mona was growing up, an aging mother often moved into the home of one of her children. Her own mother was different. She spent her final years alone in London, Ontario, while Mona worked long hours as a broadcaster in Toronto. Mona had more than enough on her plate in the 1950s, but the sense that she *should* have been caring for her mother full-time must have hovered constantly. Her guilt at not being closer to her mother probably made Mona's own aging process all the more fraught. On some level, she may have felt she did not deserve to be looked after.

Yet family were not the only ones surrounding Mona during this time. She had a lot of friends, who sometimes understood her better than we did. Ray and Pat Williams took her to hear live jazz at the Sheraton hotel. Many others dropped in to her apartment or wrote to her regularly. Mona's closest friend during this period was John Ide, the nephew of John Aylesworth. John Ide had first met Mona about ten years before, when Mona was recovering from her cancer operation. He was barely out of his teens, and at a troubled stage in his own life when he was trying to define his identity, both as an artist as a person. Though she looked – to use his word – "frightening," with her slash of red lipstick, her long, straggly hair and blotchy skin, John was drawn to Mona because of her voice, which seemed to him calm and reassuring. "She caressed you with her voice," he told me. "I'm here for you," was her message.[1]

She gave him her rapt attention for as long as it took to draw out what he needed to say and made herself available at any hour of the day or night. Mona's apartment seemed to John a haven of tranquility, with bare wooden floors, white walls, and dark pieces of furniture that reminded him of houses in Spain or Mexico. The two spent many hours together. Her stories gave him a sense of possibilities outside of the conventional, bourgeois life he had been taught to expect. There were many times when Mona seemed not to see the real people in her life, but only characters in a drama of her own invention. In John's case, she had enough imagination to see who he really was beneath the surface, and who he could become.

During my teenage years, I often felt trapped in my role as Mona's confidante, as if she had no resources other than me. Now I realised that she had pulled the wool over my eyes – all that time, she had John. Somehow, despite the hours that both of us spent at her apartment the summer of her operation, he and I never ran into each other. But when I had had to go back to school in the fall, John was still available to stand as a buffer against her fear and loneliness.

In the 1980s, John was establishing a career as a visual artist, and had created a circle of friends that resonated with his inner world. The thought of becoming a writer himself was steadily growing. At this point, his relationship with Mona took flight. He was a kind of artistic son to her, a protégé, but a true friend as well. As such, he was able to give Mona something that "her" John – with a son's needs – never had. He accepted the side of her that wanted to be away from all relationships, to live alone and be completely free of attachment. Mona embodied a strange contradiction common to many writers. She was filled with the most profound longing for companionship, coupled with an equal and opposite need for solitude. John understood and accepted this contradiction.

When I interviewed John, he said that spending time with Mona on Macpherson had encouraged him to believe in his own goals. "But why was it encouraging to see a poet of Mona's stature living in a basement at the age of seventy-six? Why would that make you feel it was a good idea to pursue a career in the arts?" "She had a way of living below the system," he answered. It was Mona's inner resources that impressed John, and her ability to draw on these no matter what else was going on. He saw the way she was able to transform what might be a squalid, depressing situation into one of triumph, purely by the force of her personality. Art came first; money came second. That was the way things worked for Mona. This was the opposite of the materialistic values that John had been taught, and which he felt obscured his real self. "She gave me transfusions of courage," he said. "She would take the fear away."

"Mona hated weakness and did not portray herself as a victim," John said. This observation took me by surprise. By the 1980s, Mona was definitely portraying herself as a victim in her conversations with *me*. But she was as intent on protecting John Ide from her victim persona as she was from any of her concerns about material things. John told me how he noticed that she was sleeping on a terribly sagging mattress. Though he had little money to spare, he bought her a new one. When he called the next day to ask her how she had slept, she answered: "That mattress was as hard as the tarmac on Farnham Avenue." This is how he learned, he said, that you must never *give* Mona anything. She needed to be on the giving end. Another time he tried to help her clean up her apartment. The dust was building up everywhere, and he was simply showing his love for her by trying to free her from the chores she hated. He started to sweep under her bed. "You'd make a very good char." She observed caustically. He put down the broom and never tried to clean for her again.[2]

Maija Beeton, another protégé, stayed in touch with my grandmother through her young adulthood, confiding in her about her travels and romantic adventures, and her early forays into life as an artist. Like John, she celebrated the very qualities in Mona that others found difficult to bear. Mona's habit of making up stories was, for Maija, magical. She was aware of my grandmother's faults, but was able to frame them in a positive way. She acknowledged that Mona could be manipulative at times, sowing discord among the people around her and then watching the ensuing drama unfold, drawing a kind of aesthetic satisfaction from other people's suffering. This was a trait I never managed to forgive. But even though Maija herself sometimes felt the sting of Mona's manipulations, she saw through them to the creative impulse that lay beneath. As Maija framed it, Mona had a mischievous streak, akin to a child's tendency to open every forbidden cupboard and drawer in the house. She felt driven to expose what lay beneath the surface of the people around her, even if this meant finding something ugly. "Mona wanted all of us to have our wildest, deepest, truest adventures ... everything she encouraged us to do was to try to find our true selves," Maija told me.[3]

My grandmother seemed most at ease when there was emotional turmoil raging around her. Maija helped me see that only at those moments did Mona feel she knew where she stood. Only then did she feel people were acting from the depth of themselves rather than pretending to be who they thought they should be. The chaos which ensued also left room for chance, for possibilities beyond people's tightly controlled idea of how their lives should unfold. She was also aware that Mona toyed with the lives of others as a way to compensate for the lack of stimulation in her own life. "She lived through us. The sad part is she didn't actually take her adventuring and get out of the house more. There were a lot of things she could have done. She limited her existence in certain ways. Early. Way earlier that she needed to."[4] Mona was cruel to some people, treating them as barely human. But for a chosen few, the experience of knowing her was to be treasured. "If you were inside her bubble she showed you a way to Nirvana. How to take pleasure in life, and how to even take pleasure in the tragedies because what you do is you revel in them. You revel in everything that you're entitled to experience because you're alive. And that was her great lesson was to take these experiences, to really try to feel them and live them and not disown them."[5]

Mona made friends among her neighbours as well. They were mostly young men who were trying to make their way in the arts. Before long, her apartment became a Mecca for all these actors and writers and their friends. Wanting a break from their busy schedules, they would stop in and visit Mona. There were not enough chairs in her room, so they draped themselves over her bed, or sat on her floor. She had an infinite appetite for listening to the ups and downs of their romantic and professional lives, and created a kind of sought-after buzz around herself. Eventually, they were all competing for her attention. Despite feeling extremely vulnerable, Mona managed to transform her basement apartment into a kind of Bohemian commune.

ॐ

More worrisome than her finances, her housing, her family relationships, and even her health was Mona's situation as a writer during this period. With others, she continued to weave magnificent tales of past glory, but the fact now stared her baldly in the face that she had still not achieved the recognition that her early talent promised. Her last book had been published over twenty years earlier. She was still hoping for another before she died, but there was no apparent way of breaking through the obscurity that had settled over her. Toronto's artistic community exploded in the 1980s, becoming not only larger, but more diverse. Nonetheless, Mona could find no place within it. Her journals from the early 1980s show her grappling with these issues. She expressed a sense of failure, a fear that she had gone as far as she could go in life, without realising her dreams. And as always, her attachment and dedication to others was seen as the reason she had fallen short. Ironically, her private jottings had as much literary merit as the chatty essays she was assembling.

April 20th
(what's o'clock) pound the spring pavement – "Bravo" we should (silently) or who would dare? Do a lot of people, I wonder, yearn to leave some record of their lives – even a very little life – never dignified by a Gov Gen's Award – nothing like that! Never a degree from a university. For what? Never a medal of Canada to wear on a length of brown twine round the neck – out of sight – no – never!

Then whence this urge: this struggling urge – to set it all down! Who will read it? There are nifty little fat books in all libraries with [unclear] bindings and seductive titles – But when you check the cards in back – they've only been taken out once, or at most twice! You feel bad for the writers! Who would look down and scuff a toe in the dust!

Then why write? Perhaps it is the search for God. No Mustard Seed safe in the pocket. You feel for it. Yup. It's still there, all right. But that's it?

You begin to wonder, to ponder, to speculate – is it all in the search, then? Are we never allowed – given passage – just this nagging urge – this pressing on and on – when no voice cries "Bravo" on you. It is Sunday morning. It is Spring as you jog past. It is April. We are tying our laces.[6]

Though there was plenty of self-pity in Mona's journals, she also used them to talk herself out of her worries, and remind herself of her greatest strength: she could take pleasure in life regardless of circumstances. This pleasure came to her through writing.

April 1986
... BK Sandwell will get me for this. He told me it was downright im-moral to write for fun, (which I always have) but the fun of finding a little secret clutch of watercress hiding under a wild country spring – gushing out of a rock at you! That type of fun! Not Disco Dancing or watching the "toob" – I know deep in inmost me that my poems are good! I have put my best into them: tried to learn each day, and set them like jewels on the page. The singing began in me, when I was born, and has companioned me, faithfully. I believe in my output now.[7]

She allowed herself flights of whimsy, and a kind of ecstatic joy in every-day things. For many years, she had used alcohol to bring her closer to these ecstatic feelings, but her hunger for the transformative moments was such that she continued to seek them out without any substance to enhance her experience.

April 27th, 1986
I just did all my ugly, messy, weeklong dishes. Hell! How I hate doing dishes. But now? I feel virtuous! The day intensifies. It is nooon. Utter summer! Sweet! I still have my NY Times to get and I want Chanel. It's a Chanel sort of Sunday!

May 10, 1986
... If I had wagon loads of gold coin I could not buy a more beautiful space than I am in this spring morning. Because I am enclosed in God's living growing Green! All trees and leaves all green leaves – dandelion bright – are mine! Je suis contente.[8]

The message of many her writings was that money could not buy happiness; indeed, Mona was certain that money stood in the way of attaining the kind of happiness she was capable of producing within herself. She denounced materialistic considerations, in herself and in others. When life became difficult, she would portray her move to Macpherson Avenue as a paring-down process. She was stripping away the last vestiges of a comfort which she felt inhibited her spiritual growth.

Sunday, May 5, 1986
When I moved here to Macpherson Manor I was still "tainted" with materialistic beliefs + habits. The "clingings". After M's disastrous "pleasure trip" to Portugal [Her friend had taken a trip to Portugal and had failed to bring Mona home a gift] I think it was stunningly brought home to me for the "forever-th" time how feckless it is to cling to material objects and soft comforts. It limits the mind and soul and even makes the body receptive to trivial "illnesses".[9]

Though she often talked herself out of her ambitions in her journals, Mona made a move toward realizing her dreams. With the help of a young woman in her building, she submitted an application for an Ontario Arts Council grant. In combination with her pension, the Works in Progress Grant would have made her comfortable for many months to come. She placed enormous hopes in this book, even as she cushioned herself against possible disappointment.

Sunday, May 5, 1986
...
Biography – Essays and Poems by Mona Gould

This is it! A meld of prose and poetry. My best! Yes! It is the key! I can now settle in to it. Forge ahead pronto pronto. Get Gov't Grant! Go for the "bundle". Poems out to the New Yorker. Yup!

And what if? What if I never have that book!
The ticker Tape parade kind of big smash all artists and writers in their secret hearts would love even once in a lifetime. The heady wine of success – after great "trying" and hurting + all the going-without a committed artist must walk thru – What if? I could have had [unclear] to

follow the "public way" of achieving them? I would have been sure of that one big explosion into fame! A seductive goal. But I would have returned to reality with an empty heart! I gave myself – my heart – my effort – to people I love + loved! It is not possible to experience both. Life has a way of making you play the "Walnut shell game" whether you want to or not. I am content with my choice. What if? What if? I never have that book? The French have a summing up for me: "C'est ne faire rien and Toujours Gaie."[10]

Her application was rejected. This gave rise to journal entries so rancorous and petty, I cannot bear to reproduce them. Deeply disappointed, personally offended, she let fly her rage at everyone close to her. Her daughters-in-law, Hetty and Ingi, were the principal targets, but even my father and I (the most sacred of sacred people) were depicted in her journals as betraying her. It was never our fault, though. She always saw the impetus as coming from someone else. My mother kept in touch with Mona during this time, and externally at least, their relationship was warm. When she took Mona to a movie or promised to knit her a sweater, my mother would be praised in Mona's journals, but was given the title of "Mommie dearest" in-between times. At one point, Mona wrote of the crushing discovery that I had had a boyfriend for three years without her knowledge. "Hetty has won!" Mona wrote. In fact, she had met him already, but seemed to have forgotten. I, on the other hand, was still squirming at the memory. "Your grandmother was *flirting* with me," he had said with disgust, afterwards. Before long he was avoiding all the Goulds assiduously, and I was happy to do my share in keeping these two powerful forces in my life apart.

Mona eventually moved upstairs, an improvement over the dark basement where she had spent more than a year. The change appeased her, briefly, but soon the old juggernaut of anger and manipulation re-established itself. In her journals, I read that she had tried to tell me about some of the dramas going on in her life. I had said I would not listen to her "gossip." This amazes me, because I have no memory of speaking to her so firmly.

After a number of confrontations with neighbours and family, she made a decision to leave Toronto entirely. She phoned John Aylesworth and declared she needed a thousand dollars for a plane ticket to Vancouver. Amazed, he agreed. She called Aylesworth's first wife, Jean, who had lived in West Vancouver for many years, and formed a plan to move in with her. The reasons she gave for going west were not clear, but they had to do with feeling slighted, feeling driven away. Her journals show that she wanted to test the loyalty of her son and regain his attention. In late June 1986 she wrote: "I am going away – for 1 reason – + 1 reason only because I love Jon + that is the most important thing in my life."[11]

Mona felt trapped: by time, obscurity, and by her own aging body. Her response was to run away. She needed a caregiver, someone she would not have to put on an act of self-sufficiency for, and someone who would be ultimately responsible in case she could not function any more. Her son was the natural one to take on this role, but that meant showing him that she had physical needs. And this was not the way Mona acted around men. Of course, with her son came a capable and willing daughter-in-law, but to depend on Ingi meant giving entirely too much power to a woman she had an uneasy relationship with, at the best of times.

In her journals, Mona chronicled how she announced to me she was moving west. Apparently, I told her in no uncertain terms that she was being melodramatic, that she did not have enough money to move to Vancouver and would not have a good enough support system once she got there. I said I would do nothing to help her with the move, an enormous undertaking that involved getting rid of most of her possessions within a month-long period. Other things had to be stored to be shipped to her later. John Ide recalled the scene of helping her pack: "When she took off to Vancouver, she took just one suitcase and her cat. A green plastic job that was filled not with clothes but with photos still with bits of tape and cat hairs on them. I know because I helped her zip it shut. 'Mona! Don't you want to take more clothes?' 'I don't need them, Darling. I need these pictures, though.'"[12] Mona was recklessly detaching herself from material things as well as from the people in her intimate circle. She felt a breakaway sense of freedom. What was there to lose? John Ide was able to appreciate the magnificence of Mona's gesture. At a time in life when so many people become narrow, cautious and closed, Mona had decided to fly off into the unknown.

Everest

During her stay in Vancouver, I would phone Mona occasionally, and write to her, but I was determined not to bow to what I saw as yet another massive play for attention. To fill me in on what I had missed, I located Jean Aylesworth in Vancouver. I had never met Jean, but had seen pictures of her wedding, when she looked like a young Grace Kelly. My grandfather, Graham, had been the one to walk her down the aisle that day. When I told Jean I was writing about Mona, and that I'd like to do an interview, she laughed with delight at the prospect of spending an hour talking about this woman who had made such a mark on her life. Although divorced from John Aylesworth many years before, she had kept in touch with Mona on the strength of her ex-husband's attachment to her and what that meant to their children. Mona had given them a great deal of help setting up their lives together in the fifties. And Jean, like so many people, loved Mona unconditionally.

Initially, Jean had greeted the idea enthusiastically of having Mona come and stay with her. She had a spare room in her apartment and was looking forward to caring for Mona. But things began to go amiss as soon as Mona's plane arrived. Jean was there to pick her up at the airport, and after a fond greeting, Mona announced it was time to pick up her cat. Cat? She had said nothing to Jean about a cat, and Jean had a strong dislike of them. But where Mona went, so did Sumi, and so Sumi took up residence in Jean's apartment. This was a source of distress to the meticulous Jean, since the cat was used to roaming in and out of cupboards and walking on the table when people were eating. Mona fed rich food to all her cats, and they were greasy to the touch. The whole apartment became full of oily cat hair.

And then, there was the matter of what Mona expected when she moved in with Jean. "I found that she was quite demanding and I found that I was making coffee or running around doing things and being a handmaiden and I'm not used to waiting on people, and Mona did like to have that way of life. To be waited on. And of course she was in a strange apartment and she would count on me to get the coffee and things like that. It came time after maybe a month that I decided it was time to look for something permanent for her, if she was planning to stay."[1]

Jean found Mona a one-bedroom apartment close by in West Vancouver. It was pleasant and clean, with a view of the sea, but there was furniture to be bought, as well as day-to-day errands to be done, and Mona did not have a car. Jean's sister-in-law, Jan, did a lot of driving for Mona. Although there was shopping in walking distance, West Vancouver was not a pedestrian-friendly place. Mona was isolated and dependent on her two friends. Eventually, Mona's cataract became "ripe" for removal, and Jean and Jan helped her through the operation. Soon it became clear that Mona's sight would never fully return. She had macular degeneration. Jean and Jan were not blood relatives, nor had they been around Mona day-to-day over the years. It was a lot to ask of them.

Jean said: "She didn't want to go out and walk to the store. She would have people bring things in. That's where the Haagen Daz came in. At that time I thought she was living on Haagen Daz ... She decided she needed a huge table. She had no furniture. I was providing her with things. As I recall I found where I could get an inexpensive bed. She needed everything of course ... My son [Rob] gave her his big soft down chair. That delighted her because ... [it] had been given to Rob by his father. Mona really cared for John Aylesworth and this had been his chair and that made it important to her. It was a great big overstuffed thing. The bed never did go into the bedroom. It was in the living room. The bedroom was used for boxes and things."[2]

Mona received visits from her brother Doug and his family, who now lived in the United States. Mona's older brother was the most practical of men, conservative in both his politics and his spending habits. Behind his back, Mona spoke witheringly of Doug's stinginess, but the sister and brother loved each other dearly. Doug's three grown children and their spouses welcomed the opportunity to get to know Mona. This was how Mona made her one and only foray into the computer age. Paul Ferrar – Doug's son-in-law at the time – determined that with her failing eyesight, Mona needed a computer to remain active as a writer. He traveled from Oregon to Vancouver with an Apple computer for Mona, and gave her lessons on how to use it. She would speak on the telephone of this "infernal machine" as if it were a malevolent creature. I had never heard the world "apple" used with such sinister connotations, apart from its early career in the Bible. From this point on, we in the east began receiving missives from Mona, created on what she dubbed The Apple II. Mona never quite adjusted to life after the carriage return. There would be line ends where there should be none, and other sections would be run together line after line with no punctuation or spaces between the words. Writing was now an act of war between Mona and the machine. The Apple II represented all the forces of conformity, of reductionism, of pettiness and aesthetic insensitivity that the modern age could muster. Mona fought on the side of romanticism and creativity, and she would always win.

Well – here we   go again, Spillage
Will crop up from time to time
Buy [sic] the horrid flukes grow less
And less! This give me great
Hope and I go on and on! Immense
Effort and concentration u
Would not believe! Whenever I
Brag about progress tiny persisy
Tent little arrows litter my
Pearly prose and prove that I am
Tenderfoot and stoopid! However en
Avant and toujours gaie I always
Say & also C(est ne faire rien!³

Eventually, Mona disconnected the thing and kept it locked in the closet as if it might get out of its own accord.

Mona also received a visit from John Ide. He had always admired the sparseness of Mona's living quarters, and this was her most uncluttered environment thus far. They talked for hours, walked by the sea, and lived on a diet of ice cream and coffee. After what had seemed an enchanted visit, she wrote to him, "Some wise man said 'friendship must be the highest form of love' – Well then! We have it – my faithful one!"⁴

None of this was enough to fill Mona's long days in West Vancouver. She was lonely. Jean said, "Mona felt there was something wrong ... Mona wouldn't have admitted it. She was so proud, and she had been such a strong woman, and she didn't really admit that it was a mistake but it had been a very big mistake. It wasn't the dream, the escape that she thought it would be. She was really running away ... She was an Ontario girl. That's what she knew, that's where she fit. It was all about Ontario, Toronto."[5] And so, in consultation with her son, Mona agreed to move back to Ontario, this time to Barrie. She had spent a little over a year in Vancouver.

Strip't bare. Mona after eye surgery. The marks
on the edges of the photograph suggest it spent
some time taped to a wall or cupboard door.

She would continue to have her own place to live, but from now on she would always be close to her children, in case she needed help. She was delighted to become a great-grandmother for the first time, to Melissa's daughter, Allison. However, being in the bosom of the family also meant compromises on Mona's part. Nothing was stated outright, but it was clear she was going to have to accept that John had a separate life, and that his primary loyalty was to Ingi. He would visit his mother regularly, but she would not necessarily be woven into the fabric of his daily life as she had once expected to be. At around that time, she began to announce that she intended to start drinking again on her eightieth birthday, but received a stern admonishment from her son that she must never touch alcohol again.

Mona grieved more for what Vancouver represented than out of any deep attachment to the place. It had been a last bid for freedom. This freedom was particularly important for Mona, since she believed artists were compromised, not just by their attachment to others, but by the practical concerns she could no longer ignore. Thus, as far as Mona was concerned, coming home also meant a blow to her artistic identity, and possibly to her work. In one journal entry, she wrote of her sadness at leaving Vancouver, with overtones of another, deeper sense of longing. She still wanted a closer connection with her son.

> Before I lose the thread – had enormous dreams! Deep down in my Inner Woman! Dream of my SeaWall existence in West Van! But Jon had come to get me + bring me home in my dream. I huddled against his lean flank like a little dog – quivering with the wrench of leaving … I was weeping (inwardly) + the nostalgia on leaving the sea rim was overwhelming – Awesome! I struggled with it but my heart was blk + empty as a bat's cave! Jon kept comforting me! Saying "I think I knew what's hurting you." + then he would stop there! And so I never found out![6]

❧

Barrie was the right size of community for Mona. During the 1980s, Toronto was relentlessly forging its reputation as a "world class city," striving to leave behind its history of WASP domination along with its reputation as "Toronto the Good." Mona had been part of that history, and now felt forgotten. Yet she still believed that all her life events should be accompanied by media attention. In Barrie, this became possible. She made the acquaintance of a local journalist by the name of Barbara Fear who drew on Mona's stories to write a feature with numerous pictures in the Sunday supplement of the Barrie newspaper.[7] She began reading to school children, convened a writers' workshop, and set up weekly readings at the IOOF, a local seniors' home. She also volunteered for the newly formed hospice. This gave her occasion to write frequently to June Callwood, who was active in setting up Casey House hospice in Toronto, and she saved Callwood's affectionate and encouraging replies.[8] In April 1992, she received an Ontario Community Service Award for her volunteer work at the IOOF. Another was to follow in 1993 from the Chamber of Commerce in Barrie.[9]

Mona's apartment was a box-like one-bedroom with less character and charm than any of her homes so far. The parquet floors were buckling in spots, the pressboard cupboards chipped and stained. The walls were uncomfortably chilly to the touch, and the concrete balcony overlooked highway 400. None of this seemed to bother Mona, whose eyesight was now dim enough to soften the apartment's depressing aspects. The building was clean and well maintained, and this was enough for her. Besides, she found a way of getting out of the house in all weathers. A restaurant across the street called Ruby Begonia's now became her second home. Each day, she would jay-walk, in leisurely fashion, across the highway and traverse Ruby's vast parking lot as if it were a street in Yorkville. It was a split-level restaurant decorated with brass railings and silk foliage which served enormous helpings and offered a buffet at noon for the business crowd. No matter how busy they were, the staff at Ruby Begonia's would greet Mona by name, seat her by the window and serve her a bottomless cup of coffee with a drinking straw. Now, she could be free of cooking when she had guests. She would offer her visitors the menu just as in the days when she was a regular at the Walrus and the Carpenter. My own response – and probably I was not alone in this – would be to thank Mona profusely for lunch while discretely handing the server my credit card. Mona also made herself known to the local taxi company. A driver was coached to do a Monday-morning run to purchase milk, coffee, ice cream, and a copy of *The New York Times*. In Barrie, she could once again pick up the phone and say, "It's Mona Gould, Dear," with no further explanation required.

Mona was not paying as much rent as she had in Vancouver, but she was still feeling a strain. A budget from the time shows that almost her entire pension was taken up with daily living. The remaining twenty-one dollars went as a down payment on what had become a prodigious credit card bill. Not accounted for in the budget were Mona's colostomy supplies, which amounted to almost one hundred dollars a month. During this time, her monthly allotment for food was only one hundred and sixty dollars.[10] Under the circumstances, it is likely that Ruby Begonia's boosted Mona's pension with a few free meals.

❧

John Ide traveled extensively throughout the 1980s and 1990s. He wrote to Mona from various places in Europe, Canada, and the Middle East, taking her with him in letters as her son had done, so many years ago. The exotic locales formed a backdrop for sober meditations on John's history and future. He had come to share Mona's fascination with memory, and her conviction that the past was as alive and vital as the present. Mona drew out his writing, and he found his voice in her listening. He wrote in a poem of Mona's beauty in old age. She was "stripped to the essentials/Skeleton thin/Edited into Poetry."[11] At around this time, he introduced her to photographer Greg Staats, who did a series of portraits of Mona draped in black fabric, looking frankly and in all the dignity of her years into the camera.

John Ide began to influence Mona's writing as well. His research into world religions fed Mona's interest in Eastern mystical thought. Increasingly, these ideas began to flavour her daily writing sessions. She prepared herself like a meditator for the moments of enlightenment she would receive through writing. The process had become central to her; the product, unimportant. "I write enough for a book every morning," she told me once, during these years. "Some of it is crap, some of it is great. And I don't care anymore."

In 1988, she wrote a poem called "Old Age to Me." Like "This Was My Brother," it came to her all at once, and said exactly what she wanted it to say.

Old age is not descent
It is Everest
It is the essence of trees
Without leaves
Strip't down
The beautiful skeleton of design

It is graphic
Luminous sky
Before midnight.
It is a concourse of eagles.
It is not austere
It is passionate.[12]

The first person she showed the poem to was John Ide. As he read it, all the stories Mona had told him, the images that had passed through his mind during the years of listening to her coalesced. Inspired by the poem, he created a multi-media piece called *Moments*, which consisted of a slide show with photos of Mona, and lines from the poem fading in and out. He also created some accompanying material for the piece: a thick book with photocopies of many of Mona's letters and clippings. This meant John was Mona's first archivist. *Moments* was presented at A Space Gallery in Toronto in the spring of 1989, as part of a group exhibition of artists' books.

The exhibition was a turning point in John's career, presenting new opportunities for him as a visual artist. For Mona, it was a balm after so many years of obscurity. In her situation, many writers would have turned inward, questioning themselves deeply and searching for ways to improve their writing. Mona, on the other hand, simply waited for the kind of recognition she believed she deserved all along. The creator of "This Was My Brother" – who received a poem whole, as if from a divine source and was then catapulted to fame by it – *this* was the person she recognized as her true self. Now, after all these years of waiting and flailing, came an opportunity for her to take on this mantle again.

The opening of *Moments* was a triumph for Mona. She walked into the room and immediately commandeered everyone's attention. The curator approached and remarked that she was a little old to be spending time in a "Parallel Gallery." In a voice intended to be heard by everyone around her she replied, "I've always loved big spaces, Dear. I lived in a loft before you were born." Mona lived for experiences like these, though they occurred only a few times in her life. The moments when she was the object of admiration were "real life," as far as she was concerned. Everything in between was an aberration. She wrote about the evening on the back of a poster for the show.

Friday the 9th April 1988

It was her day! Compleat! As if Father Gawd had said:
We will weave a tapestry of
This Day –
We will weave a scarlet cloth without a
Single flaw – a
Dropt stitch –
That she may put it upon
Her wall and
Look at it – and
Glory will be hers
Forever after.

With one spark, her ego was fully kindled again. She went on: "There was not a single flaw in my day. No bitter moment ... [the audience] sat on the floor and hung on the walls and doorways to see and murmured aloud their comments and whistled at the leg shots etc. all appreciative ... It was a wonder to me to be congratulated on [unclear] and truth of my work. But I felt right about it. Knighted. A star! For the time I felt praised for all the right reasons – earned ones. Earned it by living it all out. The bitter and the sweet!"[13]

The deep fulfillment of that evening may have discouraged Mona from trying to get "Everest" published. It was enough for her to feel the heady combination of inspiration followed by immediate attention. She did not want to risk marring the experience by inviting the possibility of rejection.

❧

Mona's second cataract had reached a point where it could be removed. Although the operation was successful, leaving her with only minor loss of vision, she began to tell people she had gone blind. She talked about this compulsively. Once she got started it was almost impossible to stop her. When I could bring myself to put aside my impatience, I recognized the metaphorical aspect of her complaints. Mona had lost a vital connection with the world: the connection of publishing and broadcasting. For years, she had had a channel by which what was *in* her could come out, a context where people could in turn respond to her. Now it was gone. She felt this as keenly as the loss of a sense, and mourned it accordingly. To declare herself blind was the only way to receive attention for this loss without ever having to acknowledge it. Ironically, her tenacity in clinging to this story alienated her further from the world. One friend of Mona's – who had health problems of her own – told me that she stopped calling because she could not bear to listen to the manifestly robust Mona talk about her blindness any more.

Mona spoke frequently of her imminent death. For years, I had found this irritating; now it strengthened the bond between us. I thought about death a lot, in those days. I was in my early thirties, and everyone around me seemed to be entering the prime of their lives: falling in love, having children, buying houses. My sister Ellen had her first child, Kalil, in 1993. But I was single by this time, having lost the relationship I had staked so much on keeping. Meanwhile – after almost two decades of remission – my mother had experienced another attack of lupus. I could not have predicted the caregiving would go on for fourteen years, but though I pretended to have the same ambitions as my friends, I knew my mother would take most of my attention for a long time to come. Beneath a determinedly youthful exterior, I felt like an archetype: the spinster looking after her aging mother. Spending so much time in hospitals changed my perspective. I was more focused on the end of life than its beginning.

With Mona, I did not have to hide my tragic view of life. I remember one visit to my father's home on Thanksgiving, in about 1994. There were about ten people there, and partway through the afternoon, everyone went for a walk in the nearby fields. Mona wanted to come along, though the terrain was rough and most people in their eighties could not have handled it. I walked with Mona behind the rest of the group. She wore her raincoat over a dress, with bare legs and knee socks. Both of us were in running shoes. I kept my arm around her, protecting her against the bitter wind, and we followed the little knot of walkers that dwindled in our vision as they left us further and further behind. At one point we stopped and looked over the gray October landscape with its touches of frost in the hollows, its steely sky. This was not the glorious autumn of Mona's poems but a desolate landscape. A few yellowish stalks of grass and some faded pines gave the only colour.

"Death," Mona said.

"Yes," I answered.

"That's the next thing I've got to do."

I said nothing and we carried on walking.

Mona had watched her loved ones succumb to various illnesses, and felt more and more alone with each loss. The death which had struck the deepest was that of Margaret Steven Tanton in January, 1991. They had been friends since childhood, and Mona wrote a poem about her feelings when she lost her oldest friend.

I speak aloud – often
I walk about my house
I go to the window
I survey my scene
I speak it aloud
Often
"Where are you now
Margaret" – to my friend
Of 77 years –

Silence
Comes
Back to
Me!14

❧

But for Mona, death was still a long way off. She had another chapter to live out. The local IOOF seniors' home, where Mona gave weekly poetry readings, had built an apartment complex which offered rent-geared-to-income. Mona placed her name on a waiting list and in 1994, moved into a large, bright apartment with a view of Kempenfelt Bay. There were also a dining room and recreational facilities on site, as well as in-house help available as needed. In Heritage Place, Mona began to thrive. The practicalities of life were taken care of. At last, she had a decent diet. Chewing had been a problem for several years but here the kitchen ground her food up for her. Nourished by more than coffee and strawberry ice cream, her skin and hair began to shine, and she lost her unwanted weight.

The staff in the building took the time to discover what made Mona tick. They would come to her door every few hours and see if she needed anything: a sandwich? A cup of tea? Or would she like them to reapply her lipstick? They understood that this "red badge of courage" as she called it, was as important to Mona as food. The visiting manicurist laid in a stock of her favourite red nail polish. Most importantly, Mona's rent never went over a third of her pension. With fees regularly coming in for reprints of her poems, she was free of the chronic anxiety about money that had dogged her since she left her parents' home at the age of nineteen. Now she could concentrate on the things that mattered to her: reading, writing, art, politics, and thought. She listened to talking books and interview programs on the radio. She developed a passion for baseball (miraculously enjoying a return of her sight for the exciting parts of the games). Most of all, she was not alone. The building was full of other retired people who had time to fill. They ate together in the dining room, dropped in for visits to each other's apartments, met each morning for a daily "coffee klatch."

When Mona moved into the IOOF, she put a definitive end to her closeness with John Ide. "Please don't come and see me, Dear." She told him, "Remember me as I was." They spoke on the phone, but she would not let him in on the details of her daily life. Mona would only let John know her as a Bohemian, living for her art, eschewing every kind of material support and comfort. Ironically, she looked better than she had in thirty years.

Mona now began to attend the church services offered in the building. This gave her an opportunity to sing, to revisit the Bible verses familiar to her from childhood, and to gather with her neighbours. She attended a pow-wow where she proudly had her photograph taken with a group of First Nations' elders. At times she referred to God as "The Creator." In her journals, she began addressing God directly, in daily prayers of thanks. "I'm a grateful sort of person," she used to say, and indeed this attitude pervaded her late journals. Each entry began with a comment on the beautiful day or how well she had slept, followed by the words: "Thank U Father Gawd, Sir!" She referred to herself as a lowly "human bean." Somehow, she had decided that her maker appreciated her "sauciness" as well as her fundamental sense of irony. From these journals, I came to understand that gratitude was something Mona had expected of herself, all her life. She considered it the proper attitude to take toward the world.

Mona often cast herself as a victim – especially late in life. Yet I began to see that her moments of bitterness and self-pity had been a source of shame to her, because she saw the failure to be grateful as sacrilege. Mona's mother had written letters complaining of loneliness and ill-health, and no doubt she was even more negative in person. Mona wrote in her journal that she feared repeating this pattern. Complaining was such a taboo that she did not distinguish between moments of self-indulgence, and times when she was fully justified in saying something was wrong, between times when she was hurt, and times when she was looking for an excuse to strike out at others. Maybe her self-pity would have become less pernicious had she been able to acknowledge and examine it.

The Heritage Place minister, John Crump, encouraged Mona in her creative pursuits. When she began her "farewell tour" speeches, he told her it was not time to think of dying yet. She still had work to do. The daily coffee klatch became the outlet for Mona's poem-of-the-day. A sign on her door displayed the epithet, "Mona McTavish Gould, Poet-in-Residence." Mona had a constituency, and could resume what she felt was her true role in life. She began to write poems on eleven by seventeen inch sheets of paper provided by the building's staff. They were breezy, rhyming verses that pleased her neighbours. She wrote on the occasions of their birthdays and anniversaries, and sometimes their deaths. Events in the building would be noted, and the security guards, cleaners, minister, doctor, and cooks thanked in verse. She kept about a thousand poems in all.

Good Morning to <u>All!</u>
We trot down to the Greenhouse
Every Morn – to touch the new
Leafage
All newly born
The tall ones the teeny ones
That smell like – corn!
It is an adventure so early and <u>all</u>
To pop out your door and go down your hall.
You might trip on an Elf or a
Leprechaun
And never turn up for
To-morrow's dawn –
So be careful and all
Of what you <u>put</u>
Your Foot
<u>On!</u>
...

As you dodge down our hall –
Give your "Good day, kids" to all – just call:
Olé, olé, olé (louder) Olé![15]

All of the poems ended with the assembled crowd chanting "Olé!" several
times. This became part the coffee klatch routine. A wholesome wake-up call
with overtones of Mediterranean bloodlust was exactly Mona's style.

This lustiness was not restricted to the coffee klatch. The handful of male
residents in the building had a lot of women to choose from, yet they tended
to gravitate to Mona. On one of my visits, we met a man in the hallway outside her apartment. Both he and Mona were wearing around their necks the
kind of alarm that someone with a health problem can press if they are in
trouble. Mona and the man hugged each other firmly, as if this were their
accustomed greeting.

"Did I set off your beeper?" the man asked.

"Most definitely," Mona answered. "Yours?"

"Always," he replied.

Mona swept past him, swinging her cane jauntily while he watched her
disappear down the hall.

ॐ

Mona continued to write in her journals, using the process to transform mundane experiences into ecstatic ones. She now understood the importance of
process, and gave it the weight it deserved. Her daily practice was, after all,
responsible for her well-being. She was living proof that creative expression
is an element in mental and physical health. She wrote:

Friday
2 pills – taken – 1st thing –
C – moved – fully! Oley!
(Thank U Gawd!)
Sun up – good day – ahead!
Oley! Oley! Oley!
Thank U Jesus-Man!
Took single new pill before lunch!
Confab with Simon (Guard) a.m.

(helpful!)
Sunday
Gordie in – early lights – Vett me.
2 tummy pills, Ensure – liquid medic.
Chores: bed etc.
Sun out –
4th floor lunch – noon! Stuff from Big Dining Room –
Still under Quarantine – other Bldg.
(illeg) feeling better at last! Good![16]

In old age, Mona freed herself from the pressure to succeed in a larger world with her poetry. She was not as famous as she had hoped, but this no longer nagged her. She had enough attention close at hand that she could let go of her far-flung dreams. She had a new way of being special: she was aging well, due in large part to her daily practice of writing. Her poetry was turning out to be a resource in her later years after all. With better nourishment and less isolation she was prodigiously healthy, mentally alert, and energetic. Now, she proudly announced her age like a pre-school child.

When I visited, she would introduce me to her neighbours and take me around to her favourite haunts in the buildings. The first stop was the greenhouse, where she sank her fingers into the dirt and stroked the leaves of all the plants. She approached this communion with the botanical world in a spirit of reverence, as if she believed her very touch as an elder was going to make the plants grow stronger and that, in turn, the strength of the plants could enter her own body. Then she would take me out on the roof deck where she would demonstrate her deep-breathing exercises. Finally, we would go to the lounge where daily, she practiced piano. I would ask her on each visit to play me what had become one of my own favourite songs:

I'll see you again
Whenever spring breaks through again.
Time may lie heavy between,
But what has been
Is past forgetting.

The functional lounge with its white linoleum floor and florescent lights was transformed into a sophisticated piano bar; such was the power of Mona's presence. Through the exhaustion that I always carried with me in those days, I reminded myself that Mona's blood also flowed in my veins. At about this time, Mona wrote a short poem in her journal:

Death Wish #1

Whose head
Do you want to live <u>on in</u>
   When you're dead!
   I choose
   Marija-Poo
   You would
   Too!
[Marija-Poo was Mona's nickname for me][17]

Mona stayed at Heritage Place until just six weeks before she died. A picture taken in the nursing home shows her singing and clapping in a group of other seniors. Her skin is papery-white. The image is frightening; this is a body in the process of shutting down. She is literally almost a corpse. But it is beautiful, too. Mona's body and face were "edited" – as John Ide had put it – to the bare essentials, and so was her life. Now, like a child who does not see any reason why not, Mona simply expressed herself in any way she could. She continued her practice of writing every day until the day before her death. The staff of the nursing home created a book for her with a series of poems, some dictated, and some in her own handwriting. She illustrated them the way she had as a child. One picture shows a landscape with a spreading tree, which also resembles a face. Another is a study of a woman with downcast eyes. The expression is angelically peaceful. During one of my last visits, she dictated a poem to me.

   I wanted to sing a sweet little song
   But all that came out was a little chirp
   More like a burp
   So to strengthen my day
   Olé Olé
   Not much of a verse
   But I have written worse·
   Olé Olé Olé

Bones

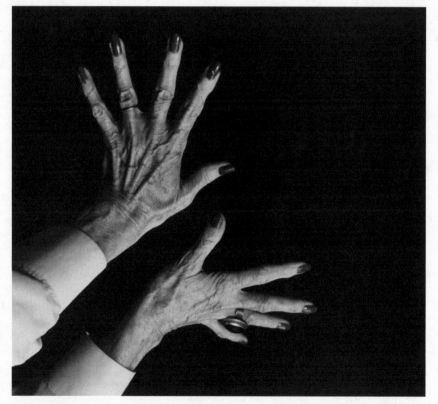

Mona's hands, photograph by Greg Staats

It ain't no sin, to take off my skin, and dance around in my bones! Mona told the story of how she used to sing this song to her mother, then flounce off to avoid the smack that would inevitably follow. Mona loved her bones. In old age, she ate little, and her bones became more and more visible: in her hands, her temples, her ankles, and wrists. She would study her hands, admiring their slimness. She loved the word *bones*, its depth and resonance.

Mona requested that she be cremated when she died; she wanted her body to be reduced to bones which would then be reduced to powder. She said she wanted to be scattered over water, but she didn't say where.

Ingi and my father visited me soon after Mona's death. I made tea while they stood side-by-side in the doorway of the kitchen, not quite crossing the threshold. There was some fumbling and arranging, some passing of an object from her purse to his hands, and then my father stepped forward, proffering a silver box. He pointed to me, and then to the box. I opened it. Inside: Mona's wedding ring, the thin band that never left her finger. Tears blurred my vision, and I looked up to see the eyes of my father and Ingi, also awash. The presence of this ring – in the box, not on her hand – made it real. The hand that wore this ring did not exist anymore. Mona was dead.

∞

One evening in June, 2003 I traveled north to Barrie. The next day, we were to scatter Mona's ashes outside Owen Sound. My father and I sat in the sunporch adjoining the kitchen of their home. It was just after dinner and the light still shone in all around us. He started to tell a story using his combination of gestures and familiar phrases. The story had to do with adversity, determination. I thought I recognized it. Whenever I went to visit, he told me about his recovery from his stroke.

"At first the thing was really bad. And he says, no, no." My father would begin the story with his head lowered, a defeated expression around the mouth. Then there would be a gradual rallying. He was in conflict with some stronger being. The being refused him something, but he set his chin and knit his brow. He would do it, anyway. He made a horizontal gesture in the air with one hand, then the same gesture with the other, slightly higher, then higher and higher, faster and faster.

"And this and this and this," he would say, indicating the steps he took to recovery.

"At first you were discouraged ..." I prompted, assuming my part in our familiar dialogue.

"No it's not!" he said, and stabbed at my knee. "This. *This* is the guy."

"Are you talking about me? Telling a story about me?"

"That's right!" My father took on a determined expression, flapped his hands as if something were flying into his face. Wind? Rain? He mimed walking in steady rhythm, against some kind of resistance.

"Are you talking about when we used to take walks together?"

"That's right! It's a great thing."

"About how I used to take long walks with you?"

"That's right!" The wind and rain again. He patted my knee urgently. "It's a great guy."

"I kept going."

"That's right. That's right."

↫

The next day we made a day-trip to Owen Sound: my father, Ingi, my step-sister Melissa, and me, in their car. My father set his chin straight, in line with the rutted earth before us. He squinted, eyes on the horizon. The box of ashes rested on his lap and he arranged his hands on either side of it, formally and symmetrically. "Let's do it," he said, every so often. The road was long and overhung with trees. Two troughs had been worn into the road, a ribbon of grass thriving between them. June: the wild power of nature at this season, persistent growth taking over every inch of ground not stressed by human tread and wheels. It was good, doing this, the four of us in the car. The connections between us were tenuous and tangled, yet we moved forward together along this honey-coloured road in the sunshine, stripes of light and shade moving across the windshield.

At last, there was the beach. The wooden dock extended over an expanse of calm, blue lake. The sun was hot, relentlessly, as it can be in June, but the breeze let us know summer had not really arrived. Ingi carried the box to the end of the dock, and my father, a copy of *Tasting the Earth*. He handed the book to me, and addressed himself to the box of ashes.

The box was sealed. This had to be got through. Inside was a thick plastic bag, fastened with a grooved strip of plastic. The box dropped away, onto the dock, and my father and Ingi struggled with the bag. There were unexpected obstacles, layers of packing between their hands and the brownish powder. Human ashes, as I'd learned, are mixed with wood from the coffin. The bones make up only a small proportion of the stuff in the bag. *The white flecks*, I thought, *those must be the bones*.

And now, a cry of surprise was torn from all of us as a single gust of wind came from behind – from the land. A shot of light dashed out across the bay. Silver! The sun reflected on the million tiny particles that now descended, broke the surface of the water and continued to fall. These were fragments of Mona's bones, catching the light. They dropped down through the water – a thicker element – their brightness magnified, and at last settled on the bottom in a phosphorescent cloud. We watched, silent, as the cloud dispersed. Gentle waves one by one spread the powder which had been Mona's body across the bottom of the lake.

My father put his hand on my shoulder, indicated the book.

"You want me to read something?"

"That's right."

"'This Was My Brother?'"

"That's right."

I held the book up, yet recited the poem from memory. He thanked me. And before we could take another breath, a commotion arrived behind us. A pickup truck was driving on to the beach with a cargo of live chickens. It was not an interruption; we had done what we came to do. We turned and made our way back to the car.

Afterword

When Mona's collection was finished, in 2004, it was appraised by antiquarian bookseller David Mason. He valued it at almost sixty-two thousand dollars. This was over fifteen times what anyone had anticipated. In no year of her life did Mona earn enough to have benefited from the tax receipt. Because of the high sum, a second opinion was called for. Robert Wright appraised the collection at close to sixty-seven thousand dollars.

In a letter accompanying his appraisal, Mason wrote, "I cannot remember another archive I have appraised where so clear a picture is given of the difficulties and range of activities which the free lance writer and editor had to cope with in Canada, especially in the period from the 1930s to the 1950s ... On top of everything else, one would have loved to meet Mona Gould. This well rounded record of a life engaged in writing and the literary scene in Canada is an important and remarkable research source."[1]

Notes

All archival materials are at the Fisher Rare Book Library, University of Toronto, unless otherwise specified.

CHAPTER TWO

1 *The Globe and Mail*, Saturday 3 April 1943. File 29.1.
2 *The Montrealer*, April 1943. File 29.1.
3 *The Hamilton Spectator*, 17 April 1943. File 29.1.
4 Letter from E.J. Pratt, 5 May 1943. File 29.1.
5 Letter from Martha E. Law (looks like), 9 October 1943. File 29.1.
6 Announcer's copy, CJOR *Limited Design for Women*, Friday 16 April 1943. File 29.1.
7 Letter from Marjorie Freeman Campbell, 17 May 1944. File 29.1.

CHAPTER THREE

1 Letter from Ruby Whitter, 14 March 1988. File 16.4.
2 E-mail from Douglas McTavish Jr, 8 December 2005.
3 E-mail from Douglas McTavish Jr, 8 December 2005.
4 Letter from Ruby Whitter, 14 March 1988. File 16.4.
5 E-mail from Douglas McTavish Jr, 8 December 2005.
6 Author interview with Phyllis Benner, December 2005.
7 Author interview with Phyllis Benner, December 2005.
8 Author interview with Douglas McTavish, Jr, December 2005.

9 Author interview with Douglas McTavish, Jr, December 2005.

10 Author interview with Douglas McTavish, Jr, December 2005.

11 Letter from Mona Gould to Douglas McTavish, 1980s.

12 Box 29.

13 *The London Advertiser*, date unknown. File 32.4.

14 File 32.4.

15 Marty, *Creative*, 120-5. Margaret Stevens, publishing under the pseudonym of Anne Reece, also had four poems in the anthology; 120–5.

16 Mona's notes beside the closely-cropped clipping attribute the article thus: Ann Elizabeth Wilson, "If a Child Has It in Him: Some Canadian Demonstrations," *The Chatelaine*, September 1928. File 32.10.

17 Durham in Marty, *Creative*. 7–8.

18 Marty, *Creative*. 17–20.

19 *The London Advertiser*, date unknown. File 32.2.

20 Beattie, in Carl S. Klinck, ed. *Literary History*, 724.

21 Author interview with Edra Ferguson, March 2004.

22 Mona Gould, "Composition," 30 November 1923. Marked by Mr MacDonald. File 7.18.

23 Letter from Nancy Durham, 17 March 1927. File 12.6.

24 Letter from Nancy Durham, 17 March 1927. File 12.6.

25 Letter from Nancy Durham, 17 March 1927. File 12.6.

26 Lang, *Women,* 166–70.

27 Mona McTavish, *St. Thomas Times-Journal*, date unknown. File 32.3.

28 Lang, *Women,* 162-8.

29 Lang, *Women,* 169–81.

30 Mona McTavish, *St. Thomas Times-Journal*, date unknown. File 32.3.

31 Lang, *Women,* 192.

32 Author interview with Edra Ferguson, March 2004.

33 File 8.10.

34 Author interview with Edra Ferguson, March 2004.

35 Box 31.

36 Author interview with Edra Ferguson, March 2004.

CHAPTER FOUR

1 The publication began as *The Chatelaine*, then changed its name to *Chatelaine* in 1931. The transition occurred during the early years of Mona's involvement with the magazine.

2 *The Canada Year Book*, 1936, 802, 814.

3 Mona Gould, journal entry, 14 August 1984. Box 44.

4 File 4.5.

5 Box 27.

6 Mona Gould, Unpublished fragment. File 8.2.

7 Mona Gould, unpublished fragment. File 8.1.

8 File 23.1.

9 Mona Gould, "Silver." Unpublished short story. File 8.1.

10 Mona Gould, "Sire," *I Run with the Fox*, 3.

11 Mona Gould, unpublished poem. File 4.1.

12 Mona Gould, "Squegee," *Every Boy's*, October 1933, 7. File 31.4.

13 "Squegee," *Every Boy's*, October 1933, 7. File 31.4.

14 Sutherland, *The Monthly Epic*, 124.

15 Letter from Alvah Beattie, 4 January 1931. File 11.3.

16 Letter from Alvah Beattie, 4 February 1932. File 11.3.

17 Letter from Alvah Beattie, 11 March 1932. File 11.3.

18 Letter from Alvah Beattie, 5 April 1932. File 11.3.

19 Letter from Irene Kon, 26 September 1932. File 11.3.

20 Letter from J. Walker, 4 August 1933. File 11.3.

21 Letter from Alvah Beattie, 12 June 1933. File 11.3.

22 Beaulieu, *La Presse*, 116.

23 Letter from Byrne Hope Sanders, 27 September 1933. File 11.3.

24 Letter from Patricia Meredith, 13 November 1936. File 11.3.

25 *The Crucible*, Vols. 1–5, holdings at Toronto Central Reference Library and at Fisher Rare Book Library. Irvine, *Editing Modernity*, 203–4.

26 Letter from Hilda Ridley, 21 July 1932. File 11.1.

27 Letter from Hilda Ridley, 21 July 1932. File 11.1.

28 Sutherland, "The Transitional *Canadian*," *The Monthly Epic*, 96–111.

29 Letter from J.L. Rutledge, General Editor, 18 May 1931. File 11.3

30 Irvine, *Editing Modernity*, 206.

31 Irvine, *Editing Modernity*, 208–9.

32 Mona Gould, "Autumn," *The Crucible* 1, no. 3, 7; "Beauty is a Hurdy-Gurdy," *The Crucible* 1, no. 4, 7; "Night Garden," *The Crucible* 2, no. 2, 1.

33 Irvine, *Editing Modernity*, 14–15.

34 Irvine, *Editing Modernity*, 205.

35 Irvine, *Editing Modernity*, 183.

36 *The Canada Year Book*, 1936, 126.

37 White, "The Corkscrew Town," *Owen Sound*, 86-92.

38 *The Curtain Call*, 1935. File 7.8.

39 File 14.3.

40 Pictures: box 28. Programs: file 23.4, file 14.3.

41 Letter from B.K. Sandwell, 13 October 1938. File 13. 2.

42 Box 20.

43 File 17.3.

44 File 4.5.

CHAPTER FIVE

1 Louÿs, *Aphrodite*, 22.

2 Mona Gould, *Tasting the Earth*, 9.

3 Mona Gould, *Full Circle*, unpublished manuscript. File 4.6. All poems in this chapter are from the same manuscript.

4 File 8.10.

5 File 23.9.

CHAPTER SIX

1 Letters from Eric Rechnitzer, 26 August and 11 September 1940. File 11.6.

2 Author interview with Dodi Robb, March 2004.

3 Letter from B.K. Sandwell, 9 December 1936. File 13.2.

4 Letter from B.K. Sandwell, 19 August 1937. File 13.2.

5 Letter from B.K. Sandwell, 19 January 1938. File 13.2.

6 Letter from B.K. Sandwell, 4 April 1944. File 13.3.

7 Letter from B.K. Sandwell, 24 July 1944. File 13.3.

8 Letter from B.K. Sandwell, 16 January 1948. File 13.3.

9 Letter from Edith Frith, Toronto Central Library, 13 June and 21 July 1977. File 13.2.

10 Pitt, *E.J. Pratt*, 58-9.

11 Scott, "Overture," 37.

12 E.J. Pratt in Pitt, *E.J. Pratt*, 184.

13 Pitt, *E.J. Pratt*, 184.

14 Nathaniel A. Benson, *Canadian Poetry Magazine*, December 1943, 9.

15 File 13.1.

16 *Canadian Poetry Magazine*, August 1943, 36.

17 File 13.1.

18 File 23.8.

19 File 13.1.

20 Panofsky, "Head of the Publishing Side of the Business," 58.

21 Panofsky, "Head of the Publishing Side of the Business," 54.

22 Letter from Eric Rechnitzer, 3 January 1942. File 23.18.

23 Inside front cover, *Liberty*, 18 November 1944. File 29.2.

24 Letter from B.K. Sandwell, 1942. File 13.2.

25 File 31.6.

26 Letter from J.N. Kelly, 10 June 1942. File 31.6.

27 File 31.6.

28 November 1944. File 31.6.

29 Letter from Margaret Christie, 23 July 1944. File 31.6.

30 Letter from Herbert Hodgkins, 2 February 1943. File 11.5.

31 Mona Gould, *Tasting the Earth*, 19.

CHAPTER SEVEN

1 Letter from Gordon Howard McTavish, 15 June 1940. File 16.2.

2 File 32.12.

3 Mollie McGee, "Colonel Piloted Ship When Skipper Killed." *The Globe and Mail*, 24 August 1942, 7, W.T. Cranfeld, filed from London, 30 September 1942. (Clipping from an unknown newspaper.) File 32.12.

4 File 32.12.

5 Radio coverage of the Dieppe raid is archived on the CBC website, including commentary from later years, and a reading of "This Was My Brother," broadcast after Mona's death. This page gives an excellent sense of how the raid was treated in the media, both immediately after the raid and in later years. See "The Contentious Legacy of Dieppe," http://archives.cbc.ca/war_conflict/second_world_war/topics/2359/

6 Mona Gould, "Peace, Peace," *Poetry Yearbook, 1936*, 11.

7 Gillmor, Michaud, and Turgeon, *Canada*, 187.

8 Letter from Alvah Beattie, 28 December 1939. File 23.7.

9 In a second version, written in the fifties (and accepted with high praise by *Gossip* magazine in 1969), Mona puts the words in the mouth of an anonymous speaker. It thus begins "She said/I am a woman ..." Mona must have found it gratifying when Paul Nowack, *Gossip*'s then editor, described the poem in his acceptance letter as: "Magnificent! You have said everything that needed to be said." Both versions of poem: File 4.2. Correspondence: File 12.3.

10 *The Windsor Star*, 25 October 1943. File 32.12.

11 Box 27.

12 *Toronto Telegram*, 19 November 1941, 8 January 1942, 28 May 1942.

13 File 2.3.

14 File 23.9.

15 Letter from Ellen McTavish, 31 March 1943. File 23.9.

16 File 12.3.

17 Letter from Douglas McTavish, 6 April 1943. File 23.9.

18 Mona Gould, "They used to say 'Never work for a Woman' … but now?" *Chatelaine*, February 1943. Box 31.1.

19 Mona Gould, *Saturday Night*, 26 September 1942. File 32.9.

20 Letter from H.D. Burns, 21 September 1942. File 11.4.

21 Author interview with John and Ingi Gould, December 2001.

22 Box 29.

23 File 13.1.

24 File 8.10.

25 Draft, file 8.7.

26 Author interview with John Aylesworth, 17 December 2005.

27 Author interview with John Aylesworth, 17 December 2005.

28 E-mail to Maria Meindl from John Aylesworth, 19 December 2005.

CHAPTER EIGHT

1 Letter from J.E. Chandler, 29 October 1945. File 11.4.

2 Letter from J.E. Chandler, date unknown. File 11.4.

3 Letter from Mona Gould to Dr F.W. Routley, 31 March 1945. File 31.6.

4 Letter from Dr F.W. Routley, 16 April 1945. File 31.6.

5 Letter from Sydney Morrell, 11 October 1945. File 11.4.

6 Letter from Sydney Morrell, 1 November 1945. File 11.4.

7 Telegrams from Graham Gould. File 14.15.

8 File 14.15.

9 File 14.15.

10 Box 27.

11 File 14.15.

12 Londerville, *Pay Services*, "1944: From the Beaches to Belgium," 151–76.

13 Graham Gould, "The Sunny Room," unpublished short story, 1950s. File 14.3.

14 Mona Gould, "You Can't Go Home Again," *Saturday Night*, 11 December 1948, 12. File 32.9.

15 File 6.2.

16 *St. Thomas Times-Journal*. File 32.11.

17 Letter from Ellen Elliott, 1 March 1946. File 23.2.

18 Letters from Winnifred Eayrs, 3, 10, 17 and 24 July 1946. File 23.22.

19 Letter from Ellen Elliott, 6 March 1946. File 11.6.

20 Letter from Ellen Elliott, 10 April 1946. File 23.2.

21 File 23.22.

22 Letter from B.K. Sandwell, 16 July 1946. File 32.11.

23 Letter from Helen O'Reilly, 20 March 1947. File 23.22.

24 *Owen Sound Sun-Times*, File 23.22.

25 *Owen Sound Sun-Times*, File 23.22.

26 File 23.11.

27 File 8.10.

28 Letter from Helen O'Reilly, 27 September 1946. File 23.22.

29 Letter from Arleigh Junor. File 12.1.

30 Letter from Arleigh Junor, 20 October 1946. File 11.6.

31 File 23.11.

32 Adele Saunders, "War Memorials, What Form?" *Chatelaine*, March 1945, 10. File 29.1.

33 Letter from Byrne Hope Sanders, 25 February 1947. File 11.6.

34 "J'O'C", *The Halifax Chronicle*, 14 December 1946. File 31.7.

35 *Saturday Night*, 24 April 1943. File 31.7.

36 Sally Townsend, *The Globe and Mail*, 21 December 1946. File 31.7.

37 *Vancouver News-Herald*, November 1946. File 23.11.

38 Letter from Bertha James, 5 December 1945 (sic). File 12.1.

39 Letter from Lettie Anne Hill, 13 January 1946. File 23.22.

40 Letter from Douglas McTavish, 24 November 1946. File 12.1.

41 File 23.5.

42 Mona Gould, "Visit," *Chatelaine*, October 1949. File 23.19.

43 Letter from Graham Gould. File 14.3.

44 Letter from Margaret Steven Tanton. File 16.5.

45 File 6.1.

46 Letter from John Gray, 8 February 1949. File 11.6.

47 Letters from Winnifred Huff, 10 August 1948, and from Lotta Dempsey, 12 October 1948. File 11.6

48 Mona Gould, "Like Going to the Moon and Just as Exciting," *Saturday Night* 27, November 1948. File 29.3.

49 Virtue, *Leonard and Reva Brooks*, 94–112; 164–80.

50 Letter from Reva Brooks, 29 November 1948. File 12.20. Mona and Reva continued to correspond. In 1963, Mona looked into the possibility of a trip to Mexico, and Reva wrote to her about local hotels where she might stay. The trip never happened, though, and Mona never saw Mexico again. Reva

died in Mexico in 2004 at the age of ninety-one and Leonard still lives there
at the time of this writing.

51 Letter from Reva Brooks, 28 July 1949. File 12.20.

52 Letter from Antonio and Salvador. File 11.6.

CHAPTER NINE

1 Letter from Margaret Steven Tanton, 1960s or 70s. File 16.5.

2 Letter from Douglas McTavish, 1992. File 16.1.

3 Letter from Dora Smith, 1990s. File 16.7.

CHAPTER TEN

1 Letter from M. Rosenfeld, 20 May 1949. File 23.11.

2 Kesten's Corner, *The Toronto Telegram*. File 23.10.

3 *Ontario College of Art and Design Alumni Directory, 2006*, ©OCAD, Toronto,
2005.

4 Letter from John Gould, "Wed nite," Fall 1948. File 15.2.

5 Nowell, *Hot Breakfast*, 23.

6 Nowell, *Joyce Wieland*, 82–3.

7 Nowell, *Joyce Wieland*, 82–3.

8 Author interview with Jean Aylesworth, December 2005.

9 Christine Sismondo, "Raising a Glass to the First Cocktail Bars," *The Toronto
Star*, 11 March 2007. "ONTARIO: Set 'Em Up!" *Time Magazine*, 14 April 1947.

10 Author interview with John Aylesworth, December 2005.

11 Author interview with John Aylesworth, December 2005.

12 Letter from John Gould. File 15.2.

13 Postcards from Mona and Graham. File 15.1.

14 Letter from John Gould. File 23.18.

15 Letter from M. Rosenfeld, 20 May 1949. File 23.11.

16 *Listen Ladies*, 26 October 1949. File 1.1.

17 File 12.2.

18 Letter from Annie Black of Hamilton. 16 March 1951. File 12.2.

19 "Kesten's Corner," *The Toronto Telegram*, date unknown. File 23.10.

20 *Listen Ladies*, 24 December 1951. File 1.6.

21 E-mail to Maria Meindl from Douglas McTavish Jr, 8 December 2005.

22 File 12.3.

23 *Listen Ladies*, 22 August 1950. File 11.9.

24 *Listen Ladies*, 16 and 30 December 1949. File 1.2.

25 Letter from G. MacGregor Grant, Rosedale Church, 14 February 1952. File 4.18.

26 Letter from Isabel Woodrow, 7 Febrary 1952. File 12.2.

27 Letter from "Mona," 16 April 1950. File 12.2.

28 Letter from M.E. Carter, Toronto. File 12.3.

29 "Radio by Gordon Sinclair," *The Toronto Daily Star*, 23 August 1952. 41.

30 Letter from Kay Heal, 20 December 1952. File 12.3.

31 "Radio by Gordon Sinclair," *The Toronto Daily Star*, 27 November 1951. 4. File 32.14.

32 Letter from Bernice Coffey of Elizabeth Arden Cosmetics, 14 July 1959. File 23.13.

33 Letter from N. Riley, 26 October 1950. File 11.7.

34 Interview with Margaret Thornton, Director of Women's Promotions for Ronald's Advertising of Canada. Possible column piece or notes toward a column. File 8.12.

35 *Carousel* fragment. File 3.14.

36 Box 28.

37 *Toronto Telegram*, 8 September 1959. File 31.7.

38 Interview with Irving Layton, *Be My Guest*. File 1.16.

39 "Radio by Gordon Sinclair," *The Toronto Daily Star*, date unknown. File 32.7.

40 "Radio by Gordon Sinclair," *The Toronto Daily Star*, 16 November 1949. 8. File 23.10.

41 Letter from Bob McStay, Royal Alexandra Theatre, 27 October 1950. File 11.8.

42 Author interview with John Aylesworth, December 2005.

43 Nancy Phillips, "Woman's View," *The Toronto Telegram*, 10 July 1959, II, 2. File 32.5.

44 "Radio by Gordon Sinclair," *The Toronto Daily Star*, date unknown. File 32.7. See also *Toronto Daily Star*, 14 September 1950, 11.

CHAPTER ELEVEN

1 Here is the full text of the poem Dodi Robb tried to quote from memory.
Love Is Not All
by Edna St Vincent Millay

Love is not all: it is not meat nor drink
Nor slumber nor a roof against the rain;

Nor yet a floating spar to men that sink
And rise and sink and rise and sink again;
Love can not fill the thickened lung with breath,
Nor clean the blood, nor set the fractured bone;
Yet many a man is making friends with death
Even as I speak, for lack of love alone.
It well may be that in a difficult hour,
Pinned down by pain and moaning for release,
Or nagged by want past resolution's power,
I might be driven to sell your love for peace,
Or trade the memory of this night for food.
It well may be. I do not think I would.

2 Author interview with Dodi Robb, March 2004.

CHAPTER TWELVE

1 Letter from Mona Clark, 5 May 1946. File 11.5.
2 Letter from John Gray, 8 February 1949. File 11.6.
3 Sally Townsend, "Whimsy." File 23.10.
4 File 23.10.
5 *Owen Sound Times Journal*, January 1947. File 23.11.
6 File 23.10.
7 Mona Gould, *Gossip*, 15.
8 Mona Gould, *Gossip*, last page (un-numbered).
9 See newspaper story, date unknown. File 31.3.
10 Panofsky, "Head of the Publishing Side of the Business," 63.
11 Irvine, *Editing Modernity*, 92. Quoting from John Sutherland, "Anne Marriott's Native Realism," rpt. in Sutherland, *Essays*, 100–1.
12 Irvine, *Editing Modernity*.
13 Century Motor Sales scripts, June 1951. File 1.12.
14 Sinclair, "Radio by Gordon Sinclair," *The Toronto Daily Star*, 5 June 1951. 4. File 31.7.
15 Letter from Mona Gould to John Gould, summer 1951. File 14.1.
16 Letter from Graham Gould, about 1952. File 14.3.
17 Graham Gould, "The Sunny Room," unpublished short story, 1950s. File 14.3.
18 Letter from Charles Miller of CBC, 16 March 1950. File 11.7.
19 The Associated Board of the Royal Schools of Music, 26 March 1951. File 11.9.
20 Column by Lotta Dempsey. File 32.5. Various columns, *The Paris Star*. File 32.14.

21 *The Paris Star*, 23 November 1951. File 32.14.

22 *The Paris Star*. File 32.14.

23 Letter from Alvah Beattie, 23 October 1952. File 11.9.

24 Letter from Anne Metcalfe, *Cats Magazine*. Pittsburgh, PA. 15 February 1955. File 11.7.

25 Letter from Keith A. Knowlton, 7 February 1952. File 11.9.

26 Letter from Keith A. Knowlton, 30 January 1952. File 11.9.

27 Letter from Keith A. Knowlton, 7 February 1952. File 11.9.

28 CBC Radio Archives: http://archives.cbc.ca/programs/942/

29 Mona Gould, "Only Human," *New Liberty Magazine* (November 1954), 9. File 10.7.

30 Letter from Ada Twohy Kent, 24 September 1954. File 11.7.

31 Sutherland, *The Monthly Epic*, 195–6.

32 Sutherland, *The Monthly Epic*, 196.

33 Sutherland, *The Monthly Epic*, 195.

34 Sutherland, *The Monthly Epic*, 198–200.

35 Anderson, *Rebel Daughter*, 124.

36 Max Braithwaite, in *The Monthly Epic*, 199.

37 *The Monthly Epic*, 199–201.

38 Letter from Mona Gould to Frank Rasky, 1954. File 11.7.

39 *The Monthly Epic*, 193.

40 *The Monthly Epic*, 196.

41 Hugh Garner, in *The Monthly Epic*, 197.

42 Letter from Jack Kent Cooke, 9 December 1952. File 11.9.

43 Letter to Alvah Beattie, Toronto, 16 February 1955. Undated reply from Alvah Beattie on back. File 11.9.

44 Stan Helleur, *Toronto Telegram*, 6 May 1955. File 32.5.

45 Letter from Jeann Beattie, 24 December 1956. File 23.11.

46 Mona Gould, "Mona Gould Talks to Lotta Dempsey," *The Royal York Magazine*, November 1959, 22–3; 28.

47 Box 24.

48 Letter from Eric Rechnitzer. 1955. File 11.9.

49 Letter from Clare Bice to Dr James McKegney. 22 February 1955. File 11.9.

50 Sinclair, "Radio by Gordon Sinclair," *The Toronto Daily Star*, 13 September 1952. 5. File 31.7. Various columns. Files 31.7. 32.5.

51 Correspondence from John Gould, 1950s. Files 15.1, 15.2.

52 Letter from Ellen Howard, late 1950s. File 14.2.

53 Letter from John Gould, early 1950s. File 15.2.

54 Letter from Mona Gould to John Gould, 1956. File 14.4.
55 Mona Gould, "The Gift." Unpublished poem. File 4.20.

CHAPTER THIRTEEN

1   Letter from Mona Gould to John Gould, fall 1956. File 14.4.
2   Letter from John Gould, 1956. File 15.2.
3   Letter from Ellen McTavish. File 14.2.
4   Letter from Mona Gould to John Gould. File 14.1.
5   Mona Gould, unpublished fragment. File 10.1.
6   Mona Gould, unpublished poem. File 4.20.
7   Letter from Mona Gould, mid-fifties. File 14.1.
8   Letter from Mona Gould, mid-fifties. File 14.1.
9   Notes by Graham Gould. File 14.4.
10 Letter from Graham Gould. File 14.4.
11 Notes by Graham Gould. File 14.4.
12 Notes by Graham Gould. File 14.4.
13 Letter from Mona Gould to John Gould, 2 September 1956. File 14.1.
14 Postcard from Graham Gould, April 1959. File 14.3
15 Letter from Graham Gould. File 14.4.

CHAPTER FOUTEEN

1   David Olson, *The World on Paper*, 124–5.
2   *The Globe and Mail*, 7 July 1958, 15.
    The Toronto Telegram, 21 July 1958, 24.
    Lotta Dempsey, "Private Line," *The Globe and Mail*, 1 July 1958. 11. File 32.
    16.
3   Mona Gould, unpublished fragment. File 10.1.

CHAPTER FIFTEEN

1   Unpublished notes. File 10. 1, 17.5, 8.18.
2   Unpublished notes. File 10.2.
3   Graham Coughtry, Robert Hedrick, and Gordon Rayner all spent time in
    Ibiza, sometimes with wives and babies in tow.
4   Elizabeth Dingman, "Getting Around," *The Toronto Telegram*, 4 July 1960,
    23. File 32.5.
5   Mona Gould, "The Iron Maiden and Me." Unpublished story, early 1960s.
    File 10.3.
6   Letter from John Gould, 4 July 1960. File 15.3.

7 Letter from Ben Ward Price, 17 June 1960. File 11.11.
8 Mona Gould, "The Iron Maiden and Me." Unpublished story, early 1960s. File 10.3.
9 "Visit to Paris," *Be My Guest* script. File 1.17.
10 "The Picasso Exhibition at the Tate," *Be My Guest* script. File 1.17.
11 *Be My Guest* script. File 1.17.
12 Unpublished fragment. File 8.18.
13 Letter from Hetty Gould, 20 October 1960. File 15.7.
14 Letter from Hetty Gould, 6 November 1960. File 15.7.
15 Letters from John Gould, 1960. File 15.3. Letters from Hetty Gould, 1960. File 15.7.
16 Unpublished fragment. File 8.18.
17 Unpublished notes. File 17.5.
18 Letters from Barry Nesbitt, CKFH, 24 October, 3 November, 24 November 1960. File 11.11.
19 Unpublished fragment. File 8.18.
20 Unpublished notes. File 17.5.
21 Letter, 19 December 1960. File 11.11. I assume this is from Eric Rechnitzer.
22 Unpublished notes. File 17.5.
23 Unpublished notes. File 17.5.
24 Letter from Gloria Harron, CBC, 30 October 1961. File 11.10.
25 Mona Gould, unpublished poem, October 1962. File 5.2.
26 Nowell, *Painters Eleven*, 2. The source of the story is given as follows: "In the late 1960s the author met Tom Hodgson and enjoyed a few martinis and parties at the Pit. This text derives from the author's personal recollections, observation and participation." 326.
27 E-mail correspondence and interview with Marjorie Harris, 16–17 November 2010.
28 CBC Archives, "Cops ban artist for 'lewd' drawings," 2 February 1966. http://archives.cbc.ca/on_this_day/02/06/ "Called Obscene, Drawings Seized." *The Globe and Mail*, 27 May 1965, 12.

CHAPTER SIXTEEN

1 Author interview with Elizabeth Barry, January 2006.
2 Author interview with Elizabeth Barry, January 2006.
3 John Gould had a solo exhibition at the Here & Now Gallery in 1963. His colleagues who also exhibited that year included Gerald Gladstone, Robert Hedrick, and Tom Hodgson.

4 E-mail correspondence and interview with Marjorie Harris, 16–17 November 2010.

5 Pearl McCarthy, "Abstracts Proved Popular," *The Globe and Mail*, 30 September 1961, 18.

6 E-mail correspondence and interview with Marjorie Harris, 16–17 November 2010.

CHAPTER SEVENTEEN

1 Mothercraft archives: ledgers, 1940s through 1960s.

2 McDiarmid, *The Canadian Mothercraft Society*, 1994.

3 Mothercraft advertising brochure. File 13.4.

4 Mona Gould, orientation address to Mothercraft trainees, 2 September, probably 1965. File 13.8.

5 Mona Gould, letter to "Judy." File 13.4.

6 Correspondence from Vera MacIntosh Bell. Files 13.10-13.12.

7 Letter from Vera MacIntosh Bell. Thursday, February 7, mid-1960s. File 13.11.

8 Copies and correspondence. File 13.6.

9 Correspondence with Jeanne Renshaw. File 13.7.

10 Pitt, *E.J. Pratt*, 49.

11 Mona Gould, "Canadian Club's 'Big Daddy,'" *Gossip*, 30 May 1964, 6–7. Box 25.

12 Letters from Peter F. Heering Junior, 22 December 1966. File 11.11, and 9 January 1967, File 11.10.

13 Letter from Lorne Duguid, 11 June 1964. File 11.11.

14 Mona Gould, "The Genteelwomanly Use of Spirits," *Gossip*, 21 November 1964, 5. Box 25.

15 Box 26.

16 Mona Gould, "Dr. Bette Stevenson, the Ontario Medical Association's Colourful Leader," *Gossip*, 5 July 1969, 4. Box 26.

17 Mona Gould, "A Sense of Values," *Gossip*, 28 September 1968, 4. Box 26.

18 Mona Gould, "Invitation to Life," *Gossip*, 4 April 1964, 8. Box 25. "A Rare Humility," *Gossip*, 2 November 1968, 4. Box 26.

19 Margaret Steven Tanton, "We are Here in a World of Loneliness," *Rapport*, November 1968, 7. File 10.11.

20 Mona Gould, "We Are Here in the World Program for Refugees," *Rapport*, March 1971, 6. File 10.11.

21 Letter from John Bruce, T. Eaton Co., 3 March 1969. File 11.11. Letter from Eric Miller, MacLaren Advertising, 4 June 1969. File 11.11.

22 Letter from Mrs Major K.C. Evendon, The Women's Inter Church Council of Canada, 27 October 1969. File 11.11.

23 Letter from George E. Marshall Jr, 4 November 1968. File 12.11.

24 Mona Gould, transcript of poem and notes. File 12.11.

25 Letter from George E. Marshall Jr, 22 November 1968. File 12.11.

26 Memorandum from Goodenough, Higginbottom, McDonnell and Colville, 5 December 1968. File 12.11.

27 Memorandum from Goodenough, Higginbottom, McDonnell and Colville, 22 January 1969. File 12.11.

28 Letter from George Marshall to Goodenough, Higginbottom, McDonnell and Colville, 12 February 1969. File 12.11.

29 Letter from Mona Gould to George Marshall, 19 March 1969. File 12.11.

30 File 12.11.

31 Margaret Steven Tanton, "This Thing Forlorn." File 16.5.

32 Letter from Mona to Margaret Steven Tanton. 13 March 1969. File 16.5.

33 Letters to Jeremy Jessel and Dodi Robb. File 13.7.

34 Letter from Barry Penhale, 17 August 1977. File 11.13.

35 Mona Gould, "Verbal Meanderings: A Collection of Recollections. Vintage Varley," *Gossip*, 30 August 1969, 4. Box 26.

36 Mona Gould, journal entry, approximately 1964. Box 19.

37 CBC Contract, April 1963. File 11.10.

38 Letter from Bette Kennedy, CKFM. 21 April 1964. File 11.10.

39 CBC Contract, 18 September 1969. File 11.10.

40 Mona Gould, unpublished poetry collection. File 7.3.

41 Mona Gould, journal entry, approximately 1964. Box 19.

42 Mona Gould, journal entry, approximately 1964. Box 19.

43 Mona Gould, journal entry, approximately 1964. Box 19.

44 Mona Gould, unpublished prose, mid-sixties. File 10.2.

45 Mona Gould, unpublished prose, mid-sixties. File 10.1.

CHAPTER EIGHTEEN

1 Letter from Mona to Margaret Steven Tanton, 13 March 1969. File 16.5.

2 Letter from Mona to Douglas McTavish. File 16.3.

3 Press release, *Gossip* Magazine, 1 May 1970. File 11.12.

4 Letter from Mona to Gerald Campbell, 11 November 1970. File 11.12.

5 File 11.12.

6 Author interview with Maija Beeton, December 2005.

7 Author interview with Maija Beeton, December 2005.

8 Mona Gould, unpublished manuscript, "Welfare Office," 1972. File 8.12.

9 Mona Gould, "You Cast So Small a Shadow," 1974. File 5.10.

10 E-mail to Maria Meindl from James McTavish, 26 December 2005.

11 Author interview with John Aylesworth, 17 December 2005

CHAPTER NINETEEN

1 Mona Gould, journal entries, spring 1967. Box 19.

2 Mona Gould, journal entry, Sunday 10 September; probably 1967. Box 19.

CHAPTER TWENTY

1 Author interview with John Aylesworth Ide, December 2005.

2 Author interview with John Aylesworth Ide, December 2005.

3 Author interview with Maija Beeton, December 2005.

4 Author interview with Maija Beeton, December 2005.

5 Author interview with Maija Beeton, December 2005.

6 Journal entry, 20 April, probably 1986. Box 34.

7 Journal entry, April 1986. Box 34.

8 Journal entries. 27 April and 10 May, 1986. Box 34.

9 Journal entry, 5 May 1986. Box 34.

10 Journal entry, Sunday, 5 May 1986. Box 33.

11 Journal entry, 22 June 1986. Box 34.

12 E-mail to Maria Meindl from John Ide, 9 December 2005.

CHAPTER TWENTY-ONE

1 Author interview with Jean Aylesworth, December 2005.

2 Author interview with Jean Aylesworth, December 2005.

3 Mona Gould, Notes. File 14.29.

4 Mona Gould, "For John Ide." File 15.11.

5 Author interview with Jean Aylesworth, December 2005.

6 Journal entry, 1 January 1989. Box 45.

7 Barbara Fear, "That's Mona at the Mike: A Poet Becomes a Pioneering Broadcaster on a Dare," *The Huronia*, 22 September 1991, 11–13. Box 32.9.

8 File 12.12.

9 File 14.26 and box 43.

10 Budget, early 1990s. File 14.27.

11 Letter from John Aylesworth Ide, 15 July 1986. File 15.2.

12 Mona Gould, "Old Age to Me." File 7.2.

13 Notes, 9 April 1989. File 7.20.

14 Mona Gould, untitled tribute to Margaret Steven Tanton. File 16.6.

15 Mona Gould, unpublished Poem, mid-1990s, box 48.

16 Notes, mid-1990s. File 14.27.

17 Journal entry, approximately 10 May 1993. Box 41.

AFTERWORD

1 Memorandum to the Thomas Fisher Rare Book Library from David Mason, 27 July 2004.

Bibliography

Anderson, Doris. *Rebel Daughter: An Autobiography*. Toronto: Key Porter Books, 1996

Beattie, Munro. "Poetry (1920–1935)." In *Literary History of Canada: Canadian Literature in English*, edited by Carl F. Klinck, 723–41. Toronto: University of Toronto Press, 1965

Beaulieu, André, et al. *La presse québécoise des origins à nos jours. Vol 6: 1920–1934*. Québec: Les Presses de l'Université Laval, 1973

Dominion Bureau of Statistics, General Statistics Branch. *The Canada Year Book, 1936*. Ottawa: J.O. Patenaude, King's Printer, 1936

Gillmor, Don, Achille Michaud, and Pierre Turgeon. "A New World Order." In *Canada: A People's History* Volume Two, 185-236. Toronto: McClelland and Stewart, 2000

Gould, Mona. *Tasting the Earth*. Toronto: Macmillan of Canada, 1943

– *I Run with the Fox*. Toronto: Macmillan of Canada, 1946

– *Gossip*. Toronto: Gossip Magazine, 1949

Irvine, Dean. *Editing Modernity: Women and Little-Magazine Cultures in Canada, 1916–1956*. Toronto, Buffalo, London: University of Toronto Press, 2008

Lang, Marjorie. *Women Who Made the News: Female Journalists in Canada, 1880–1945*. Montreal and Kingston: McGill-Queen's University Press, 1999

Livesay, Dorothy. *Journey with My Selves*. Vancouver: Douglas and McIntyre, 1991

Londerville, J.D. *The Pay Services of the Canadian Army Overseas in the War of 1939–45*. Ottawa: The Runge Press (for The Royal Canadian Army Pay Corps Association), 1950

Louÿs, Pierre, *Aphrodite [ancient manners]*. Translated by Willis L. Parker. New York: Illustrated Editions Company, 1932

Marty, Aletta, ed. *Creative Young Canada: Collection of Verse, Drawings and Musical Compositions by Young Canadians from Seven to Twenty Years of Age.* With a forward by Agnes Delamoure. Toronto: J.M. Dent and Sons, 1928

McDiarmid, Norma J. *The Canadian Mothercraft Society: An Embodiment of Practical Idealism and Philanthropy.* St Catharines, Ontario: Lincoln Graphics Ltd, 1994

Milford, Nancy. *Savage Beauty: The Life of Edna St. Vincent Millay.* New York and Toronto: Random House 2002

Nowell, Iris. *Hot Breakfast for Sparrows: My Life with Harold Town.* Toronto: Stoddart, 1992

– *Joyce Wieland: A Life in Art.* Toronto: ECW, 2001

– *Painters Eleven: The Wild Ones of Canadian Art.* Vancouver: Douglas and McIntyre, 2010

Olson, David. *The World on Paper: The Conceptual and Cognitive Implications of Writing and Reading.* Cambridge: Cambridge University Press, 1994

Panofsky, Ruth. "'Head of the Publishing Side of the Business': Ellen Elliott of the Macmillan Company of Canada." *Papers of the Bibliographical Society of Canada.* 44:2 (Fall 2006), 45–64

Pitt, David G. *E.J. Pratt: The Master Years 1927–1964.* Toronto, Buffalo, London: University of Toronto Press, 1987

Sandwell, B.K., ed. *Poems for the Interim: A Selection of Twenty-four Poems by Nineteen Canadian Authors Published during 1945–46 in "Saturday Night,"* Toronto: Consolidated Press Ltd, 1946

Scott, Frank. *Overture,* Toronto: The Ryerson Press, 1945

Sutherland, Fraser. *The Monthly Epic: A History of Canadian Magazines.* Toronto: Fitzhenry and Whiteside, 1989

Virtue, John. *Leonard and Reva Brooks: Artists in Exile in San Miguel de Allende.* Montreal and Kingston: McGill-Queen's University Press, 2001

White, Paul. *Owen Sound: The Port City.* Toronto: Natural Heritage/Natural History Inc., 2000

WEB SITES

Canadian Communications Foundation
http://www.broadcasting-history.ca/index.html

CBC DIGITAL ARCHIVES
http://archives.cbc.ca/programs/